Adiel Sherwood

BAPTISTS

HISTORY, LITERATURE, THEOLOGY, HYMNS

General Editor: Walter B. Shurden is the Callaway Professor of Christianity in the Roberts Department of Christianity and Executive Director of the Center for Baptist Studies, Mercer University, Macon, Georgia.

John Taylor, *Baptists on the American Frontier: A History of Ten Baptist Churches*
   Edited by Chester Young
Thomas Helwys, *A Short Declaration of the Mystery of Iniquity*
   Edited by Richard Groves
Roger Williams, The Bloody Tenant of Persecution for Cause of Conscience
   Edited by Richard Groves
   Edwin Gaustad, Historical Introduction
James A. Rogers†, *Richard Furman: Life and Legacy*
Lottie Moon, *Send the Light: Lottie Moon's Letters and Other Writings*
   Edited by Keith Harper
James Byrd, *The Challenges of Roger Williams: Religious Liberty, Violent Persecution, and the Bible*
Anne Dutton, *The Influential Spiritual Writings of Anne Dutton: Volume 1: Letters*
   Edited by JoAnn Ford Watson (Fall 2003)
David T. Morgan, *Southern Baptist Sisters: In Search of Status, 1845-2000* (Fall 2003)
William E. Ellis, *"A Man of Books and a Man of the People": E. Y. Mullins and the Crisis of Moderate Southern Baptist Leadership* (Fall 2003)
Jarrett Burch, *Adiel Sherwood: Baptist Antebellum Pioneer in Georgia* (Winter 2003)
Anthony Chute, *A Piety Above the Common Standard: Jesse Mercer and the Defense of Evangelistic Calvinism* (Spring 2004)

ADIEL SHERWOOD

BAPTIST ANTEBELLUM PIONEER IN GEORGIA

by

Jarrett Burch

Mercer University Press
Macon, Georgia

ISBN   0-86554-788-2
        0-86554-890-0
MUP/H595   P258

© 2003 Mercer University Press
6316 Peake Road
Macon, Georgia 31210-3960

First Edition.

∞The paper used in this publication meets the minimum requirements of American National Standard for Information Sciences—Permanence of Paper for Printed Library Materials, ANSI Z39.48-1992.

Library of Congress Cataloging-in-Publication Data

Burch, Jarrett, 1971-
  Adiel Sherwood : Baptist antebellum pioneer in Georgia / by Jarrett
Burch— 1st ed.
     p. cm.
Includes bibliographical references and index.
  ISBN 0-86554-788-2 (alk. paper)
  1. Sherwood, Adiel, 1791-1879. 2. Baptists—United States—Clergy—Biography.
3. Baptists—Georgia—History—19th century. 4. Georgia Baptist
Convention—History—19th century. I. Title.
  BX6495.S47B87 2003
  286'.1'092--dc22

                                                          2003016025

*To all the Baptists
who call Georgia home.*

CONTENTS

ACKNOWLEDGMENTS

The successful completion of this work is largely due to the love of Georgians for their past and Baptists in particular for their history. A few years ago, I walked into the special collections of Mercer University for the first time looking for a topic to research. I had one antebellum leader on my mind but was soon redirected toward an individual I did not know existed—Adiel Sherwood. Susan Broome, Arlette Copeland, and Robert Gardner, all supervisors of this area in Mercer's Jack Tarver Library, provided me much assistance for the next few years. Indeed, their department became my home away from home for quite some time.

Additional help, support, and correction came from many areas of Baptist life. I am greatly indebted to Tom Nettles of Southern Seminary for his expertise in Baptist thought and practice. Other professors in church history and theology helped in the composition of this text. A special word of thanks is to be extended to Greg Wills, Bruce Ware, and Craig Blaising. The late Marvin W. Anderson also inspired the early stages of research. Daniel Sanders, a former researcher of Sherwood, provided me with much bibliographic research as well as J. A. Orehosky, a descendant of Sherwood. I appreciate the help of several libraries such as the James P. Boyce Centennial Library at The Southern Baptist Theological Seminary, and the special collections of George Washington University, Duke University, University of Georgia, and Georgia College and State University.

Former professors of the author deserve credit for developing an interest in Adiel Sherwood, a Georgian pioneer and Baptist organizer. Hutch Johnson of Gordon College, Wayne Mixon, formerly of Mercer University, and the late William I. Hair of Georgia College and State

University were men who aroused my interest in antebellum Georgia life. James Leo Garrett, Jr., and H. Leon McBeth, both of Southwestern Seminary in Fort Worth, Texas, led me in studying the historical and theological roots of the Baptists in the South.

Finally, I am thankful for the help from my personal and church families who sustained much of this writing and research. To my parents and family, thank you so much for your encouragement. To my present pastorates, Bethany and Mount Moriah Baptist churches of Washington County, Georgia, thank you so much for your support.

Jarrett Burch
Eastman, Georgia
July 2003

PREFACE

The reader may ask: Why read a book about a Georgia Baptist before the Civil War? Many historians and historical readers may not see the validity of studying such a character of the past. Viewing Georgia Baptists as belonging to either the larger umbrella of the Southern Baptist Convention or as dissenting congregations of the SBC, the reader may not feel drawn to reading a historical account of these people. After all, are not Georgia Baptists those people who have excessive denominational meetings, who speak on every apparent social issue of morality, and who argue on issues of education and Baptist polity? Well, yes… and that is precisely why this book should be read.

The movement of antebellum religion into Georgia followed the paths of human migration into the state while adapting to the environment of the area. Early concerns such as Sunday schools, temperance societies, protracted meetings, and ministerial education while outside influences later filtered into Georgia Baptist life in particular and Georgian society in general. Men such as Adiel Sherwood helped to inject these reforms although many frontier peoples resisted such developments.

To understand Georgia religious life, the roots of such beliefs and practices can explain much of the rationale for present-day attitudes and customs. By gazing at early pioneer efforts of Georgia Baptists, we can see the early divisions of this religious group of people who helped form the Southern way of life we presently know. I hope you enjoy reading this book of a man who fell in love with Georgia and the Baptists who lived there.

1

INTRODUCTION

In 1867, Augustus B. Longstreet, a Georgia lawyer and Methodist who wrote the well-received *Georgia Scenes*, asked the aged Baptist preacher Adiel Sherwood a rhetorical question. "The war made sad havoc of my estate, but it left me enough to live comfortably on, and God be praised, and God be praised for so much. Have you as much?"[1] Writing from Oxford, Mississippi, to Saint Louis, Missouri, this Methodist layman who helped Sherwood found the Georgia State Temperance Society forty years earlier really stated the same story for both men. The destructive forces of Sherman's March through Georgia had sent Longstreet to Mississippi and Sherwood to Missouri, separating them from the antebellum world in which they did much good.

The founders of institutions and movements in history are often forgotten. Their names usually survive longer than their thoughts or actions. This is especially true for the historical figure of Adiel Sherwood. Today, his name appears on the face of a building on Mercer University's campus in Macon and on a few collegiate awards in three Baptist colleges. Georgia history books mention his name as the author of four editions of the *Gazetteer of Georgia* (the first statistical book in Georgia). Yet, this individual's other writings and his pioneer efforts

---

[1] Samuel Boykin, *History of the Baptist Denomination in Georgia: With Biographical Compendium and Portrait Gallery of Baptist Ministers and Other Georgia Baptists* (Atlanta: James P. Harrison and Company, 1881) 351.

have largely been forgotten. Few recall his influence on the institutions and ideas he promoted. Sherwood founded the first Baptist Sunday school in Georgia and the first local temperance society in the state. He functioned as the leading revivalist preacher during the Great Georgia Revival of 1827. He initiated the organization of the Georgia Baptist Convention in 1822, and he organized a school that later became Mercer University.

Adiel Sherwood has suffered the same demise as other aspects of Southern religion. Most religious historians in the past century have analyzed the sociological dimensions of religion in the South, bypassing the issues of faith and religious fervor as meaningless subjects. Truly, the histories following the Civil War glamorized the growth of denominational Protestantism to a distasteful degree. The aftereffect resulted in assigning religious history to denominational historians and excluding it from general history. For most of the latter twentieth century, Southern religion received a negative treatment from secular historians with a secular explanation at best. Ecclesiastical and denominational developments in the South have been explained as reactions to sectional or social problems. Lately, historians have retraced the value of belief in Southern society. These historians have rediscovered the value of religion in Southern life as a contributing aspect toward defining Southern identity. Could it be possible that one's beliefs force the individual to change his or her society rather than society shaping the importance of religion?

When analyzing the growth of religion in the antebellum South, a microstudy involving a state denomination and one of its prominent leaders can accomplish much in defining the larger picture of a trend. In Georgia before the Civil War, the Baptists, like their Methodist brethren, experienced phenomenal growth. At the beginning of the nineteenth century, less than one hundred Baptist churches existed in Georgia. By the end of the Civil War, the Baptist denomination in Georgia competed with the Methodists as the largest religious group in the state. Through the use of revivalist methods and organizations, Georgia Baptists helped form Southern society.

Before the Civil War, Georgia experienced a series of revivals that increased the importance of religion and expressed itself through denominational growth and organization. In the colonial era, the mild effects of the First Great Awakening in the 1740s led to the formation of Whitfield's orphan's home in Bethesda and the immigration of New England converts into Southern regions. After the Revolution, the Second Awakening in the first decade of the 1800s sent revival preachers into the mountains and frontier borders of Georgia. Between the time of the Creek Wars of 1818–1819 and the Civil War, the state of Georgia saw a phenomenal growth in denominational churches that preached the revivalist message of conversion. Presbyterian, Methodist, and Baptist churches outdistanced their Episcopal and Catholic rivals, leaving their impression on secular society.

From 1818 to 1845, Baptists in Georgia grew from a few associations of churches to a strong state denomination that supported a new Southern convention. When Baptists of the South met in Augusta in May 1845, the denominational structure and identity of Georgia Baptists already existed, and it contributed to the formation of the Southern Baptist Convention. For the next sixteen years, the Georgia Baptist Convention helped shape the national organization as an example of a missionary group of benevolent and revivalist churches. When the Civil War began in 1861, the Southern Baptist Convention modeled the smaller state conventions, with Georgia being one of the oldest.

The Importance of an Individual in Georgia Baptist Life

Adiel Sherwood is a nearly-forgotten figure in the history of Baptists in the South, as well as the general study of Southern religion. Belonging to the same era as Baptist pioneers such as Jesse Mercer, Luther Rice, and J. M. Peck, Sherwood left a unique impression on his denomination that is noticeable upon closer examination. His companions described him as a humble man by nature, intentionally self-conscious of receiving praise. His own literary works reflect this trend. He published several monographs refuting the positions of Roman Catholics and Protestants who practiced infant baptism.[2] His greatest work, *Notes on the New*

---

[2] Sherwood's polemic against the advocates of infant baptism can be found in the following: *The Jewish and Christian Churches; or the Hebrew Theocracy and Christian Church Distinct Organizations* (St. Louis: T. W. Ustick, 1850), and *The True and*

Testament, compiled the quotes of contemporary exegetes on every passage of the New Testament, providing a distinct perspective of New Testament studies in antebellum America.[3] However, the larger corpus of his writings is found in Baptist periodicals. From his coming to Georgia in 1818 to his death in St. Louis, Missouri, in 1879, Sherwood wrote in every Baptist paper applicable to his location. Baptist papers in New York, Kentucky, Virginia, North Carolina, Georgia, and Missouri printed his short columns on topics including cultural reflection, Baptist ecclesiology, biblical doctrine, and New Testament exposition.

In recent scholarship, Sherwood's influence on Georgia Baptists in particular and Southern Baptists in general has received only marginal recognition. Two journal articles from a Georgia Baptist journal have discussed his interaction with Georgia Baptists.[4] In a small Southern Baptist journal, Robert Baker also wrote a brief article on Sherwood.[5] Yet, within the larger context of Southern Baptist history, Southern Baptist historians have largely forgotten Sherwood and his impact on the state and national level.[6]

Spurious Churches Contrasted (Philadelphia: King and Baird, 1845). He also wrote sections within books promoting Baptist principles. See Robert Fleming, *An Essay on the Baptism of John with an Introduction by Adiel Sherwood, D.D.* (Athens GA: W. C. Richards, 1849); J. B. Jeter, J. M. Pendleton, and A. Sherwood, *The True Mission of Baptists* (Sherwood wrote pt. 2, "The Mission of Baptists," 31–75) (Nashville: South-Western Publishing House, 1859).

[3] Adiel Sherwood, *Notes on the New Testament, Practical and Explanatory* (New York: Sheldon, Blakeman and Company, 1857).

[4] Two articles can be found in the formerly-printed *Viewpoints* journal. See W. J. Carswell, "Adiel Sherwood," *Viewpoints: Georgia Baptist History* 2 (1969): 93–107; and Daniel P. Sanders, "Frontier to Forefront: Adiel Sherwood and the Shaping of Georgia Baptists, 1818–1841," *Viewpoints: Georgia Baptist History* 12 (1990): 31–46.

[5] Robert A. Baker, "Big Little-Known Southern Baptists: Adiel Sherwood," *Quarterly Review* 37 (January–March 1977): 17–22.

[6] Of the five SBC histories already discussed, only Robert Baker and B. F. Riley mention Sherwood. Baker makes the connection between Sherwood and the development of a state convention (see *The Southern Baptist Convention and Its People 1607–1972* [Nashville: Broadman Press, 1974] 132–33). Benjamin Franklin Riley, the banned historian of the convention, stated, "In 1818, there removed from New England to Georgia, a minister and teacher of exceptional ability, who was destined to play no small part in the early Baptist annals of that state. This was Adiel Sherwood, who was trained in the best of New England schools, and to whose natural gifts were added the forces of

Sherwood's contemporaries recognized his formative influence on Georgia Baptist development. First, the historians of Georgia Baptist life recognized him as a founder of their convention. Second, colleagues, students, and converts also noted his efforts and work.[7] Even as late as the 1880s, historians noted Sherwood's historical significance. William R. Williams noted Sherwood's pioneer efforts in secular and theological education.[8] Thomas Armitage of New York, who wrote a voluminous and well-received Baptist history, gained access to much of his information on Georgia through Sherwood's manuscripts. He recognized Sherwood as "one of the most godly men in America." He also asserted:

> Georgia owes much to him for its pre-eminence as a Baptist State, especially in that zeal and intelligence which have made our Churches and ministry so strong within its bounds. No one else has exerted so wide and healthy an influence in advancing

---

culture and those of a consecrated heart. Without hesitation the cultured New Englander adjusted himself to the novel conditions in the South, and with a philosophic calmness entered into the turbulence which he found existing between the progressive elements of the denomination and the anti-missionaries" (Benjamin Franklin Riley, "A History of the Southern Baptists" [James P. Boyce Centennial Library, Southern Baptist Theological Seminary, Louisville; n.p., n.d.], microfiche, 308).

[7] More histories have been written on the Georgia Baptist Convention than on any other Southern state convention. The impact of Sherwood on its foundational identity has been documented, second only to Jesse Mercer. The first two histories were based on Sherwood's own compilation of Georgia Baptist history. His former student, Jesse Campbell, wrote *Georgia Baptists: Historical and Biographical*, rev. ed. (Macon: J. W. Burke and Company, 1874) while Sherwood was still living. The first official history was based on Sherwood's manuscripts. See Samuel Boykin, *History of the Baptist Denomination in Georgia*. Two later histories also mention Sherwood's impact. See B. D. Ragsdale, *The Story of Georgia Baptists*, 3 vols. (Atlanta: Executive Committee of the Georgia Baptist Convention, 1938); and James Adams Lester, *A History of the Georgia Baptist Convention* (Atlanta: *Christian Index*, 1972).

[8] William R. Williams, *Lectures on Baptist History* (Philadelphia: American Baptist Publication Society, 1877) 328. The closest friends and students of Sherwood who documented his efforts in Georgia Baptist life include the following: Mrs. A. P. Hill, *The Life and Services of Rev. John E. Dawson, D.D.* (Atlanta: Franklin Steam Printing House, 1872); S. G. Hillyer, *Reminiscences of Georgia Baptists* (Atlanta: Foote and Davies Company, 1902); Jeremiah B. Jeter, *Memoir of Abner W. Clopton, A.M.* (Richmond: Yale and Wyatt, 1837); George A. Lofton, "Memorial Sermon of Dr. Adiel Sherwood: Delivered at Third Baptist Church, St. Louis, Mo. Oct. 12, 1879" (n.p., n.d.).

our cause there excepting his true yoke-fellow, Rev. Jesse
Mercer, whose apostolic wisdom, zeal and spirituality have
rendered him immortal.[9]

Evidently, from the comparison between current histories and
Sherwood's contemporary audience, Adiel Sherwood has been forgotten.
The life of Sherwood represents an early link between Northern
evangelicalism and Southern denominationalism. Coming from an area
of interdenominational cooperation, Sherwood directed the efforts of one
denomination in one state that later influenced a national convention. As
a writer, pastor, and organizer, his interests in Georgia influenced the
interests of subsequent leadership in the national convention. However,
Sherwood's relation to the larger American Baptist life and thought
before entering Georgia flowed from his personal religious experiences
and his religious world in New England. A few Northern influences
followed Sherwood from New England to Georgia, influencing the local
developments of the denomination in Georgia.

THE EARLY LIFE OF ADIEL SHERWOOD

Life began for Adiel Sherwood in the region of New England and the
state of New York. On 3 October 1791, Adiel Sherwood became the
firstborn male child of his parents, Adiel and Sarah Sherwood. The elder
Adiel, a Revolutionary veteran and personal friend of George
Washington, owned a small farm in Fort Edward, New York. As a
farmer, the father provided a living for his children, due largely to the
frugality of his wife. Both parents possessed the faith of evangelical
religion, and both instilled into the future preacher the sense of discipline
and pious belief.

As the young Sherwood grew into adolescence, he dedicated
himself to the duties of school and religion. Most of his early life, he
attended country schools in the winter and worked on the farm in the
summer. When he later moved off to boarding school, he still found time

---

[9] Thomas Armitage, *A History of the Baptists; Traced by Their Vital Principles and
Practices, from the Time of our Lord and Savior Jesus Christ to the Year 1886* (New
York: Bryan, Taylor and Company, 1887) 772.

to return each harvest season to work on his father's estate. His father owned only a few slaves, which was permissible in early New York life, but it took the efforts of father and sons to ensure the success of their work.

During his earliest years, Adiel Sherwood lived within a family that practiced the type of church life that many of that day called "evangelical religion." Dating back to the beginning of the first Great Awakening and the writings of Jonathan Edwards, the Baptists that sprung from New England Congregationalism frequently looked at their inner lives. They encouraged the lost to seek conversion by analyzing their human affection for God. Under the conviction of sin, sinners trusted in God's grace and then testified to this assurance at their places of worship. Through public declaration, converted sinners openly attested God's work of grace and, in Baptist life, followed it with believer's baptism by immersion. This method of conversion was the popular form of Sherwood's day, and it touched his own life in a certain way.

New England Baptists practiced the custom of inquiring about salvation as a congregation. In 1808, Sherwood's pastor, Elder Harrington, publicly asked members of the Baptist church to relate their former feelings of conversion, and then he opened the inquiry to the entire congregation. For the next two years, Sherwood wrestled with the thoughts of conversion and salvation, wondering if his soul could be saved from sin and damnation. During this time, he continued to hear the testimonies of church members and the private discourses of conversion experiences from women who visited his mother. Upon hearing that faith was the hope of salvation that could be felt through trusting God, the young Adiel clung to the same hope. Though he did not experience a sudden change in disposition, he did begin to live a life of obedience, attending to the duties of his newly-acquired faith. In February 1810, he related his type of conversion experience to the Baptist church and Elder Harrington baptized him in the cold, icy waters of a local creek.

In December 1810, Sherwood enrolled and moved to Granville Academy in Granville, New York, to review his former studies in order to pursue a law practice. Beginning a custom that would continue throughout his life, Sherwood chose a private household as a place of residence. During his two-year tenure, at times he resided with a merchant, but mostly he stayed with the rector of the school, Dr. Salem Town, a Congregationalist. When summers arrived, he journeyed back to the family farm to labor in the day and study at night. When the customary two-month winter break began, he would teach at a local school or start his own.

In November 1813, Sherwood began his studies at Middlebury College in Vermont with the hope of being a lawyer. Moving to the small town, he joined the local Baptist congregation and boarded with its pastor, Dr. Kendrick. During this time, he seriously thought of abandoning his legal studies to become a preacher. Finding time to steer his education toward the pulpit ministry, Sherwood also continued to work on his farm and to teach every winter break. At Middlebury, he met many ministerial students who later shared in his missionary work in Georgia. In 1814, he met Luther Rice for the first time, beginning a friendship that would continue for two decades.

Spending three years at Middlebury College, Sherwood moved in fall 1815 to Union College in Schenectady, New York, in order to improve his personal health and satisfy his father. The distance between the former school and his farm, as well as the severe cold weather in Vermont, had not agreed with his weak lungs, which were highly susceptible to pneumonia. During fall term 1815, he experienced a bout with weakened lungs that delayed his entrance into Union College until the following spring.

The next three years brought numerous changes into Adiel Sherwood's life. His health improved along with the happiness of his father. By spring 1817, Sherwood completed his studies under Eliphalet Nott and T. C. Brownell. Upon graduation from Union, he returned to Fort Edward to open his own school, but within months he grew restless from teaching and farming.

Looking toward more theological education, Sherwood had two choices: go to Dr. Staughton in Philadelphia or Andover Theological Seminary. Most young Baptist ministers moved to Philadelphia to learn from the well-respected preacher, since the Baptists had not yet organized a theological school. However, the new theological school for Congregationalists at Andover appealed to some Baptists. Formed in reaction to the growth of liberalism and Unitarianism, this evangelical school existed as a viable alternative to which the New England Congregational churches could send their ministerial students.

In fall 1817, Andover accepted Adiel Sherwood as a new student of high standing. He came with letters of recommendation from Dr. Eliphalet Nott, Bishop T. C. Brownell, and Professor D. H. Barnes, all of Union College. These letters introduced him to three important men living near Andover: Dr. Thomas Baldwin, Rev. J. M. Winchell, and Prof. Moses Stuart. Baldwin would introduce the young Sherwood to a lifelong desire for home missions. Winchell motivated him to spread evangelical literature such as hymnbooks and gospel tracts. Stuart inspired the desire to study the New Testament in the original Greek.

Sherwood only studied at Andover for a year, never receiving a degree from the institution. However, local Baptist ministers and members of the school introduced him to the new form of missionary work of the day. Sherwood became an itinerant fund-raiser and organizer of missionary societies, with the purpose of promoting missions within his denomination. During these early years, denominational leaders worked closely with other evangelical ministers, pooling their resources together without eliminating the distinctions of sectarianism.

In summer 1818, Sherwood toured New England to bolster support for Dr. Baldwin's *Baptist Missionary Magazine*, as well as to start mite societies to fund missionary work. He discovered an antimissionary spirit in all forms of Baptist life. He noted that the Freewill Baptists of the district were just as opposed to funding missionary work as the regular Baptists. The summer experience opened a new possibility in Sherwood's life. Through raising support for missions, he realized the need to awaken Baptists to the need for evangelism. Also, he knew that warmer weather agreed with his health. When Georgia was mentioned as a good location for a Baptist teacher-preacher, he extended his tour to the South.

SHERWOOD: A NORTHERN INFLUENCE ON SOUTHERN RELIGION

The influence of Northern evangelicalism on Southern religion appeared early in American religious history. Within Baptist life before and after the Triennial Convention of 1814, connections existed. In 1696, William

Screven's congregation from Kittery, Maine, moved to Charleston, South
Carolina, beginning the first Baptist church in the South. During the
Great Awakening, New England Congregationalists, later called Separate
Baptists, converted to Baptist principles and migrated to the South,
forming the earliest Baptist churches in Virginia, North Carolina, and
Georgia. The beginnings of American Baptist involvement in missions
started with the conversion of Adoniram and Ann Judson and Luther
Rice to Baptist convictions, signaling another Northern influence on
Southern religion.

With the rise of organized missions, Baptists in the North looked at
the South as a mission field, just as they viewed the far countries of Asia
and Africa. Adiel Sherwood represented the generation of Baptists in the
North who migrated to the South after the beginning of the Triennial
Convention and before abolitionism became an issue of separation.
Sherwood's influence on Southern religion took the form of a theological
agenda, not a social one. Between 1814 and 1845, Sherwood represented
the last generation of Northern preachers who migrated to the South to
advocate a theology and practice of missionary Baptists that excluded a
social agenda toward American slavery.[10]

The form of Northern evangelicalism influencing Adiel Sherwood
came from three figures: Andrew Fuller, Moses Stuart, and Thomas
Baldwin.[11] Andrew Fuller, British pastor and theologian, advocated a
new theological emphases popular among Baptists who supported
missionary activity. He promoted an activist view of the Christian faith,
called "duty-faith," and stressed a view of Christ's atoning work on the
cross that was unique in Reformed thought. Moses Stuart, Professor of
Sacred Literature at Andover, provided Sherwood with a biblical

---

[10] Although the conversion of the slaves continued as an issue for Northern
abolitionists, the social issue of freeing slaves annulled many efforts to present the
gospel. The moral crusade of abolitionism blurred the individualistic revivalism of the
Second Awakening. After 1845, a concerted effort to convert slaves through catechetical
instruction and preaching accelerated in the South.

[11] Julia Sherwood lists several men who served as spiritual influences on Adiel
Sherwood: Moses Stuart of Andover, Thomas Baldwin of Boston, and James M.
Winchell. However, Winchell only served as a young friend to Sherwood. See Julia L.
Sherwood and Samuel Boykin, *Memoir of Adiel Sherwood, D.D.* (Philadelphia: Grant
and Faires, 1884) 90–93.

literalism that minimized confessional categories. Stuart advocated the practice of developing scriptural answers to theological opponents without using categories common among systematic theologians. Stuart popularized this methodology in refuting heretical notions such as Unitarianism. Thomas Baldwin, pastor of Second Baptist Boston, founded in 1802 the Massachusetts Baptist Missionary Society, which challenged the formation of other societies to promote the cause of home and foreign missions. Sherwood served initially as an employee of this society when he entered Georgia.

Andrew Fuller (1754–1815), through the 1785 publication of his popular tract *The Gospel Worthy of All Acceptation*, convinced many English Baptists to present an open invitation to all their hearers.[12] Fuller defended and promoted general invitations of repentance by appealing to the moral inability of the sinner as the hindrance toward repentance and faith. This position was a mediating option between antinomianism and legalism.[13] Later, through the publication of Fuller's theological works in

---

[12] David Benedict, a Northern Baptist reflecting upon a fifty-year ministry, stated, "Forty years ago large bodies of our people were in a state of ferment and agitation, in consequence of some modifications of their old Calvinistic creed, as displayed in the writings of the late Andrew Fuller, of Kettering, England. This famous man maintained that the atonement of Christ was general in its nature, but particular in its application, in opposition to our old divines, who held that Christ died for the elect only. He also mad a distinction between the natural and moral inability of men" (*Fifty Years Among the Baptists* [New York: Sheldon and Company, 1860] 135). Benedict also asserted, "Our old Baptist divines, especially those of British descent, were generally strong Calvinists as to their doctrinal creed, but few of them felt at liberty to call upon sinners in plain terms to repent and believe the gospel" (136).

[13] Fuller saw the attempt of equating natural inability (the lack of a natural propensity to follow God's law) with moral inability (the lack of following God according to a change of the heart) as a dangerous position. The theological result could either be licentiousness toward God's revealed law (antinomianism) or a dangerous legalism that excludes a change in the heart. See Joseph Belcher, ed., vol. 2 of *The Complete Works of Andrew Fuller* (Harrisonburg VA: Sprinkle Publications, 1988) 392. The doctrine of the sinner's inability to believe, being divided into natural and moral categories, dates back to Jonathan Edwards, Sr. In his *On the Freedom of the Will* treatise in section 4, Edwards distinguished between natural and moral inability as they relate to natural and moral necessity. His final argument rested on the observation that moral inability is the only inability that requires divine intervention. A change in the moral nature of the heart (i.e., regeneration) restructures the natural inability of man and the two forms of necessity. See vol. 1 of *Works of Jonathan Edwards* (Peabody MA: Hendrickson Publishers, 1998) 10.

America, mission-minded Baptists possessed a theological text that defended a missionary rationale of calling on sinners actively to repent. Many Baptists in America adopted "Fullerism" as it was called and used his theology as a justification for doing mission work in the 1820s. Sherwood promoted the same theological emphases as Fuller in his promotion of mission causes in Georgia.

Moses Stuart (1780–1852), Professor of Sacred Literature at Andover Theological Seminary, advocated a biblical literalism separated from confessionalism. Educated and converted at Yale College under Timothy Dwight, Stuart held the belief system that many considered evangelical Calvinism. This early nineteenth-century version of Edwardsean theology attempted to avoid the pitfalls of scholasticism at the expense of evangelism.[14] The early Andover Seminary epitomized a synthesis of scholastic and evangelical Calvinism, the theological and the practical. Yet, Stuart's greatest influence on his students would be in the area of biblical science. Taking the historical and grammatical approach

---

Within the following New England Congregational generations, evangelical Calvinism pushed the idea of moral inability as a mediate position that embraced a strong view of God's sovereignty as well as a positive view of man's ability to trust God for salvation when God prepares the heart. Many Baptists followed the same trend under the writings of Andrew Fuller, but within three groups: the Gillites, the Fullerites, and those who believed the differences between Fuller and Gill to be greatly exaggerated.

[14] Only one monograph has made it into print concerning Stuart. See John H. Giltner, *Moses Stuart: The Father of Biblical Science in America* (Atlanta: Scholar's Press, 1988).The appointment of a Unitarian professor to Yale College forced New England Congregationalists to form another seminary (i.e., Andover). However, it began as a union among extremes in the Calvinist camp. Two forms of orthodox Calvinism existed at Andover: those given to metaphysical thought and those given to revivalism. See John H. Giltner, "The Fragmentation of New England Congregationalism and the Founding of Andover Seminary," *Journal of Religious Thought* 20/1 (1963–1964): 27–42. Other evangelical Calvinists later departed from Calvinism completely, abandoning the doctrines of imputation, human inability, and a limited atonement. These theological shifts have received much discussion from American religious historians such as David Wells and Mark Noll as they have revisited the work of Frank Hugh Foster. See Frank Hugh Foster, *A Genetic History of New England Theology* (Chicago: University of Chicago Press, 1907); Mark Noll, "The Contested Legacy of Jonathan Edwards in Antebellum Calvinism," in *Reckoning with the Past* (Grand Rapids: Baker Books, 1995); David F. Wells, "The Debate over the Atonement in 19th-Century America," in *Bibliotheca Sacra* 144 (1987–1988): 123–43, 243–53, 363–76.

to interpreting the Bible, he pioneered a trend in America to interpret biblical texts without imposing a systematic theology or confessional framework on the text.[15] Although he remained true to his Calvinist heritage, his nontheological approach to theological debates made him appear unorthodox on occasion. From 1817 to 1818, Adiel Sherwood studied under Moses Stuart, who continued many approaches to biblical studies as his teacher, but within a Baptist context.

Thomas Baldwin (1753–1826), pastor of Baldwin Place Baptist Church in Boston from 1790 to his death, established the Massachusetts Baptist Missionary Society and published the *Massachusetts Baptist Magazine*.[16] Both promoted the earliest causes for missions in American Baptist life. Known for his prolific pen on Baptist distinctives, Baldwin also favored the formation of a national denomination based on an associational or conventional model.[17] Though Sherwood belonged to the First Baptist Church in Boston (no Baptist church existed at Andover), his pastor, being close to his own age, did not serve as a mentor. Dr. Baldwin of Second Baptist encouraged him in his efforts in the missionary society.[18]

Certain aspects of Northern Baptist life therefore can be considered as formative elements of Adiel Sherwood's thought. He adopted Andrew Fuller's theology. He considered the biblical training he received from Moses Stuart to be invaluable. Later, his lecture table would also center on New Testament studies. By being associated with Thomas Baldwin for a few years, Sherwood received an adequate, practical training in

---

[15] Stuart's greatest blunder occurred when he refuted the new spokesman for Unitarianism, William Ellery Channing. Stuart answered Channing's synopsis of Unitarian belief, evident in the publication of the sermon delivered at the ordination of Jared Sparks (1819), titled "Unitarian Christianity." Stuart's *Letters to Rev. William E. Channing* confronted Unitarianism with the claims of Trinitarian orthodoxy, using a strict biblicism without a systematized approach. Subsequently, Stuart drew fire from strict Calvinists as he appeared to subordinate the essence of the Son to that of the Father. See Bruce M. Stephens, "Breaking the Chains of Literalism: The Christology of Moses Stuart," *Covenant Quarterly* (August 1992): 35–40.

[16] William Cathcart, "Thomas Baldwin, D. D.," in vol. 1 of *The Baptist Encyclopedia* (Philadelphia: Louis H. Everts, 1881) 63–64.

[17] William Wright Barnes, *The Southern Baptist Convention 1845–1953* (Nashville: Broadman Press, 1954) 4–5.

[18] Sherwood and Boykin, *Memoir*, 87–94.

Baptist principles. Baldwin's influence would direct Sherwood toward seeing all Baptist causes as equally valid and worthy to be the focus of a denomination, not separate societies.

At the end of summer 1818, Sherwood resigned his post as agent of the Massachusetts Baptist Missionary Society in order to move temporarily to Georgia. He entered the Southern state as a former fundraiser and schoolteacher. Sherwood still had not delivered a regular sermon, received ordination, or established a church. These efforts would come later, but he did arrive in Georgia with a burden to educate children and to see the improvement of morals in church members.

2

SUNDAY SCHOOL AND TEMPERANCE IN GEORGIA

Adiel Sherwood entered Georgia for medical reasons, but he also moved to the state with missionary purposes in mind. His earliest work in Georgia was not the establishment of new churches, associations, or state denominational works, but the propagation of interdenominational concerns. He cooperated with the Presbyterians and Congregationalists, some of whom, like him, moved to Georgia from New England. Within the Baptist denomination in Georgia, Sherwood advocated and enacted the beginnings of benevolent societies that later became instrumental aspects of the state convention.

The formation of Sunday schools and temperance societies in Georgia contained a theology that would help define the identity of missionary Baptists. Sherwood established the first Baptist Sunday school (sometimes referred to as Sabbath school) at Trail Creek Baptist Church in Clarke County on 4 July 1819. Although two other Sunday schools in Georgia predate Sherwood's, they were predominantly interdenominational. One school existed in Augusta, while a more popular one functioned in Savannah.[1] He also established the first local

---

[1] Sherwood's memoir quoted his diary as stating the motion for establishing a Sunday school. The day the Sunday school was established was also recorded: "I reached Athens about 3 o'clock P.M., having lost my hat in crossing the river. July 3D.—I visited several of the brethren at Trail Creek church and spoke to them on the subject of Missions,

temperance society in Georgia at Eatonton in July 1827.[2] This local
society led to the establishment of the Georgia Temperance Society in
1828.

Several areas of inquiry appear in the formation of Sunday schools
and temperance societies that preceded the Great Georgia Revival of
1827. First, these efforts displayed the early interdenominational
cooperation among Baptists, Presbyterians, Congregationalists, and
Methodists that did not interfere with internal denominational growth.
Second, both endeavors signaled Sabbatarian violations that all
denominational leaders recognized. Third, early interdenominational
efforts actually strengthened denominational unity. Adiel Sherwood
transmitted Northern evangelical, interdenominational practices into vital
components of a Southern denominational institution.

SUNDAY SCHOOL FOR GEORGIA BAPTISTS

In October 1818, Adiel Sherwood entered Savannah harbor, willing to
work for God within the Baptist denomination. He stated this purpose in
his journal.

> My lungs were then very weak, and several persons advised
> me to seek a milder climate. Professors Stuart and Porter had

---

staying with Bro. Atkinson. Sabbath, July 4th, 1819.—By request Rev. Dr. Brown
attended with me at Trail Creek church. After hearing the children recite in the Sabbath
School, the constitution of the Missionary Society was read, and some remarks were
made explanatory of its objects" (Sherwood and Boykin, *Memoir*, 131). A Sunday school
reportedly existed in Augusta in connection with the Richmond Academy before 1818.
Yet, it was not a Baptist Sunday school. The Augusta Baptist Church was founded in
1817 and then ceased to meet much of 1818. On 22 May 1819, the church called W. T.
Brantly, recently returned from Beaufort SC. He began preaching to the church fall 1819
and reorganized the entire church on 20 January 1820. See Anna Olive Jones, *History of
the First Baptist Church, Augusta, Georgia 1817–1967* (Columbia SC: R. L. Bryan
Company, 1967) 8–13. Lowell Mason in Savannah, a Presbyterian, spent many years
supervising the Sunday school at First Baptist Church of Savannah. In both cases, these
schools existed as interdenominational efforts. To distinguish Sherwood's pioneering
work from Mason's, Sherwood established a Sunday school for a Baptist church that
existed for a purely Baptist constituency.

[2] Sherwood and Boykin, *Memoir*, 231. This assertion holds the greatest weight of
proof.

been South once or twice, and they urged this course upon me with force. Rev. Dr. Caldwell requested me to visit Waynesboro, Ga., and assist him in an academy, where he had taught the previous winter. Dr. Baldwin gave me letters to Rev. Messrs. Sweat, Wynn and Johnson; Mr. Winchell gave me a letter to Mr. Jesse Mercer; Mr. Jer. Evarts gave me one to Mr. Wm. T. Brantly; and Dr. Morse gave me one to Dr. Kollock. A son of Dr. Morse was my companion on the voyage, and a most intimate friend: he began to teach the academy in Savannah, but, I think, remained only a few months.[3]

If one looked carefully at Sherwood's grantors and receivers of his letters of recommendation, the purpose of each, although not stated, was evident in the names. Thomas Baldwin, founder of the Massachusetts Baptist Missionary Society, recommended Sherwood to those active in the Savannah Missionary Society. In the Georgia Baptist denomination, Jesse Mercer and W. T. Brantly served as the most influential leaders of that time. Dr. Henry Kollock, pastor of First Presbyterian in Savannah, introduced Sherwood to Georgia academy life and missionary opportunities.

Sherwood's cooperation with other denominations actually furthered the Baptist cause when he entered Georgia. The Savannah Missionary Society (a mixture of Congregationalists, Presbyterians, and Baptists) provided missionary-minded Baptists with a means of founding benevolent institutions.[4] This society's purpose centered on the propagation of the gospel at home and later abroad (and should not be confused with the Savannah Baptist Society for Foreign Missions, established in 1813).[5] In this domestic arena, the interdenominational

---

[3] Ibid., 89–90.

[4] Samuel Boykin, *History of the Baptist Denomination in Georgia: With Biographical Compendium and Portrait Gallery of Baptist Ministers and Other Georgia Baptists* (Atlanta: James P. Harrison and Company, 1881) 78–80.

[5] The Baptist society must have disappeared when W. B. Johnson left the Savannah pastorate in 1815. Benjamin Screven served as pastor from 1815 to 1819 and James Sweat from 1819 to 1822. James Sweat served on the Savannah Missionary Society Board of Trustees.

society established institutions of benevolence in order to foster a revival of religion where duties of Christianity had become lax.[6]

Lowell Mason, an instrumental figure in the Savannah Missionary Society, founded the first Sunday school in Georgia. At Savannah, the children of the city met at First Baptist, to be led by a Presbyterian minister.[7] Students of hymnody recognize the name of Lowell Mason. He completed his musical composition of "From Greenland's Icy Mountains" in 1824 in Savannah. He also composed the music for "When I Survey the Wondrous Cross" and "Safely through Another Week" during his stay in Savannah. Yet, his greatest efforts in promoting the causes of the Savannah Missionary Society have been largely forgotten. Mason and Sherwood sailed together in October 1818 to Savannah, as Mason returned from a Northern visit and Sherwood entered Georgia for the first time. They knew each other, and both promoted the organization of Sunday schools and worked for the Savannah Missionary Society.[8]

Sherwood's work did not include Savannah, but his immediate destination of Waynesboro, Georgia. He delivered a sermon before the Baptist congregation in Savannah in early November, making it his first sermon in Georgia. Soon after, he moved to Waynesboro via Augusta. Traveling up the Savannah River from Savannah to Augusta, he rode by horse to his destination. In Augusta, he met the aged minister Abraham Marshall, as both of them preached at the Richmond courthouse. From November 1818 to May 1819, Sherwood served as instructor at the

---

[6] "The Savannah Missionary Society was formed on the first day of January 1818…. It was rendered necessary by the spiritual wants of so many parts of our state, that are destitute of the regular administration of the word and ordinance of the gospel" (Margret Freeman Lafar, "Lowell Mason's Varied Activities in Savannah," *Georgia Historical Quarterly* 28 [1944]: 125–26).

[7] Margret LaFar stated, "In the winter of 1815–16, the Savannah Sabbath School, as often as not referred to as the Sunday School, was formed with Lowell Mason as superintendent. He continued to hold that office until his removal from the city in 1827. This interdenominational Sunday School, open for all those who were interested, was, until 1822, the only Sunday School in the city" ("Lowell Mason's Varied Activities," 116).

[8] Sherwood and Boykin, *Memoir*, 96.

Waynesboro Academy in Burke County.[9] During this time, he functioned as the guest preacher at various Baptist churches but maintained his correspondence with the Savannah society.

His efforts as school instructor to Waynesboro children were not fruitless. In 1818, the Savannah Missionary Society employed several domestic preachers to raise support for missions and establish benevolent societies, such as Sunday schools. Pliny Fisk, the first foreign missionary of the organization, visited Sherwood in February 1819. Traveling through Georgia, Fisk attended meetings and preached, noting after one particular meetng that "a number of Christians seem most earnestly engaged in prayer for a revival of religion."[10] Later serving as the missionary from the society to Jerusalem, Fisk documented the work Sherwood had already begun in Waynesboro. Young people were Sherwood's first concern.

Within a few months, Sherwood established the first Baptist Sunday school at Trail Creek Baptist Church, near Athens, Georgia, on 4 July 1819. Julia Sherwood quoted from her father's diary, documenting the first Baptist Sunday school in Georgia.

> June 26th—I attended a meeting at Trail Creek church. Bro. Isham Goss, the pastor, preached a long sermon. In conference, Bro. Malone, with whom I had passed several days, introduced a motion that something should be done by the church, either by establishing a Missionary Society, or a Tract Society, in order to further the Gospel.... He [Goss] seconded the motion of Bro. Malone, and I made a few remarks on the different subjects discussed and endeavored to explain the nature and importance of Sunday Schools, concluding by the promise to meet the young

---

[9] "In 1801, only six academies had been incorporated in the State. These were in Savannah, Augusta, Sunbury, Louisville, and in Burke and Wilkes counties" (Adiel Sherwood, *A Gazetteer of Georgia* [Macon GA: S. Boykin, 1860] 143).

[10] "Savannah Missionary Society," *Christian Watchman and Baptist Register* (Boston MA), 6 May 1820, 2. Julia Sherwood documented this in her work by quoting Sherwood's February journal entry (Sherwood and Boykin, *Memoir*, 104).

people there on the first Sabbath in July, to establish a Sunday School.[11]

The day that the Sunday school was established was also recorded:

> I reached Athens about 3 o'clock P.M., having lost my hat in crossing the river. July 3D.—I visited several of the brethren at Trail Creek church and spoke to them on the subject of Missions, staying with Bro. Atkinson.
> Sabbath, July 4th, 1819.—By request Rev. Dr. Brown attended with me at Trail Creek church. After hearing the children recite in the Sabbath School, the constitution of the Missionary Society was read, and some remarks were made explanatory of its objects.[12]

Assisting the pastor, Isham Goss, Sherwood may have organized this Sunday school in a similar pattern as the Congregationalists and Presbyterians in Savannah and Augusta, though no information beyond the date has thus far appeared concerning this Sunday school. Most members of this church constituted First Baptist Church of Athens in 1830, dissolving the Trail Creek Church.

Two weeks after Pliny Fisk's report, the *Christian Watchman and Baptist Register* announced the ordination of Adiel Sherwood to the gospel ministry as an evangelist. The Sarepta Baptist Association in Georgia related to the New York newspaper that Sherwood was approved by the Board of Missions to the Georgia Association to be "set...apart to the great work of an Evangelist."[13] Apparently, the ordination consisted of appointing Sherwood as a traveling preacher—functioning as an ordained minister without a congregational charge. The Bethlehem church served as the body that commissioned Sherwood to preach throughout Georgia. During the next twelve months,

---

[11] Sherwood and Boykin, *Memoir*, 130.

[12] Ibid., 131.

[13] *Christian Watchman and Baptist Register,* 20 May 1820, 2.

Sherwood traveled the newly settled regions of Georgia that lay between the Ocmulgee and Oconee rivers, specifically Wilkinson, Laurens, Twiggs, and the adjoining counties.[14] By May 1821, Sherwood resigned his post as an agent of the Savannah Missionary Society.[15] Within this year, Sherwood married Anne Adams Early, the recent widow of the late Governor Peter Early, while taking charge of the Hermon Academy in Oglethorpe County and serving as pastor of Freeman's Creek Church in Clarke County. Sherwood would continue to live on the Peter Early estate for five years. In 1822, his wife died shortly after childbirth and was buried in the Greensboro cemetery with the infant. In 1824, he married Emma Heriot of Charleston, South Carolina, and they both lived on the Early estate near Scull Shoals until their move to Eatonton in 1827.

THE EDUCATION OF CHILDREN

In October 1820, Sherwood delivered a sermon (later to be printed as a circular) to the Sarepta Baptist Association. Within this discourse, he set forth his beliefs about Sunday school education. First, he stated that education is important. "The youthful mind is continually on the stretch for knowledge. Our Children, even in their earliest years, will learn something. If lessons of valuable instruction are not presented to them, they will learn that which will taint their minds and corrupt their actions."[16] Second, he noted the mixture of apathy and resistance of his listeners to the education of children. Sherwood asserted, "But some have said, 'we will not attempt to control the opinions of our children, but leave them to adopt such as they choose.' This sentiment never had seat in the heart of a Christian parent."[17]

Sherwood introduced the importance of education not from a literal, biblical standpoint, but from an argument of moral sentiment. He observed that Christian education changed individuals.

---

[14] Sherwood and Boykin, *Memoir*, 183–84.

[15] Ibid., 200.

[16] "Circular," *Minutes of the Sarepta Association* (Augusta: William J. Bunce, 1821) 7.

[17] Ibid., 8.

> Our Children have passions which must be subjugated,
> desires which must be moderated in their early years. The lash
> will not do this.... In a Christian education, we teach them to
> regard the consequences of their actions and that all of these
> must be referred to the day of judgment; that though a present
> gratification is grateful to the natural feelings; yet these must be
> moderated and kept within the bounds which the scriptures
> prescribe.[18]

Christian education also has revolutionized communities. Sherwood
saw Sunday schools as transformers of community morality.

> Contrast in your minds the appearance of two
> neighbourhoods, in one of which the children have shared a
> Christian education; in the other they have not. In the former, as
> a general thing, you find them submissive to authority, dutiful to
> parents, respectful to old age, affectionate. Here family altars are
> erected, and on them morning and evening is offered the incense
> of prayer. In the latter you find them ungovernable, undutiful to
> parents, disrespectful of old age, saucy, Sabbath-breakers,
> profane.[19]

Not only is education important, but the Christian also has a duty to teach
children. From the Old Testament, Sherwood recognized the importance
of the Hebraic law as binding Old Testament believers to the training of
their children. He stated, "God commands it. 'And thou shalt teach them
(the commandments) diligently unto thy children, and shall talk of them
when thou sittest in thy house and when thou walkest by the way and
when thou liest down and when thou risest up.' (Deut. 6:7) Is the
Decalogue binding upon you? So is this verse."[20] A view of complete
human depravity taught in the New Testament drives home the

---

[18] Ibid.
[19] Ibid., 9.
[20] Ibid., 10.

importance of making the child aware of his or her sin. Sherwood stated, "We have been the means of their natural existence; we have brought them into the world sinners, in a state of spiritual death, enemies to God, 'children of wrath.'...We can not, to be sure, make them innocent, but since we have communicated depravity to them, we can use our exertions to weaken this depravity by imbruing their minds with Christian sentiments and make them moral."[21]

Sherwood concluded his subject with the classical method of answering the prominent objections of his opponents. Many object to Sunday school in that it cannot convert children. Only God can do this task. Sherwood answered, "God is the author of this and He is pleased to use the insignificant means of Christian education to convert them."[22] Yet, the second objection carried more weight in theoretical and practical applications: "The teaching of our children to repeat the Scriptures before they are enlightened from above to understand their spiritual meaning will make them speculative Christians." However, Sherwood noticed the improbable nature of this argument. "It virtually charges God with inconsistency. He commands to educate them, but we, as if wiser than God, apprehend evil from it! His commands, rather than our notions of the probable moral good or evil to be effected are our guide."[23]

Regardless of theoretical objections from opponents, the moral and biblical arguments pointed to the practicality of Christian education. Churches meeting once a month break the Sabbath three times a month. They do not see the importance of or the duty behind studying the Bible. Sherwood concluded his argument by insisting that the gospel claims, "It is lawful to do good on the Sabbath Day." If this is so, "then take them [children] to the house of God with you and you will lessen one of the crying sins of the land, Sabbath breaking. They may be taught also in Sabbath Schools, an institution which has been blessed of God to the salvation of many souls, both of children and parents."[24]

---

[21] Ibid.
[22] Ibid., 11.
[23] Ibid.
[24] Ibid.

Nathan Beman and the Missionary

Adiel Sherwood's dislike of Sabbatarian violations fueled his promotion of Sunday schools. His thoughts on Sabbatarian strictness and Sunday schools resurfaced in 1821 and 1822 in a small newspaper in Hancock County, Georgia. During these years, he submitted his reactions to frontier irreligion, pushing for Sunday schools and the attendance to Christian duties through the *Missionary* newspaper. Edited by Nathan Beman, a New England native recently residing in Georgia, this periodical became the vehicle for transmitting New England values in Georgia.

Nathan S. S. Beman moved to Georgia on two occasions to combat consumption. Graduating from Middlebury College and serving as pastor of Third Presbyterian in Portland, Maine, Beman attempted to escape his native Northern climate in 1811 and in 1812. When he arrived in Georgia for the second time, he assumed the pastorate of the Madison Presbyterian Church (Cumberland Presbytery) in Madison, Georgia. Beman left this position in 1813 to serve as a pastor and to teach at Mt. Zion Academy in Hancock County. By 1819, Beman, along with Isaac M. Wales and Benjamin Gildersleeve (Beman's academy student), formed a partnership among themselves, appointing Gildersleeve as the editor of their new enterprise, the *Missionary*. On 30 May 1821, a new partnership between Beman and Jacob P. Norton and Ebenezer Cooper, known as the N. S. S. Beman Company, came into existence, making Beman the editor of the newspaper. For exactly a year, Beman posted his editorial comments every week. By spring 1823, Beman left Mt. Zion to assume the pastorate of First Presbyterian Church in Troy, New York.

Owen Peterson, the prime authority on Beman, claimed that the *Missionary* represented an early Beman who did not concern himself with slavery as an institution but who emphasized the establishment of Sabbatarian laws and practices. Peterson stated:

> One of the causes for which Beman labored most vigorously was the suppression of violation of the Sabbath. For one accustomed to the unremitting Calvinistic piety of New England day of worship, he found Sunday in Georgia a disquieting experience. Believing that Sunday had been set aside

exclusively for worship, Beman rebelled against the Georgian's treatment of the Sabbath as a day for social intercourse.[25]

During Beman's editorship, Adiel Sherwood submitted several articles that occupied the first page with each printing. Reminiscent of the 1820s forty years later, Sherwood identified himself as the writer under the pseudonym, Richard Orderly. As Orderly, Sherwood wrote critiques of Georgia's people and institutions. Instead of merely criticizing, he intended to use sarcasm as a method for inciting reflection and change.

Sherwood wrote at least six major pieces under this name within a year. At least three can be isolated as articles setting forth purposes for establishing Sunday schools. One scrutinized the backward nature of the local minister. Another utilized the visit of a European guest as a point of comparison to Georgia natives. Finally, the deplorable condition of the country schools and their schoolmasters received a scathing analysis from Richard Orderly.

On 31 December 1821, Richard noticed the nonaggressive spirit of his minister in an article titled "My Minister." When members of the church directed any question concerning the formation of societies for missionary or educational work toward the pastor, he "invariably repeats the fable of the cat and rat—'It may be meal,'etc."[26] To Richard Orderly, the spirit of inertia and suspicion of new methods possessed his minister. He noted:

> One of our members had been down to Augusta, and attended the Sabbath School there, and the monthly concert for prayer. He had the proficiency in Scriptural knowledge made by the pupils in the former, and had caught a little of the fervor of spirit exhibited in the latter, and on his return made bold to

---

[25] Owen Peterson, "Nathan S. S. Beman at Mt. Zion," *Georgia Historical Quarterly* 49 (1965): 163. Peterson wrote the biography of Beman two decades after publishing this article. See *A Divine Discontent: The Life of Nathan S. S. Beman* (Macon GA: Mercer University Press, 1986).

[26] Richard Orderly, "My Minister," *Missionary* (Hancock County GA), 31 December 1821, 1.

mention it—the old gentleman exclaimed, "What shall we come to when such a passion for new things gets hold of the people—our children will become head-christians, and religion will be unknown among us." He so far possesses the affections and confidence of the church that not a member will knowingly offend him. Should any one propose an innovation, though it be ever so small, he would be denounced as heterodox, and expelled from the church.[27]

This reference pointed to new resistance in Baptist life over the matter of Sunday schools. Confronted with circular arguments that sustained inaction, Richard merely denounced his minister's ideas.

On 4 February 1822, Richard wrote an article titled "My Guest." Entertaining a guest from Inverness, Scotland (home not of the "most eloquent divines," but of "many evangelical, orthodox and profound divines"), Richard took him to visit a church officer at his home. Speaking of this experience, Richard Orderly saw disorder and biblical illiteracy as the awful condition of parishioners:

> Whether it was because we were present, that prayers were made, I cannot say; but from the disorder of the children, and their gazing when the Bible was read, and their quarreling to see who should be nearest the fire, one might suppose, they were not used to such things. His Bible too, dear me! Was found after a long search in a dark closet, and it was so disfigured by the dirt and pictures made by some mischievous children, that it was scarcely legible.[28]

Although not speaking of Sunday schools, the author communicated the picture of a household where the Bible was a strange object. The lack of biblical instruction was evident with children who were not taught to be orderly and reverent.

---

[27] Ibid.

[28] Richard Orderly, "My Guest," *Missionary*, 4 February 1822, 1.

On 8 July 1822, Richard heightened his attack on disorder by centering his critique on field schools and schoolmasters in "My Schoolmaster." Typical of any desire for respectability, the term *field school* could be equated with *academy* in some places in Georgia. The academies in Savannah and Augusta were places of classical learning with high demands.[29] Yet, deeper in the Georgia interior, the term *academy* would often be applied to a regular country or field school. These institutions were local schoolhouses with a local population of students. The term *academy* in this case only elevated the concept of the school, while devoid of any practical application.

Perhaps Richard Orderly wrote the article as an autobiographical, reflective essay concerning his opinions of schools and fellow instructors. He depicted the horrible actions of a student custom:

> It will be necessary to apprize you low-country folks, that from time immemorial, a custom has obtained with the children in schools here, to assemble early at the school house on the commencement of Christmas holy-days, and prevent the master from entering until he shall have promised to give them so many play days, and to treat them to so much whiskey! This is called "barring out."—However, if this does not succeed to bring him to terms, they have their strips of bark ready, and they catch and tie him until the promise is made, and means for the whiskey produced.[30]

In this case of Georgia life, Richard equated the actions of intemperance with the lack of religion. He asserted, "We have tried, by the establishment of a Sabbath school, to counteract its influence, to stop its progress;—but like the waters of our widest and deepest rivers, it

---

[29] Some sources used the term *academy* sparingly. The *Christian Index* only lists Savannah and Richmond (Augusta) Academies by this name in 1833. Other *academies* within the Georgia interior were embracing the manual labor system on farms of vast acreage. See "Georgia," *Christian Index*, 18 May 1833, 307.

[30] Richard Orderly, "My Schoolmaster," *Missionary*, 8 July 1822, 1.

bursts away every barrier." Neither churches nor parents were active in instructing their children in godly discipline.[31]

One likely reason for the inadequacy of Sabbath instruction might have been the inattentive efforts of parents both with Sabbath instruction and in holding their children's schoolmasters to a Christian level of morality. In fact, most schoolmasters in the field schools did much to destroy many efforts of the church to educate children in Christian values. They spent weekends "at the grog-shop," drinking and inviting their students to join them. Richard commented on the irony that students followed such corruptive role models, and he accused their parents of not protecting them.[32]

In all three articles, Richard Orderly connected the acts and incidents of irreligion to the lack of those responsible for the education of children in attending to their duty. The minister downplayed modern inventions and subsequently did nothing for his congregation's well-being. The homes of church members were without biblical instruction and reverent practices. Likewise, the schools that children attended did not possess moral teachers but instructors who spoke and acted against religion. With these criticisms, Richard Orderly left the remedy open. The progress of Georgia Sunday schools developed within a decade after their introduction.

A THEOLOGY FOR SUNDAY SCHOOL

Adiel Sherwood's promotion of Sunday school continued during the era of the Great Georgia Revival of 1827. The period of 1827 to 1829

---

[31] In 1860, Sherwood reminisced in a more jovial and less urgent manner than in 1822. He recalled, "The pupils, instead of the teachers, governed part of the time. If they desired a holiday and it was not granted, the doors of the house were barred, and windows fastened so the teacher could not enter till he promised. Sometimes they demanded a treat, and if he would not 'fork over' they rolled him over or took him to the nearest water and ducked him! Then came holiday or the treat, when all would march to the dram-shop, till the boys were satisfied. The teachers, too, that is, many, made it a practice to drink from Friday night till Monday morning, and occasionally take the bottle to the school in order to cool off!" (Adiel Sherwood, "Reminiscences of Georgia: Number 16: Old Field Schools," *Christian Index*, 28 November 1860, 2).

[32] Orderly, "My Schoolmaster," 1.

marked the height of the revival. Involved with the increase in baptisms were the rise of Sunday schools as a means for calling Baptists to their churches on the Christian Sabbath. According to Sherwood's thought, the Sunday school involved the concerted efforts of parents and teachers in educating children of their lost condition and the remedy of salvation. This summarized the theology of Sunday school.

Sherwood printed an account of a child's conversion during this time, illustrating the need for parents to be concerned with the spiritual education of their child's soul. Set within the Georgia revival movement, this story, originally printed in the *Baptist Tract Magazine*, was also printed in the *Christian Index*, serving as a tool for furthering revival awareness. In an article titled "Little Jane Bussey," Sherwood related his encounter with a child.

Stopping at Mr. Bussey's house during a lengthy journey, Sherwood delivered an informal sermon to the family before he slept for the night. Becoming a regular friend of the family, he returned on two other occasions: "In the December succeeding I called at Mr. B's for dinner and while it was in preparation, I found an opportunity for conversing with one of his older daughters on the subject of religion, and saw during our conversation a little girl listening with intense interest, and then suddenly retire, as I afterwards learned, lest I should converse with her."[33] In January 1828 (a month later), Sherwood stopped to preach at the Bussey house again and heard of a startling testimony from the grieving father, unaware of the demise of little Jane Bussey:

> I made a short exhortation, and while several were gathering around me for prayers, the old gentleman, being deeply affected, arose and detained us a minute with the following narration: "I have just buried my little daughter, and she has left the following message for you: 'Tell Mr. S. that I hope to meet him in heaven. His preaching here in October called up my mind to religious subjects, and I have found Jesus precious to my soul.' She went

[33] Ibid.

out of the world," continued her father, "in the strong hope of a blessed immortality."[34]

    Using this illustration, Sherwood concluded with two prominent points concerning Christian education of children. First, he hoped the illustration would encourage ministers to be constant workers in their field, inside and outside the church building. Second, he stressed the importance of parents to attend to the conversion of their children's souls. He stated, "Many a child has been under the convicting influence of the Holy Spirit, without being conscious what it was which gave them uneasiness; whereas, if the parents had frequently called up the subject of salvation, wholesome instruction might have been communicated, and the child would have unbosomed all its sorrows in answer to your affectionate inquiries."[35] In summary, Sherwood saw the lack of interest of ministers and parents in the education of their children in regard to spiritual matters as the root of the problem of irreligion.

    In another article several years later, Sherwood equated the institution of Sunday school with preaching, an explicit means of the gospel that most Baptist churches recognized.[36] The two means only differed in their mode of presentation. Sunday schools existed to transmit the gospel to children, who cannot understand adult discourse. He stated, "Many children, it is true, enjoy the privilege of attending public worship, but it is evident that few have minds sufficiently capacious, to be benefited much by the exercises which they there witness."[37]

    For Sherwood, Sunday schools were the epitome of religious liberty and religious sanctity. He claimed that the reading component and the moral application of Sunday schools made children better American

---

  [34] Ibid., 206–207. Sherwood completed the narrative: "The subject of the foregoing account was 14 years of age, though one would have supposed her to be not more than ten from her size. She died in Putnam County, Ga. January 4, 1828" (208).

  [35] Ibid., 209.

  [36] "One of the means, which he [God] is employing at the present day, to enlighten the world, is the preaching of the gospel; he therefore, who is contributing, in any manner, to its dissemination, is engaged in his service" (A. S.[Adiel Sherwood], "The Sunday School Institution," *Christian Index*, 6 May 1834, 71).

  [37] Ibid.

citizens. Sunday schools prepared the heart for revival. He admitted, "Almost all the revivals of religion, that have taken place at the north within a few years past, have owed their origin to the instrumentality of Sunday Schools."[38] They also strengthened the view of a strict Sabbath. Children and adults attended the assembly of God on the Christian Sabbath and subsequently were absent from ungodly locations on the Sabbath.

Sherwood made this final application under the pseudonym Melanchthon—the quiet reformer of the church. He posited the following propositions against monthly meetings and for weekly services:

> 1. Our monthly meetings have no scripture to sustain the practice. The primitive practice was a weekly meeting; but ours is monthly, and therefore is only one fourth right.
>
> 2. They produce indolence in religious matters. The answer, that they can attend meetings elsewhere, three or four hours being not more than 10 miles distant does not obviate the difficulty; for though they can, few only do it, and many who do, seem to go rather as a matter of recreation, to greet friends, etc., than to worship God.
>
> 3. It engenders a disregard for the Sabbath. While the family is allowed to lounge about 3 Sabbaths in each month, they will inevitably contract habits of indolence, and will, at home, trench upon the sacredness of the Sabbath, by labour and amusements.
>
> 4. Its tendency is to make us undervalue our souls.
>
> 5. We have no promise of God that his presence will be with us.[39]

Melanchthon saw the prominent objection to weekly meetings being the lack of obtaining preachers. Supposedly, Southern churches could not obtain a preacher every Sunday, so they would not meet. The continual assembly of the people to have Sunday school remedied this practice. "That is no excuse," claimed Melanchthon. "Preaching is not

---

[38] Ibid.

[39] Melanchthon, "Sabbath Monthly Meetings," *Christian Index*, 23 June 1835, 3.

indispensable to the worship of God. We should feel the duty to assemble in God's house, preacher or not. Let us meet, read our bibles, instruct our children and servants, and thus by example point the way which leads to heaven."[40]

The utility and theology of Sunday schools solved the problem of Sabbatarian violations. The formation and progress of Sunday schools in the early decades of Georgia Baptist life annulled the effects of godlessness on the Georgia frontier. Conversely, it provided young people with a location other than the drinking houses (or the dram shops, as they were called). In a positive manner, Sunday schools inculcated the gospel into young minds and strengthened Sabbatarian belief. The establishment of Sunday schools preceded the Georgia revival but strengthened it. They served as positive innovations toward increasing religious conviction.

THE EARLY TEMPERANCE MOVEMENT IN GEORGIA

Adiel Sherwood often associated Sabbath day violations with the spirit of intemperance. From his perspective, those absent from God's house usually frequented the public drinking houses. Sherwood saw the excessive drinking behavior of Georgians as godless and uncultured. Therefore, he countered this behavior by forming the first temperance society in Georgia and began to write against all forms of alcoholic consumption.[41] With his efforts toward temperance, Georgia Baptists became aware of the terrible effects of strong drink and formed societies to combat it religiously within their denomination and legally within their communities.[42]

---

[40] Ibid.

[41] Sherwood did not address the issue of fermented wine used during communion in his writings.

[42] Studies in the antebellum temperance movement in the South have been lacking. Secular historians who study this topic with an interest in the rise of abolitionism can miss the point of Southern denominationalism in this movement. The North moved toward combining the issues of the abolition of slavery with temperance, thereby making temperance more of a political problem than a social and religious one. The South inevitably retreated from temperance during the latter antebellum era, as it became a

Georgia residents recognized their propensity to consume alcohol. Intemperance served as an object of a joke but rarely as a cause of alarm. The use of alcoholic beverages did not become a subject for printed sermons. Moderation, according to the later advocates of abstinence, was rarely advocated. One writer growing up in Georgia before the early temperance movement described his own family and pastor in the following manner:

> My parents were from "Old Virginia," and of the Baptist persuasion. My father was—what was called—"an old peach brandy Baptist;" by which I mean, he made peach brandy, kept it on his side-board, took a drink before breakfast and dinner, and asked every one who came to his house to do the same, particularly the preachers, who drank, and as they drank; became more happy and fervently religious. In my Simplicity I did not then know what was the matter, but I have long since learned better. I don't care if the sprit, which increased their religious demonstrations, did come out of my father's decanter, they were, nevertheless, good men and Christians.[43]

Before 1827, a general distinction existed between moderation and abuse, but no literature in periodicals attacked the general use of alcohol. Temperance societies within a short period developed into abstinence societies. However, from the earliest records, alcohol for medicinal purposes continued to be a part of temperance constitutions.[44]

H. A. Scomp provided the greatest resource in analyzing Sherwood's impact on the antebellum temperance movement in

---

secular or interdenominational movement. After the Civil War, the issue of temperance remained alive in the yearly temperance reports of Baptist associations.

[43] Garnett Andrews, *Reminiscences of an Old Georgia Lawyer* (Atlanta: Cherokee Publishing Company, 1984) 9.

[44] Since temperance societies centered on one issue and did not necessarily require a faith-oriented membership, the use of alcohol in the Lord's Supper did not become an issue.

Georgia.[45] In *King Alcohol in the Realm of King Cotton*, Scomp pointed to three sources that justified his opinion that Sherwood established the first temperance society in Georgia. Resting his decision on J. H. Campbell's *Georgia Baptists* (1874), Boykin's *History of the Baptist Denomination in Georgia*, and Julia Sherwood's *Memoir of Adiel Sherwood, D.D.*,[46] Scomp saw Sherwood as the originator of this movement. The central point of reference came from Sherwood's journal in his memoir, where he stated:

> During the meeting at Eatonton, we formed a small "Temperance Society," composed, I think, of Thomas Cooper, J. Clark, A. Richardson, myself, and perhaps three more. In the succeeding April of 1828, at the meeting of the State Convention at Monticello, I requested Abner Clopton, then agent of the Columbian College, who was in Georgia, to write a constitution, and on Tuesday we organized the "Georgia State Temperance Society," Gen. Shorter, president; E. Shackleford, secretary; A. Sherwood, treasurer. After this I was the secretary of the society, and continued so until I left the State for Washington City—a period of five or six years.[47]

---

[45] H. A. Scomp, *King Alcohol in the Realm of King Cotton* (Blakely GA: Blakely Printing Company, 1888). A more recent work cited Scomp but only made a passing reference to this era. See Mrs. J. J. Ansley, *History of the Georgia Woman's Christian Temperance Union from its Organization, 1883 to 1907* (Columbus GA: Gilbert Printing Company, 1914) 26.

[46] Jesse H. Campbell stated, "The first society was organized in Eatonton in July, 1827." See *Georgia Baptists: Historical and Biographical* (Macon GA: J.W. Burke and Company, 1874) 18. See also Sherwood and Boykin, *Memoir*, 231–32; and Boykin, *History of the Baptist Denomination,* 178–79. Mrs. J. J. Ansley stated, "Although the Baptist Church at that time contained no law against the members using alcohol as a beverage, it was the first church in Georgia to organize a society to create temperance sentiment. At Eatonton, Georgia, in July, 1827, Dr. Adiel Sherwood, of the Eatonton Baptist Church and Dr. J. H. Campbell, of Columbus, Georgia, (Baptist Church), organized the first temperance society in the State. Rev. Abner W. Clopton, of Virginia, a Baptist minister of remarkable power, drafted the Constitution…one year later, April, 1828, at Monticello, Georgia, the organization of the State Temperance Society was accomplished" (*History,* 26–27).

[47] Sherwood and Boykin, *Memoir*, 231. Sherwood assumed the pastorate at Eatonton in 1827, leaving it in 1836. In 1860, he returned to this pastorate for two years.

Scomp reinforced Sherwood's impact on the Georgia temperance movement by placing it within a larger context. In its first annual meeting on 14 November 1827, the American Temperance Society, organized in Boston on 10 January 1826, listed all other societies allied with its cause. Noticeably, Georgia is absent from the 1827 roll. In a sense, this could point to an independent existence of the Georgia society from the American Temperance Society, placing more emphasis upon Sherwood's involvement as a lone influence upon the Georgia society.[48]

Sherwood undoubtedly knew of the current movements coming from Boston, his prior residence.[49] All of the New Divinity men (those who adapted Jonathan Edwards's evangelical Calvinism to reconcile moral responsibility with divine sovereignty) gravitated toward moral reform. Timothy Dwight and Moses Stuart taught students to seek revivals and moral reform. The generation that followed these men gravitated toward the temperance movement and subsequently the abolition movement.

The difference between Sherwood's pioneering work and the New England clergy would be the lack of any apparent connection between Georgia and the national movement. Sherwood did not ally the Georgia organization with the national one because it was a local concern. This omission of Georgia from the national temperance roll confirms the idea of interdenominational work in Georgia not being initiated by a Northern platform.

---

[48] Scomp, *King Alcohol,* 234–36.

[49] "Though the pattern of southern temperance would soon diverge sharply from that in the North, the South's early participation in temperance reform closely paralleled the northern in timing and inspiration. In October 1826, just a few months after the organization of the American Temperance society in Boston, the Virginia Society for the Promotion of Temperance was established. By 1831 the temperance movement in the South had strong support in Virginia and Georgia, and there were societies in every state except Louisiana. As in the North, temperance sentiment developed most strongly among the adherents of evangelical religion. Methodists and Baptists, especially, carried the brunt of the early missionary work in the southern states. In both Virginia and Georgia the state temperance societies actually grew out of the active concerns of members of the states' Baptist conventions" (Ian R. Tyrrell, "Drink and Temperance in the Antebellum South: An Overview and Interpretation," *Journal of Southern History* 48 [November 1982]: 486).

The early temperance movement in Georgia also stressed the role of the Baptists as the earliest reformers rather than the typical acclamation given to Congregationalists or Presbyterians as initiates of reform. Scomp realized the difference between the Georgia temperance movement and other state historical developments. He asserted, "Beyond all question, the Baptists are entitled to the chief honor in the introduction of temperance societies into Georgia. For several years they were the chief supporters of those institutions."[50]

ABNER CLOPTON'S INVOLVEMENT WITH SHERWOOD

After Sherwood formed a local temperance society in Eatonton in July 1827, he requested the assistance of Abner Clopton of Virginia, agent for Columbian College, to compose the constitution for the Georgia Temperance Society in April 1828. Before the writing of the constitution, Clopton left a record of his opinion of the temperance movement in progress in Eatonton where Sherwood served as pastor. Writing to Elder De Witt on 16 January 1828, Clopton stated:

> I have hardly any room to inform you, that in Eatonton, where the brethren have done so much for the college, almost every member of the church is a member of the temperance society; and brother H—[Hubbard] and myself never saw there, during a stay of three days, one drop of spirits; and though it was court-day, we saw not a solitary instance of intemperance. I hate to make invidious comparisons, lest I should offend those nice feeling brethren who cannot join among us.[51]

Dying before the temperance movement fully achieved its goals, Abner Clopton left an impact on the Georgia temperance movement as he did for the same in Virginia.[52] Professor Shelton Palmer Sanford of

---

[50] Scomp, *King Alcohol*, 236.

[51] Jeremiah B. Jeter, *A Memoir of Abner W. Clopton, A.M.* (Richmond: Yale and Wyatt, 1837) 199.

[52] Scomp included a quotation from Clopton's nephew, Judge A. W. C. Nowlin of Richmond who delivered an address titled "The Origin and Originator of the Temperance

Mercer University wrote a letter to H. A. Scomp concerning the impact of Clopton on Georgia Baptists.[53] He related his recollections as a young boy when Clopton entered Georgia:

> His first appearance in Georgia was at Bethesda church in "Old Greene." He preached one Saturday, but said nothing about temperance in his sermon. After service he was invited home, by one of the prominent deacons of the church. Arriving at home, the good deacon was horrified to find the decanters all empty, and he lost no time in apologizing for the oversight. "Bro. Clopton," he said, "you must really excuse me—I have not a drop of whiskey in the house—it is the first time I have been out in twenty years, but I have just sent a boy on horseback after some, and it won't be over a half hour before he gets back." Mr. Clopton, with his ready tact and good sense embraced the occasion so opportunely offered, and "preached unto him" temperance.
>
> Clopton then began his temperance mission in earnest, and although only a mere lad, I remember what a flutter he created in the community about Greensboro; and particularly among church members. He was regarded as utterly heterodox, and I remember a good old lady, who, after listening to one of his sermons on temperance, remarked, "What a pity that so good a

---

Movement in Virginia and the Southern States." Clopton's conversion to total abstinence consisted of a small shock in affections. Nowlin asserted, "While sitting one day at dinner, he was informed that a female of respectable connections with whom he had been well acquainted, and for whom he entertained high esteem, had been carried home in a state of beastly intoxication. He was astounded. Dropping his knife and fork, he resolved instantly and solemnly, to use ardent spirits no more.... Desirous of extending the benefits of this resolution, Mr. Clopton formulated the plan of a temperance society" (Scomp, *King Alcohol,* 238).

[53] Beginning in 1842, S. P. Sanford served as professor of mathematics and astronomy at Mercer University in Penfield. He taught for more than forty years and served as Sunday school superintendent and deacon of the Penfield church. His father, Vincent Sanford (born in 1777), migrated from Virginia to Greensboro GA in 1810. Vincent Sanford served as a founding member of the Greensboro church in 1821.

man and so excellent a preacher as Mr. Clopton, should destroy
his influence, by talking so much about temperance."

Clopton started a Total Abstinence Society in Greensboro,
and although small in numbers, yet that society served as a
rallying point for many years, and was productive of much good.
My father was among the original panel.[54]

Scomp claimed that Clopton did not follow the example of Northern
evangelicalism.[55] This assertion would ally Sherwood, not with Northern
trends, but with a Southern trend toward reformation. If this was true, it
would be probable that the temperance movement in the South followed
more along a denominational trend rather than an interdenominational
trend between Baptists and Congregationalists. Either perspective cannot
be sustained beyond statements such as Scomp presented. In regard to
the question of origin and influence, the lack of any other documentation
would point to Sherwood's connection with Clopton and their interaction
being an interest within their denomination.

Sherwood certainly gave Clopton most of the credit for organizing
temperance societies. Whether or not the idea originated from the North,
Clopton delivered the foundations for procedure. Sherwood recognized
Clopton as one of the exciting leaders involved in the Great Georgia
Revival.

---

[54] Scomp, *King Alcohol*, 237.

[55] Within the Nowlin source, Scomp separated Clopton from Northern trends. He
quoted Nowlin as saying, "Mr. Clopton had never then heard of the existence of any
similar organization, and to him belongs the undisputed honor of having originated the
plan and formed the first Temperance Society ever formed in Virginia or the South. I
have ascertained by my investigations into this subject, that a similar society was formed
in the State of New York in 1808, but its very existence was hardly known outside of a
few counties in that State, and it is quite certain it had never been heard of in this section
of the Union. This does not in the least detract from the credit and distinction due to Mr.
Clopton for the more extensive and successful movement originated by him in 1826. And
I will also mention the fact just here, that the American Temperance Society was
originated in Boston, Mass., in the same year, but its founders and that of the Virginia
Temperance Society were entirely ignorant of each other's acts" (ibid., 238–39).

Few strangers ever excited more attention, and a deeper interest, than did Abner W. Clopton, in his visits to Georgia. He came among us, as the agent of the Columbian College, in the winter of 1828, during a powerful revival of religion. With all the warmth of a zealous minister of the cross, whose soul was wrought up to the highest pitch, he entered into the work, and evidenced an interest so intense for the salvation of sinners, that it may be safely asserted, he preached "not in the words which man's wisdom teacheth; but which the Holy Ghost teacheth."[56]

Also, Sherwood saw the influence of Clopton in the temperance cause in Georgia, applauding him for sketching the constitution of the temperance society. Sherwood noted that many people "were induced to put away the poison" of alcoholic drinks after hearing Clopton.[57]

Regrettably, the original constitution of the Georgia State Temperance Society cannot be located.[58] Yet, the local societies that followed the founding of the state organization modeled their constitutions after the larger one. By looking at the local constitutions, one can see the larger picture of the state organization.

The Jasper County Temperance Society with Cyrus White serving as secretary appeared in the *Columbian Star* as one of the first local societies in Georgia. From this printed constitution, several articles can highlight the organization's position on the consumption of alcohol. The first three articles illustrate the typical platform of early societies.

---

[56] Jeter quoted Sherwood's opinion in *Memoir of Abner W. Clopton, A.M.*, 215.

[57] Ibid., 216–17.

[58] Scomp interjected, "The Virginia State Society preceded that of Georgia by about a year and a half, though the formation of local societies in Georgia was begun in advance of the State Society. It is most likely that the two State constitutions were identical, or at least, not essentially different. The author has searched, or has had searched, every nook in Georgia, where there seemed to be any probability of finding a copy of the Georgia Temperance Constitution, but he has thus far failed to find it" (Scomp, *King Alcohol,* 240–41).

Article 1st. This Society shall be known by the name of the Jasper County Temperance Society, auxiliary to the Georgia Temperance Society.

Article 2nd. The members of this Society believing that the habitual use of ardent spirits, is destructive to the constitution, reputation, and property, do agree that we will abstain from their use entirely, except as a medicine, in bodily infirmity, and that we will not provide spirits for our friends, nor for persons in our employ.

Article 3rd. From and after the first Monday in January next, we will not vote for any candidate for an office, who shall be known to treat with ardent spirits, with a view to gain his election.[59]

Representative of the earliest societies, the original platform held to a total abstinence from strong drink with the exception of using the substance as a medicine. Later, the exception of alcohol as a medicine would be dropped in order to be consistent.

THE GEORGIA STATE TEMPERANCE SOCIETY

The Georgia State Temperance Society founded in 1828 with Clopton as the author of the constitution and Sherwood as the promoter of the temperance cause began to meet on a yearly basis, always at Milledgeville, Georgia's last antebellum capital. Although a few local societies preceded the state organization, the Georgia State Temperance Society fostered the foundation of additional local societies.

Adiel Sherwood served as secretary of the state society. In 1831, he published a list of questions for the local societies to answer and return to the state organization. These statements illustrated the aggressive nature of the temperance movement.

1. How many members in the county?

---

[59] "Jasper County Temperance Society," *Columbian Star* (Philadelphia), 26 December 1829, 405.

2. How many gallons of Spirits are sold from 1st of January, 1830, to 1st January 1831? And how will that quantity compare with the quantity sold, say, in 1825 or 26?

3. How many drunkards have been radically reformed since the formation of the State society in May 1828?

4. How many families have ceased the use of ardent spirits, except as a medicine?

5. How much more money has your county expended for ardent spirits, than for science and religion, including preaching the gospel, the education of your children, and all the benevolent operations of the age?

6. How much more does it pay for spirits than for taxes?[60]

An additional leader of the temperance movement in Georgia lent much of his support to Sherwood. Augustus Baldwin Longstreet, known later for the *Georgia Scenes*, a sketch of Georgia frontier tales in the 1830s, experienced conversion during the Great Georgia Revival of 1827.[61] Wishing to follow the command of believer's baptism by immersion, he asked Sherwood to baptize him. Sherwood declined—knowing that Longstreet wanted to remain in the Methodist Church and pointing to the Baptist belief of denominational separation from Pedobaptist practices.[62] If Longstreet wanted to be a member of the Methodist Church, a Baptist would not baptize him. Later, Longstreet found a Methodist pastor to baptize him, but this incident did not harm his long friendship with Sherwood. As a Methodist and a lawyer, Longstreet helped organize efforts for temperance in the state. By 1832, the Georgia State Temperance Society reorganized under a new constitution with Longstreet as president and Sherwood as secretary.[63]

The 1830s constitute the height of activity of the Georgia State Temperance Society. In fact, this society ceased to function when Sherwood left in 1836 to teach and raise money for Columbian College

---

[60] "Georgia Temperance Society," *Christian Index*, 19 March 1831, 192.

[61] See John Donald Wade, *Augustus Baldwin Longstreet: A Study of the Development of Culture in the South* (New York: Macmillan Company, 1924) 110–11.

[62] Sherwood and Boykin, *Memoir*, 231.

[63] "Georgia Temperance Society," *Christian Index*, 19 January 1833, 41.

in Washington, DC. The rise of temperance societies during the Georgia revival of 1827 culminated in a state organization, motivated by theological concerns, practical moral applications, and political expectations. During the decade of the 1830s, Sherwood's thoughts and convictions on the temperance issue reflected the state temperance society's position on the consumption of alcohol. His views on this subject agreed with the same position as other Georgia Baptist leaders such as W. T. Brantly, Jesse Mercer, and C. D. Mallary.

THEOLOGICAL DEBATE OVER TEMPERANCE IN GEORGIA

The rise of temperance in Georgia on the local level paralleled an interstate debate in the Baptist newspaper subscribed to by Georgia Baptists. In 1827, W. T. Brantly of the *Columbian Star* (later titled the *Christian Index*) began to promote the interests of temperance. Originally, Brantly served as pastor of Georgia and South Carolina churches but moved in 1824 to the Baptist church in Philadelphia upon the death of Henry Holcombe, the church's pastor. Assuming the pastorate of the Philadelphia church, W. T. Brantly labored extensively in the ministry of this church and its academy. In 1827, he assumed control of the Washington paper, previously controlled by Baron Stow and Luther Rice, and moved it to Philadelphia. The paper's original purpose of promoting the interests of missions and education in Baptist life continued under Brantly, but under a more scholarly pen.

Serving as editor from 1827 to 1833, W. T. Brantly injected several changes into the paper. First, he began to include more information concerning events in Georgia and South Carolina. Second, Brantly included discussions on social evils along with Baptist concerns in missions and education. Being in favor of temperance and concerned with his former state, Brantly promoted the cause of temperance in Georgia.

While Sherwood and Clopton organized temperance societies, Brantly initiated a temperance discussion between a Georgia Baptist leader and himself. Jesse Mercer, a Baptist pastor in Georgia, dominated many aspects of Georgia Baptist growth. As a leading figure in the churches he served, the associations and conventions he moderated, and

the efforts for which he attempted to unite Georgia Baptists, Jesse
Mercer was often perceived as the father of most Georgia Baptist causes.
Earlier in life, he and his father, Silas Mercer, established or helped form
early associations and meetings of correspondence in Georgia Baptist
life.[64] After his father's death, Jesse Mercer continued the same zeal in
leading Georgia Baptists. From the foundation of the Georgia Baptist
Convention, Mercer served as moderator and stood as the authority of
any new issue in Georgia Baptist life; therefore, Georgia Baptists looked
to Mercer as the authority on the temperance cause. During the earliest
years (between 1827 and 1831), Mercer stood with the traditional Baptist
position—alcoholic beverages should be used in moderation. With the
rise of temperance societies, Mercer addressed this position to Brantly. In
1829, Mercer delineated his position to editor Brantly in a letter,
providing two reasons for using strong drink:

> 1st. I have not yet been convinced that the use of spirits is in
> itself a sin. Convince me of this and I will be a member, or come
> to the desired result. But, 2d. I have been in bad health for years
> past, as you know, and after using many celebrated and prepared
> medicines, without effect, to restore the tone of my intestines,
> several of the most eminent physicians, at different times and
> places, recommend the habitual use of Cogniac brandy.[65]

Brantly, although a close friend to Mercer, utilized the paper to
refute Mercer's position on the point of "causing a brother to stumble."
Understanding that alcohol could serve as a medicine, Brantly
nonetheless saw alcohol as a poison. Using an analogy, Brantly asserted,

---

[64] Most of Georgia's early growth stemmed from the Separate Baptist tradition.
Settlers such as Silas and Jesse Mercer, Separate Baptists from North Carolina, did much
to populate Georgia with Baptist settlers. The founding of Mt. Enon College and the
Georgia Baptist Association (the first Georgia Baptist association) along with Jesse
Mercer's long history of participating in numerous Baptist ecclesiastical functions made
Jesse Mercer the major figure of Georgia Baptists as early as the first decade of the
1800s.

[65] "Letter to the Editor from Washington, Georgia," *Columbian Star*, 19 September
1829, 188–89. This quotation was later reprinted in Mercer's memoirs. See Charles
Dutton Mallary, *Memoirs of Elder Jesse Mercer* (New York: John Gray, 1844) 225.

"I have a good vessel and steerage, and am an expert sailor, and can therefore cruise about in Brandy Bay without being drawn into the whirlpool of intemperance, but some of my less skilled neighbors, seeing me sail so pleasantly, may be tempted to go a pleasuring upon the same deceitful Bay, and may be lost. If my examples encouraged them to the venture, I should have cause of regret."[66] This argument convinced Mercer to abandon the use of ardent spirits, even as a medicine. In 1834, a year after Mercer gained possession of the *Christian Index*, he established the *Temperance Banner* in Penfield, Georgia, a paper dedicated to the cause of halting the trafficking of strong drink.

Between the time of Brantly's early advocacy of temperance and the formation of a Georgia temperance paper, W. T. Brantly published several articles that pointed to the development of a temperance position, moving from moderate usage of alcohol to the total abstinence of it as well as the political overthrow of its circulation. In July 1829, Brantly printed early reactions to the temperance platform in the pages of the *Index*, especially the excitement of the readers over the phrase "individuals are fatally wedded to their bottles." A reader inquired from editor Brantly concerning this phrase, wondering if it actually described individuals that did not belong to a temperance society. "What is the natural construction of such an expression? Is the world to believe that all the people in Georgia, saints and sinners, old and young, male and female are uniting in temperance societies, and that those who do not unite are 'fatally wedded to their bottles'?"[67] The writer in criticizing the push for temperance saw the church as the only temperance society.[68] Already, the founding of temperance societies collided with the idea of the exclusivity of morality to be found only in the church.

---

[66] Mallary, *Memoirs*, 226–227. "Brandy Bay" also became a prominent word used in Mallary's allegory against alcohol in "Adventures of Prince Alcohol on Brandy Bay," published 1829–1831 in the *Columbian Star/Christian Index*.

[67] "Temperance Societies Admonished," *Columbian Star,* 11 July 1829, 29.

[68] "I am a friend to temperance societies, though not a member of one, and I find many of my brethren who think it rather degrading to a Baptist to join himself to a society of this kind. They are of the opinion that every religious society is a temperance society, and are therefore desirous that the religion of Christ should have all the credit of making people temperate" (ibid.).

Fraternal organizations collided with the Baptist concept of the church. When morality and spiritual awareness of moral issues began to be promoted by extra-ecclesiastical groups, some Baptists (later assuming the name Primitive Baptist) argued against such institutions. They saw such societies as organizations that had no warrant in Scripture, as institutions that circumvented the explicit commands of the Bible. Yet, Baptists who did organize such institutions never argued that these societies were explicitly commanded as institutions or assumed the role of churches in spiritual matters. These organizations only furthered the religious cause of sobriety through their organization.[69] Temperance society members hoped to band the American people together to support the cause of temperance and to arrest the use and spread of strong drink.

Early moral justifications for total abstinence began to appear by 1830. In Wilkes County, Georgia, a speaker tackled the problem through the concept of *intemperance*. Gluttony differed from drinking in that "the appetite for ardent spirits with the inebriate has no bounds." Intemperance produces "scenes of wretchedness, poverty, misery and disgrace." The only recourse to stop the spread of intemperance is to train up children to be abstainers.[70]

In 1831, Brantly included the results from numerous local temperance society meetings in Georgia but placed a special emphasis on a meeting at Bethesda Baptist Church in Greene County. At this meeting, Sherwood along with other Georgia Baptist leaders clarified popular misconceptions usually attached to the use of strong drink. Temperance leaders noticed that the objections against the temperance platform had abandoned biblical concepts, and the opposition had attached superstitious benefits to the consumption of alcohol. The conference answered three notable inquiries.

---

[69] Another writer responded to the July article, "I will agree that every member that belongs to the church ought to be temperate. We do not wish to Christianize the Church over again; we do not expect to accomplish our object in the Church, nor do we expect to accomplish it out of the Church among the present middle aged and the aged; especially when some of the Clergy write in such unfriendly terms; our great object is to hide the intoxicating liquor from our children by not using it ourselves as a luxury" ("Temperance Societies Admonished," *Columbian Star,* 15 August 1829, 108).

[70] "Temperance," *Columbian Star*, 17 April 1830, 246–47.

1st. Is not the temperate use of spirits conducive to health, especially where persons are exposed to heat and cold and wet and in all vicissitudes of weather? And is it not one of God's blessings to man?

2nd. Is not the temperate use of spirits profitable in inspiring cheerfulness in enabling persons to bear more fatigue and do more labor?

3rd. If the temperate use of spirits is conducive to health and wealth, by invigorating the physical and mental powers, and by affording cheerfulness of mind, does it not follow, as a matter of course, that it is conducive to happiness?[71]

The prominent answers of Sherwood, Mercer, and a few other respondents centered on the phrases "One of God's Blessings" and "cheerfulness." Noting that strong drink came not from God but from the exercise of human effort in using fermentation, the assembly of Georgia Baptists did not see strong drink as a blessing. Likewise, they admitted that alcoholic beverages did produce a sense of "cheerfulness." Yet, this form of cheerfulness forced a rational being into "burning his furniture and his house and to beating his wife and children—a cheerfulness, which would evince itself in a loud laugh and in shocking obscenity and curses of the funeral of a broken-hearted wife."[72]

By 1832, the Georgia Temperance Society shifted from promoting moderation to adopting a total abstinence platform. With Sherwood as secretary, the society announced the hope for ridding itself of all inconsistencies. "The obstacles in the way are professing Christians and temperate drinkers. These latter seem not to discover that though they drink but little and that too in private, they do more to uphold the cause of drunkenness than ten times the number of sots."[73]

The early temperance movement in Georgia (as a statewide movement) dissolved with the departure of Sherwood from the state in

---

[71] "Temperance Cause Advancing," *Christian Index*, 1 October 1831, 213.

[72] Ibid.

[73] "Georgia Temperance Society," *Christian Index*, 19 January 1833, 41.

1836, even though he returned in 1839.[74] Two developments point to this failure of the temperance movement. First, the Georgia Temperance Society targeted the repeal of the Georgia Liquor License law in 1838. When unable to do so, the temperance movement moved into the private arena of changing personal morality. This "Moral Suasion" era continued until after the Civil War when women began to use political means to change public sentiment.[75]

Second, the decline of Mercer's paper, the *Temperance Banner*, into a literary magazine paralleled the movement itself. Only a few issues of this pre-Civil War periodical are extant today.[76] As noted in Mallary's work, the *Temperance Banner* began in Washington, Georgia, printed by Jesse Mercer.[77] Within a few years, it moved to Penfield and became a paper independent from the Baptists but published by Baptists, such as Benjamin Brantly, son of William T. Brantly, Sr. In 1850, it reached a circulation of 5,000.[78] By the late 1850s, John H. Seals published it in Penfield and changed the name to the *Literary and Temperance Crusader*. In 1859, new owners moved it to Atlanta, where it became a fashionable literary magazine.

In 1845, Benjamin Brantly of Penfield published the final work and most succinct statement of Sherwood on the question of temperance in Georgia, with President J. L. Dagg of Mercer University providing the

---

[74] Scomp stated, "To Dr. Sherwood, more than to any one else, is the inception of temperance societies in the State undoubtedly due, and he remained Secretary of the State Society until his removal from the State in 1836. The man who searches the files of old Georgia newspapers of those days will meet very often with calls to 'Temperance Societies,' signed by Adiel Sherwood. In fact, Dr. Sherwood seemed so essential a part of the State Society that after he left Georgia, the Society went down, and ceased meeting at all" (Scomp, *King Alcohol*, 284).

[75] Ansley, *History,* 26–27.

[76] One researcher composed a short history of this paper. See Bertram Holland Flanders, *Early Georgia Magazines: Literary Periodicals to 1865* (Athens: University of Georgia Press, 1944) 160–63.

[77] Mallary stated, "[Mercer] established a temperance paper, which, though sustained at a pecuniary loss to himself, had considerable circulation, and was the means of doing much good. The paper was transferred with the Index office to Penfield, where it is now published by Mr. Benj. Brantly, not however, as the paper of the Convention, but as his own individual concern" (Mallary, *Memoirs,* 227).

[78] Flanders, *Early Georgia Magazines*, 161.

introduction. Adiel Sherwood appealed for the abolition of the license
law in Georgia, assessing it as a means of great evil. The Georgia license
law required government regulation of all spirituous liquors in the form
of a license, and the restriction of alcoholic beverages from slaves or
"free persons of color," without the consent of an owner, guardian, or
overseer.[79] Sherwood preferred the abolition of all legal means to sell
alcohol. With the prohibition of liquors, those guilty of felonies and
misdemeanors could be prosecuted according to the means that caused
them to commit such atrocities.[80]

CONCLUSION

Sunday schools and temperance societies shared a reciprocal relationship
in Sherwood's mind. The center of both efforts lay in Sabbatarian belief.
Georgia residents often forsook the Lord's house and frequented
drinking houses on the Sabbath. Sherwood saw an opportunity to remedy
these two forms of desecrations. As a pastor, he instilled the truths of
God's word and taught total abstinence from alcoholic beverages,
envisioning both endeavors as certain means for preparing the heart for
revival.

The early Sunday school and early temperance movements in
Georgia shared a common development. Both efforts originated ideally
or organizationally from Northern, interdenominational attempts. Yet,
they swiftly became denominational concerns when Adiel Sherwood
initiated them. The Georgia Sunday school movement began in Savannah
under Lowell Mason as an interdenominational attempt to educate
children. The early Georgia temperance movement included prominent
Protestant churches in the state and their leaders. Yet, when Sherwood
started his first Sunday school, it became an adjunct ministry of the local
church. When he established the first local temperance society in the
state, he relied on the support of Baptists such as Abner Clopton.
Although the issue of temperance became a larger social issue and the
Georgia Temperance Society included both members of sectarian and

[79] Melancthon [Adiel Sherwood], *An Essay on the Defects of the License Law, Now Existing in Georgia* (Penfield GA: Benjamin Brantly, 1845) 3.
[80] Ibid.

nonsectarian organizations, the issue continued to be a vital component of the state convention. Associations and the state convention promoted the cause of temperance, regardless of its growth and decline as a social issue in the larger public.

In summary, Adiel Sherwood introduced, defined, and organized two prominent benevolent societies in the state of Georgia. Within a denominational context, he introduced a Sunday school and a temperance society, but both societies related to the larger evangelical world. They were sustained longer within a denomination when individuals like Sherwood urged the scriptural importance of Sunday schools and temperance societies. The Bible demanded that God's people impart the wisdom of Scripture to children. It also instructed Christians to refrain from drunkenness and to keep their weaker brother from stumbling.

3

THE GREAT GEORGIA REVIVAL OF 1827 AND THE PRIMITIVE BAPTISTS

In the South during the 1820s, denominational structures began to materialize beyond the associational level in Baptist life. The impetus for such organization revolved around foreign and domestic missions. The thrust into missionary work changed the theological focus of many American religious groups, including the Baptists. As proponents of foreign and domestic mission work promoted missionary theology and practice, they encountered antimissionary thought and theory on the American frontier. Division over missions and revival meetings (i.e., protracted meetings) within Baptist life marked this era as a time of transition. Controversy over revivalism and missionary societies divided Baptists into missionary and antimissionary organizations. This controversy spanned the eastern seaboard and the western frontier, and it would be difficult to pinpoint its effect on a specific location by using broad definitions that fit the whole. Studies of general historical movements tend to omit the smaller exceptions. By examining a smaller section of early nineteenth-century religious life, one sees that the details of this aspect of frontier revivalism emerge with greater clarity.

Adiel Sherwood changed the theological focus of Georgia Baptists through his advocacy of revivalism and missionary theory. He provided a theological framework to his readers in denominational newspapers, justifying missionary activity and revival emphases through biblical and historical examples. His involvement in a major revival movement in Georgia as a preacher and a polemicist gave him the arena to assert his theological understanding of revivalism, missionary activity, and the relationship of his thought to his opponents' viewpoint.

In April 1818, Adiel Sherwood, as a student of Andover Seminary, wrote his sister telling her of his burden over her spiritual well-being. Unknowingly forecasting his future theological aim, Adiel explained to Elizabeth the connection between duty and repentance:

> Most of the causes for the sickness and darkness among Christians can be traced to *omission of duty* and corruption of crime, thus producing an alienation in the affections, (though I hope there is no need of the remark) let me advise you to read Fuller's "Backslider"—Could that book be more universally circulated and read, I have the fullest confidence, that we should not find *so many meagre, despairing souls* turning back, stopping, lingering along the road to heaven.[1]

Influenced by the evangelical thrust of Andrew Fuller, Sherwood's earliest letters and newspaper articles accentuated the theme of *duty faith*. Sherwood believed, like Fuller, that faith was a moral duty. Mirroring a similar transition Fuller made in England, Sherwood took the revivalist theology of Jonathan Edwards, which claimed that unconverted people lacked the moral ability to exercise faith. Even though God alone could bestow this moral ability, all sinners had a duty to believe. If God did change the disposition of the heart, the new believer had the duty to keep the Lord's commandments as his new disposition urged. Just as sinners had a duty to repent, the believer had the continual duty to believe and work out his or her salvation. Sherwood followed Fuller in adopting Edwardsean Calvinism.

Within months, Sherwood left Andover Seminary to move temporarily to the state of Georgia as a missionary for the Savannah Missionary Society. His doctor recommended that he should move to a

---

[1] Adiel Sherwood to Elizabeth [Fellows], Andover MA, 23 April 1818, Georgia Baptist History Depository, Jack Tarver Library, Mercer University, Macon GA.

warmer climate, away from the chill of New England that weakened his lungs. Georgia suited this temporary need. In his mid-twenties, Sherwood entered Savannah harbor with recommendations from mentors such as Thomas Baldwin and Moses Stuart to present to Georgia Baptists. Within the next two years, he formed a close attachment to Jesse Mercer and other leading Georgia Baptist ministers and made Georgia his home and mission field.

During the 1820s, Baptists in America gravitated toward denominational structures beyond the associational level. The impetus and purpose behind such organization revolved around foreign and domestic missions. Proponents of foreign and domestic mission work promoted missionary theology and practice through their new societies and agencies, while they encountered antimissionary thought and theory on the American frontier. Division over missions and revival meetings (i.e., protracted meetings) within Baptist life marked this era as a time of transition. Controversy over revivalism and missionary societies divided Baptists into missionary and antimissionary organizations from the eastern seaboard to the western frontier. In the history of Georgia and the missionary Baptists of the state, Adiel Sherwood played a prominent role in refuting opponents of missions and revivals, while he encouraged revivalist thought and practice.

Between 1819 and 1827, Sherwood busied himself as an academy teacher during the week and a pastor on Sundays. In 1819, he established the first Baptist Sabbath school in Georgia. In 1820, he drafted a proposal for a future state of correspondence between all Georgia Baptists, leading to the foundation of the Georgia Baptist Convention in 1822.[2] He traveled with Georgia Baptist leaders such as Jesse Mercer to the meetings of the Triennial Convention and its Board of Managers, becoming a trustee of the newly constituted Colombian College.[3] His

---

[2] Sherwood did not submit it himself because he felt himself to be an outsider (Julia L. Sherwood and Samuel Boykin, *Memoir of Adiel Sherwood, D.D.* [Philadelphia: Grant and Faires, 1884] 182).

[3] His first Triennial Convention meeting was in 1823, the year of his ordination. According to attendance reports, he regularly attended each three-year cycle until 1844. He missed the 1826 meeting, and he served on the Board of Managers from 1829 to 1845.

pastorates during this early period, normally quarter-time or half-time churches (churches meeting either once or twice a month), included Freeman's Creek in Clarke County; Greensboro (1821–1832), which he and Mercer organized; New Hope in Greene County; Eatonton (1827–1837); Milledgeville (1827–1834); Macon (1829); Monticello (1829); and Indian Creek (1831–1833).[4]

In 1827, while Sherwood served as pastor of the churches of Eatonton, Greensboro, and Milledgeville, a revival of religion began in these churches that affected the associations and churches of central Georgia. Beginning in the Eatonton church and the Ocmulgee Association, conversions within the next two years totaled over sixteen thousand.[5] For the calendar years of 1828 and 1829, baptisms rose drastically, never again to reach the same proportion in the state of Georgia.[6]

THE GREAT REVIVAL OF 1827

Though not limited to the state of Georgia, many Georgia Baptist historians name this era the "Great Revival of 1827" or the "Great Georgia Revival" due to the lack of any subsequent revival that equaled or surpassed it.[7] This revival can be traced to the Baptist church in

---

[4] William Cathcart, ed., "Adiel Sherwood," in vol. 2 of *The Baptist Encyclopedia* (Philadelphia: Louis H. Everts, 1881) 1053.

[5] This figure represented the total amount of baptisms reported from several associations in the state. The Baptists in Georgia from 1814 to 1845 grew from 16,299 to 47,151 in membership. See Robert A. Baker, *The Southern Baptist Convention and Its People 1607–1972* (Nashville: Broadman Press, 1974) 131.

[6] This phenomenon can be seen in the reports of the associations. Ocmulgee Association reported 1,772 baptisms in 1828 and 810 in 1829. The Georgia Association, the first association in the state, reported 1,761 in 1828 and 708 in 1829. See Samuel Boykin, *History of the Baptist Denomination in Georgia: With Biographical Compendium and Portrait Gallery of Baptist Ministers and Other Georgia Baptists* (Atlanta: James P. Harrison and Company, 1881) 178.

[7] Sherwood titled it "The Great Revival." See Rev. A. Sherwood, "The Life and Times of Jesse Mercer," *Christian Index* (Macon GA), 15 June 1863. Samuel Boykin and B. D. Ragsdale titled it "The Great Revival of 1827." See Boykin, *History of the Baptist Denomination*, 177; B. D. Ragsdale, vol. 3 of *Story of Georgia Baptists* (Atlanta: Executive Committee of the Georgia Baptist Convention, 1838) 3:43. Harold J. McManus defined it in the following manner: "A period of nearly two years

Eatonton and the Ocmulgee associational meeting of 1827, with the
testimony of Adiel Sherwood providing a detailed account. In July 1827,
he held a protracted meeting at his church in Eatonton. By the end of the
year, Sherwood baptized "about one hundred persons" into the
fellowship of his church.[8] The greater aspect of the revival occurred two
months later at the associational meeting.

When the Ocmulgee Association met at Antioch church, Morgan
County, in September 1827, the audience did not meet as delegates to an
associational meeting but as spectators at a protracted meeting. Several
preachers delivered sermons over a period of days. Designated as the
first speaker, Adiel Sherwood delivered a sermon titled "Great is Diana
of the Ephesians." One spectator recalled hearing the sermon: "[It was]
enunciated in the speaker's own original, peculiar style, when an old
colored person, sitting at the rear of the pulpit, commenced shouting with
all her strength of lungs. The demonstration seemed ill-timed and
uncalled.... The effect of this outburst was ludicrous. There was a
perceptible smile upon the faces of the congregation, and a trying-to-
look-proper expression upon the countenances of the ministers."[9] He
continued, "As the minister warmed into his subject, treating it wisely in
his concise, nervous way, uttering solemn truths softened by pathetic
touches, the Spirit of the Lord seemed to move upon the hearts of the
people. In the close of the services, while the congregation stood to sing
the last hymn, an invitation was given to persons desiring the prayers of
God's people to come up to 'the altar.'"[10]

At this point, the altar call consisted of the call of God's people to
ask for the salvation of their loved ones as well as an examination of
their own salvation. Sherwood stated, "Probably four thousand persons

---

characterized by a great increase in baptisms reported by the churches and an accelerated
interest and participation in missions, benevolences, educational work, temperance, and
Bible and Sunday school societies, since referred to by Georgia Baptists as the Great
Revival of 1827" ("Revival of 1827 [Georgia]," in vol. 2 of *Encyclopedia of Southern
Baptists* [Nashville: Broadman Press, 1958] 1160).

[8] Sherwood and Boykin, *Memoir*, 226. Lengthy meetings were common for Baptists,
even among later Primitive Baptists.

[9] Mrs. A. P. Hill, *The Life and Services of Rev. John E. Dawson, D.D.* (Atlanta:
Franklin Steam Printing House, 1872) 20.

[10] Ibid., 21.

rushed forward for prayer, after I concluded my sermon; and we spent two hours praying for sinners in different parts of the congregation."[11] In an article five months later, Sherwood described the meeting to a Virginia paper: "Convicted persons, who could not approach near the stand to hear the prayers, would crowd around ministers in various parts of the immense congregation, and there beseech an interest in their petitions. Three or four groups could be seen at a time bowing down in the dust."[12] James Clarke, a wealthy Baptist lawyer and planter of Putnam County, attended the Antioch protracted meeting as well. He reminisced forty years later of the meeting, recalling the event as a strange work of grace. He noted:

> Seldom has there been a meeting for the worship of God where the prayers of His people seemed so fervent for the conversion of souls; and seldom has there been in this, our beloved Southern land, a meeting where there were such copious effusions of Divine grace, or more signal trophies of Divine glory. Even the first day's service witnessed an earnest and numerous application of convicted and mourning souls for the prayers of Christians.[13]

From this point onward, Sherwood became a more active organizer of revival meetings and benevolent societies (i.e., Temperance, Mite, and Bible). During the year of 1828, he traveled over 3,000 miles within the state to preach 333 sermons in 40 counties.[14] Sherwood recognized the limitation of revival in that it comes when God desires it, but he habitually urged the duty of Christians to attend to the beginnings of a blessing. He recalled, "When I look back to those times, I am broken down under a sense of unworthiness, and cannot allow anyone to offer praise, or even hint it to me. But I hope never, in time, to forget that day;

---

[11] Sherwood and Boykin, *Memoir*, 227.

[12] Adiel Sherwood, "Eatonton, Ga.," *Religious Herald* (Richmond VA), 8 February 1828, 2.

[13] Hill, *The Life and Services of Rev. John E. Dawson*, 23.

[14] Hansford D. Johnson, "Adiel Sherwood," in vol. 2 of *Encyclopedia of Southern Baptists*, 1199. These figures were often quoted by Sherwood's coworkers.

and I feel assured that, if I ever reach heaven, there will be occasions which will frequently call it to remembrance."[15] Unfortunately, the revival dissipated by 1832, but it left in its wake many new societies dedicated to the spread of the gospel.

The Great Georgia Revival of 1827 has received as much notice as Adiel Sherwood, the leading revivalist of this movement. Although the revival was not limited to Baptists or to Georgia, Georgia Baptists experienced a phenomenal surge in converts, proving it to be a work of divine origin to many people. Yet, the most diligent preacher of this period exercised means or measures that proved to be hotly debated among some mission-minded Baptists and all antimission Baptists. Very little research, however, has been done on this particular movement. By looking at the revival of 1827 in Georgia, the historian can enlarge the picture of the larger revival movement in America. What kind of measures did Sherwood utilize? What were the highlights of the revival? What were the perceptions of missionary Baptists? How did the issue of revival mold the advocates and opponents of revival? These questions can open a new window into a forgotten time of God's work.

NEW MEASURES IN THE EARLY NINETEENTH CENTURY

Historians of American revivalism have noticed the shift in emphases between the first and second Great Awakenings. The latter revival era relied on demanding physical action of the repentant more than the former. From the 1801 Cane Ridge Revival in Kentucky through the campaigns of Charles G. Finney, new revival methods appeared in prolonged revival meetings, changing the spiritual topography of America. The prolonged meetings themselves seemed like an invention. Churches of different denominations met together, stressing spiritual unity, not denominational differences. Within the meetings, activist Christianity took control. The exhortations of the preacher stressed immediacy and demanded the audience to respond with a decision for Christ without delay. The moment of decision counted. Revival

---

[15] Sherwood and Boykin, *Memoir*, 227–28.

preachers, for good or ill, demanded action after delivering their sermons.

Charles G. Finney, the noted evangelist of this era, summarized the most debatable "new measures," new revivalistic methods, utilized in revival meetings. In his *Lectures on Revivals of Religion*, Finney outlined three innovations in revivals: *anxious meetings, protracted meetings,* and the *anxious seat*.[16] Finney admitted that all three measures had a philosophical purpose behind them, rather than a biblical mandate or example. All three functioned as means or methods to convert sinners. The *anxious meeting* consisted of a form of personal evangelism. Whether the meeting place consisted of a private home or a place near an open meeting, the concept involved individual discussion and decision. Finney provided two modes of conducting anxious meetings:

> (a) By spending a few moments in personal conversation and learning the state of mind of each individual, and then in an address to the whole, take up all their errors and remove their difficulties together.

> (b) By going round to each, and taking up each individual case, and going over the whole ground with each one separately, and getting them to promise to give up their hearts to God. Either way they are important, and have been found most successful in practice. But multitudes have objected to them because they were new.[17]

The types of *protracted meetings* were not as specific. To Finney, churches and religious communities simply extended services beyond their Sabbath. The only concern of revivalists should be the appropriate time and location for the community.

In a revival meeting, the *anxious seat* (or *bench*) became a popular method of calling sinners to make a decision.[18] When a revival speaker

---

[16] Charles G. Finney, *Lectures on Revivals of Religion* (New York: Fleming H. Revell Company, 1868) 248.

[17] Ibid.

[18] This practice predated Finney's ministry. One article claimed that the anxious seat came from a Baptist preacher, Jeremiah Vardeman (1775–1842). See "Origin of the

called on his audience to repent, he would request those seeking prayer for conversion to sit in a seat near the pulpit. With the audience praying for the individual, the occupant of the anxious seat waited and prayed for a converted state.[19] Although Scripture did not prescribe this practice, the concept had a biblical basis. The sinner waited for God's salvation. Yet, opponents of the practice saw the manipulation evident in the practice. The sinner could make a decision based on popular encouragement, not the leading of the Holy Spirit.

NEW MEASURES IN THE GREAT GEORGIA REVIVAL

New measures and measurable growth appear together in sources relating to Sherwood and the Georgia Revival of 1827. Within his earliest report of the revival at the Ocmulgee Association at Antioch church, Sherwood related the interpretation of the meeting. He stated, "Human instrumentality has been wonderfully blessed, and though Christians know that God alone can change the current of their will, they have been as active as if it depended on their exertions."[20] Throughout the next few years, Sherwood implemented the new measures while maintaining a Calvinist theology, his methods sometimes seeming to

---

Anxious Seat," vol. 9 of *The Baptist Memorial, and Monthly Record,* ed. Enoch Hutchinson (New York: Z.P. Hatch, 1850) 229. Although this claim cannot be verified, Vardeman was a popular revival preacher between 1810 and his death. He established Baptist churches in Bardstown, Lexington, and Louisville KY. In 1828 he conducted a revival in Cincinnati at which more than 100 were converted. He supposedly baptized over 8,000 people during his ministry (Cathcart, "Rev. Jeremiah Vardeman," in vol. 2 of *Baptist Encyclopedia,* 1188).

[19] Finney listed two philosophical advantages of the anxious seat: (1) When a person is seriously troubled in mind, everybody knows that there is a powerful tendency to conceal it. (2) Another bearing for the anxious seat is to detect deception and delusion, and thus prevent false hopes (Finney, *Lectures on Revivals of Religion,* 253).

[20] *Religious Herald,* 8 February 1828, 2. Sherwood also reported the following figures for the first six months of the revival: "Eatonton, 72; Liberty, 55; Little River, 36; Hephzibah, 71; Rocky Creek, 123; Bethlehem, 68; Antioch, 61; Monticello, 37; Salem, 40; Sharon, 49; Smyrna, 20; Sardis, 23; Bethel, 36; Padanaran, 20; Murder Creek, 34; Greensboro, 31; Holly Spring, 20; Island Creek, 50; several other churches, 111; Total, 1022. The greater portion of these has been baptized by six or seven ministers" (*Religious Herald,* 8 February 1828, 2).

contradict that theology. By looking at his revivalist actions in Georgia, this tension can be verified.

Later in his life, Sherwood recognized several eras of revival within the state, but he noticed a fifteen-year gap between 1812 and 1827. He also realized that new measures did not appear in the state before 1820.[21] Sherwood admitted that Jesse Mercer did not appreciate the new measures, although Sherwood did.

> Mr. Mercer never adopted the practice of inviting unconverted persons to be prayed for, as is the custom with most ministers, in protracted meetings. He would pray and weep over those that requested it; but thought it was carrying things too far to exhort sinners and ask them up to certain seats. Such measures were not employed in his early ministry, not much by the Baptists of this State till after 1820, though they had been by the Methodists; hence he questioned the propriety, fearing that animal excitement would preponderate and spurious conversions be the result.[22]

Upon entering Georgia in 1818, Sherwood interpreted the first indication of religious excitement as a fanatical phenomenon. In October 1820, Sherwood attended the Sarepta Association meeting in Ruckersville.[23] While Jesse Mercer delivered one of the sermons for the meeting, Sherwood noticed several individuals who "were affected with what is called the *'jerks'*—a peculiar twitching of the hands and

---

[21] "Mercer's Times may be regarded as the *age of revivals* in colleges: such a thing was never heard of in any European college nor in those of America till the Nineteenth century was ushered in—very few known till after the war of 1812.... Now, it is a common occurrence. The three *general* revivals in Mercer's day were in 1801, 1804, 1812 and 1827" (Rev. A. Sherwood, "Life and Times of Jesse Mercer, Chapter V," *Christian Index*, 21 August 1863, 1).

[22] Rev. A. Sherwood, "Life and Times of Jesse Mercer, Chapter IV," *Christian Index*, 15 June 1863, 1. C. D. Mallary dedicated a few pages to this topic in his biography of Mercer, *Memoirs of Elder Jesse Mercer* (New York: John Gray, 1844) 72–73.

[23] At this meeting, he submitted the first proposal to form a state convention.

feet—the nervous system much affected by religious influences or animal excitement."[24]

Before 1827, Sherwood concentrated on the well-being of his denomination. He helped establish the state convention, Sunday schools, and temperance societies. Yet, his motivation behind strengthening his denomination concerned preachers and their preaching. He wished for strong exhortations that placed a demand upon the hearer. He recalled such a concern occurring in 1823. After a meeting of the Georgia Association Mission Board, he discussed new methods of delivery with other ministers. He remembered, "After business was over, a minister's meeting was proposed, that is, that friendly criticisms should be made on the exercises, manner, faults, and defects of each minister.... [Later] All retired up stairs except Mr. M. [Mercer]; but the brethren were so much interested in the new exercises, as they all lodged in one large room, that they kept talking till a late, very late hour."[25] The subject of exercises could have ranged from practical preaching techniques to the debatable methods of revivalist preachers. Sherwood never criticized the methods he employed. He believed in strong exhortations that demanded a response, knowing this practice could easily be mistaken as being unorthodox or Arminian. In fact, he firmly perceived that his opponents could not tell the difference. He once stated, "But we suspect that many mistake practical preaching for Arminianism, not knowing the true import of the term. Everything but absolute election is Arminianism with them."[26]

---

[24] Rev. A. Sherwood, "Life and Times of Jesse Mercer, Chapter IV—Continued," *Christian Index*, 22 June 1863, 1.

[25] Rev. A. Sherwood, "Life and Times of Jesse Mercer, Chapter IV—Continued," *Christian Index*, 29 June 1863, 1.

[26] "Life and Times of Jesse Mercer, Chapter IV," *Christian Index*, 15 June 1863, 1. Jesse H. Campbell did allude to one aspect of Sherwood's earlier preaching. He stated, "In early life he was somewhat given to *controversial preaching*, in which he sometimes indulged in a degree of asperity of language towards his opponents. Later in life he has pursued a different course, and the writer has heard him express regret for what he considered unwise and unprofitable in this particular" (*Georgia Baptists: Historical and Biographical*, rev. ed. [Macon GA: J.W. Burke and Company, 1874] 417). However, Sherwood never admitted to this charge in any of his writings.

Sherwood preserved a recollection of a few other meetings that followed the 1827 Ocmulgee associational meeting. The few examples of the continuing revival represented a mixture of divine and human action. In 1828, when the Georgia Association held its session, a crowd gathered at a private residence. A preacher (perhaps Sherwood) exhorted the crowd to repentance and concluded the message with the hymn "Amazing Grace." Sherwood stated, "A number rushed forward for prayer without invitation."[27] At a meeting in March of the same year, Sherwood held an open meeting in which he mentioned several new measures. After his sermon, he encountered a distraught woman.

Invitation was given to the serious to be prayed for; a few came forward and while there was a pause in the exercises, a mother in Israel, who had a large family present, arose and poured forth an exhortation enough to melt "a marble heart," closing with something like these words: "I see my neighbors and their children desiring prayer, but not one of mine—all under God's wrath." "Go and bring them" responded the preacher.—Away she went through the congregation, weeping and beseeching her own children but she could persuade very few of the younger ones—the older refused.[28]

As late as 1833, Sherwood reported similar experiences and results, although according to the record of baptisms, the revival ended in 1830. During the middle of his debate with the antimissionary Baptists, Sherwood found time to describe a camp meeting conducted by the Sharon church in the Flint River Association.[29]

On the Sabbath, some hundreds were desirous of prayers, but the most intense feeling was on Sunday night. When the invitation was announced, so many rushed forward and crowded

---

[27] Rev. A. Sherwood, "Life and Times of Jesse Mercer, Chapter IV," *Christian Index*, 15 June 1863, 1.

[28] Ibid.

[29] Within a year, this church would be expelled from its association. The antimissionary element controlled the Flint River Association for several years.

up the passage, that not half who desired could get near the stand. Several shouted aloud as having found forgiveness; this increased the zeal of ministers, and also the anxieties of mourners. Yes despair was depicted in some countenances. "Ah! Thought many a mourner, such an one, who has been convicted only a few days or weeks, has found the Lord precious; but I, who have come here year after year, am growing worse and worse, I shall never be forgiven." Some of the ministers went and prayed at several places in the out-skirts, with those who could not reach the center. Exhortations, prayers, singing, shouts and groans, continued for three hours, and then in the tents till after 10 o'clock P.M.[30]

Evident in most of the cases that Sherwood reported, he and the other ministers apparently utilized all three measures outlined by Finney. The anxious meeting can be seen at the 1827 Antioch meeting when small groups clustered together to pray. Visiting homes as he did at the Georgia Association in 1828 also constituted a type of anxious meeting. Every revival meeting seemed protracted, extending beyond the Sabbath.[31] Georgia Baptists utilized the traditional custom of associational meetings that met three days of a weekend and then extended it beyond the three days for a "protracted meeting." This both signified their lack of cooperation with other denominations and the unity of local Baptist churches.

---

[30] A. S.[Adiel Sherwood], "Sharon Camp Meeting," *Christian Index*, 12 November 1833, 71.

[31] Joshua Lawrence, editor of the *Primitive Baptist,* gave a scathing but typical review of protracted meetings by the Primitive Baptists. Responding to the *Christian Index*'s praise of extended meetings, Lawrence declared, "They next decried the *Holy Spirit* by customs designed to aid him or do his work, such as protracted meetings, anxious seats, submission chairs, the professors singling out each his particular sinner to pray for; thereby exciting their animal sympathies, and then announcing them as the spiritual seed, the regenerate" (editor [Joshua Lawrence], *Primitive Baptist* [Tarsboro NC] 24 June 1837, 188.

In most of the narratives, individuals came forward to find "the Lord precious."[32] They "came forward" to "desire the prayers of God's people." Sherwood did not view the practice of a sinner's walking forward at the end of a sermon as constituting an act of saving faith or repentance, but rather the sinner stepped forward to discover if God would save him or her. Hence, the audience's prayers were valuable to the meeting. Although there is no mention of an anxious seat (or bench), the front of the assembly was the anxious area. Therefore, the debatable aspect of Sherwood's form of revivalism to traditional Baptists consisted of whether or not sinners should be exhorted toward an active response within the meeting (i.e., asked to step forward for ministers to pray for them).

The new methods within revival meetings that demanded open repentance became allied with other forms of open reformation. Temperance societies and local mite societies, which promoted foreign and domestic missions, surfaced in Georgia Baptist life during this same time. When the antimissionary Baptists protested the methods of revival, they also protested all other innovations of the time. They pitted explicit biblicism against innovation, marking their new denomination as a different body while claiming the original identity of the Baptists.

Before Sherwood's theology of means can be studied, an analysis of the historiography of the Primitive Baptist movement would be helpful in exploring the precise nature of the opposition he encountered.

THE REACTION OF ANTIMISSIONISM: HISTORIOGRAPHICAL PROBLEMS CONSIDERED

Before an appraisal or judgment can be delivered concerning the Primitive Baptists in Georgia, the previous models of interpretation in regard to this American phenomenon must be considered. The agitation between missionary and Primitive Baptists spanned a period of about ten years (1827–1838).[33] During this time, missionary Baptists accelerated

---

[32] Sherwood used this term repeatedly, making it probable that this was his pulpit expression for those coming to the altar.

[33] The period of antimissionism can be dated back to the entrance of Luther Rice's tour in Georgia in 1816 and the rejection of his appeal for money in several Georgia

the promotion of education, missions, and benevolent societies while the Primitive Baptists strengthened their opposition to these methods by separating from missionary Baptists at the church and associational level. Due to the consistent separatist mentality of the Primitive Baptists, once the break was complete, interaction between the two bodies of Baptists was confined to neighboring churches and family relations.[34] The future exceptions to this rule would be the migration of Baptists of the South to western regions and the brief appearance of the 1880s Gospel Missionism in Southern Baptist life.

PREVIOUS THESES FROM A REACTION MODEL

In 1960, Raymond Taylor in his doctoral research presented several interpretations of the antimission movement as a phenomenon of reaction to the Triennial Convention.[35] Taylor noted W. W. Sweet's model of antimissionism as a "peculiar frontier Baptist phenomenon" in which Primitive Baptists were lower-class frontier settlers who suspected authority and elaboration.[36]

---

associations. Yet, the antimissionary Baptists as a group did not appear until after the circulation of the "Strictures of the Kehukee Association" in 1827. Therefore, the period of measurable agitation must be from 1827 to the final restructuring of Georgia associations in 1837 and 1838.

[34] See W. W. Barnes, *The Southern Baptist Convention 1845–1953* (Nashville: Broadman Press, 1954) 114.

[35] Raymond Hargus Taylor, "The Triennial Convention, 1814–1845: A Study in Baptist Cooperation and Conflict" (Th.D. diss., Southern Baptist Theological Seminary, 1960) 89. The terms *antimission* and *antimissionary* will be used to refer to the Primitive Baptist movement. The author recognizes two other branches of antimissionism often mentioned in Baptist histories: the Two-Seed-in-the-Spirit/Parkerite sect and the Campbellite movement. However, the term *antimission* can be deceptive. Several other Baptist groups are antimissionary as denominations. The Old Regular Baptists and the General Association of Baptists (Duck River Associations of Baptists) do not like the title, but they do not send missionaries. The National Association of United Baptists of America has a progressive wing that sends missionaries from an associational level. The Fundamental Baptist Fellowship, centered in Denver CO does not sponsor missions as an organization.

[36] See William Warren Sweet, ed., *Religion on the American Frontier 1783–1830*, vol. 5 (New York: H. Holt and Company, 1931) 67. This has been the accepted understanding for many church historians in the twentieth century.

Taylor also interpreted Primitive Baptists as reactors to "Hard Times." He pointed to the only two journal articles concerning Primitive Baptists to appear in the first half of the twentieth century. According to a statistical study, Harry L. Poe in 1939 saw the rise of Primitive Baptist membership to be directly related to war and economic depression. He pinpointed their appearance shortly after the War of 1812 and a rise in their membership after traumatic American events (Panic of 1837, Civil War, Spanish-American War, and World War I).[37] In 1951, Ira Hudgins voiced a similar opinion by adding 1819 as another time of economic depression and a better starting point for the appearance of Primitive Baptists.[38]

THE DILEMMA OF HISTORICAL APPRAISAL

The major problem in assessing the natural origins of Primitive Baptists is not centered on the issue of theology versus practice as much as the perspective of historians. The only concerned audience in the debate has been either Primitive or missionary Baptists. Secular historians and non-Baptist church historians have marked the debate off as a curious, whimsical, or irrelevant exercise.[39] To Primitive and missionary Baptist historians, theology and practice continue to be important in proposing a functional definition of each body. Yet, most definitions of identity are determined by the denominational affiliation of the historian. Therefore, two historical perspectives in identifying Primitive Baptists exist at this point: a history from within and a history from without.

---

[37] Harry L. Poe, "The History of the Anti-Missionary Baptists," *Chronicle* 2/2 (April 1939): 64.

[38] Ira Durwood Hudgins, "The Anti-Missionary Controversy Among Baptists," *Chronicle* 14/4 (October 1951): 159.

[39] Bertram Wyatt-Brown summarized the secular historiographical dilemma in regard to this topic: "In the first place, secular historians are not very familiar with antimissionism. Most frequently, accounts of it appear in church histories, especially those filiopietistic denominational volumes that celebrate the triumph of godliness for nineteenth- and twentieth-century churchgoing readers" ("The Antimission Movement in the Jacksonian South: A Study in Regional Folk Culture," *Journal of Southern History* 36 [November 1970]: 502).

The internal dimension of Primitive Baptist identity possessed several scholarly defendants, historians who either belonged to or formerly identified with the Primitive Baptist denomination. C. B. Hassell compiled a history of the Primitive Baptist churches that continues to be the historical book sufficient for those of his denomination. Within this text, Hassell made frequent arguments against the emergence of New School methods as the abandonment of primitive or original Baptist principles. He based most of his arguments on one primary source—David Benedict's *Fifty Years Among the Baptists*, one of the oldest testaments to eighteenth-century American Baptist life. He aimed at establishing a Baptist identity with the Primitive Baptists as the original Baptists.[40]

Two university dissertations appeared in the 1950s, arguing for the historical legitimacy of the Primitive Baptist as representing the original customs of Baptist life. Entering the arena with a positive perspective of Primitive Baptists, Byron Lambert of the University of Chicago promoted the aspect of American freedom as the force behind the development of Primitive Baptists. Lambert provided the first doctoral dissertation defending Primitive Baptists from a secular standpoint. Although he defined himself as an admirer of Hassell and an enemy of B. H. Carroll, Jr., he qualified his opinion of the two. Hassell erred by pointing to the wrong heroes of the antimission movement and Carroll was unaware of Hassell's book. Lambert's thesis also included a rediscovery of the "real" proponents of the antimission movement.[41]

In 1959, Julietta Haynes of the University of Texas completed research in this field by outlining the history of the Primitive Baptist

---

[40] C. B. Hassell, *History of the Church of God, from the Creation to A.D. 1885; including especially the History of the Kehukee Primitive Baptist Association,* completed and revised by Sylvester Hassell (Middletown NY: Gilbert Beebe's Sons, 1886). Ira Hudgins noted that John Leland also gave historical fuel for the Primitive Baptist cause in his outspoken opinions against the New School methodology ("The Anti-Missionary Controversy Among Baptists,"153). Of course, Hudgins mentioned the testimony of John Mason Peck, the frontier preacher and educator, who was an outspoken opponent of the Old School and its total lack of any methods (a source neglected by Hassell) ("The Anti-Missionary Controversy Among Baptists," 162).

[41] Byron Cecil Lambert, "The Rise of the Anti-Mission Baptists: Sources and Leaders, 1800–1840" (Ph.D. diss., University of Chicago, 1957) vi–vii.

churches from the split with missionary Baptists to the mid-twentieth century. She based her research largely upon Primitive Baptist periodicals, ignoring missionary documents as revisionist and unsympathetic. Haynes provided the first modern scholarly study dedicated to the more current history of Primitive Baptists. Her approach, although in agreement with Lambert, sought to be more descriptive of Primitive Baptists than polemical.[42]

An external history of the Primitive Baptist movement existed alongside the internal one. Similar to the motif of "winner-take-all," most of what is known and available came from missionary Baptist historians. This did not mean that missionary Baptists misrepresented the Primitive Baptists, as much as they were unsympathetic toward them. B. H. Carroll, Jr., wrote the first (and only) monograph to be dedicated to the origins of the antimissionary Baptists from a missionary perspective.[43] Taking more of a regional approach, Carroll centered his discussion on the conflict in the antebellum western frontier of Kentucky. Later historians of Baptist history follow the same discussion of antimissionism by isolating the movement to Carroll's three players, Parker, Taylor, and Campbell.[44]

The value of Carroll's historical work as an external history accomplished his purpose of isolating the key figures in the antimission movement according to a region. Carroll centered his argument on where he thought the division was most vital. Although he utilized an area to define the larger context of the division, interpreters of his work have made his region the source of the division. If this is the perceived interpretation, subsequent historians have been mistaken. The frontier territory of the Ohio River Valley may have been a central location for

---

[42] Julietta Haynes, "A History of the Primitive Baptists" (Ph.D. diss., University of Texas, 1959).

[43] B. H. Carroll, Jr., *The Genesis of American Anti-Missionism* (Louisville: Baptist Book Concern, 1902).

[44] See Baker, *The Southern Baptist Convention and Its People 1607–1972*, 148–59 and H. Leon McBeth, *The Baptist Heritage* (Nashville: Broadman Press, 1987) 371–80. Both authors listed the triumvirate of antimissioners, but McBeth included Joshua Lawrence as a fourth person, the central agitator whose pamphlet agitated the response of Sherwood in Georgia.

other antimission sects (Campbellites and Parkerites), but the Primitive
Baptists appeared in greater numbers elsewhere.

Key elements of a larger picture are isolated in a regional history,
even for internal historians. John Crowley recently published a
monograph taking this approach by isolating one geographical area
heavily populated by Primitive Baptists and telling their story. He
sympathized with the Baptists in the destitute regions of south Georgia,
south Alabama, and northern Florida where they existed as the original
population of settlers.[45] Within this work, he did not apply the regional
history of coastal Primitive Baptists to the larger American context, but
he did isolate vital aspects of Primitive Baptist identity that the larger
Primitive Baptist community shared.

In summary, Primitive Baptists or scholars who grew up within a
Primitive Baptist congregation have conducted most of the scholarly
work concerning Primitive Baptists. If recent trends remain true, the
research world will see more work coming from this group of Baptists.
Nevertheless, their stated identity (as a denomination separated from all
human inventions) has fluctuated as they have articulated it to the outside
world. Both theology and practice were reasons for their break with
missionary Baptists. Only later scholarship took into account
sociological dimensions, downplaying the original point of disagreement.
A shift back to the original thesis can be ascertained in the latest
dissertation on the subject. James Mathis of the University of Florida
recently took the approach of Hassell combined with a negative view of
nineteenth-century American democracy. He resurrected Hassell's work,
providing its legitimacy to the larger historical interpretation.[46]

---

[45] John G. Crowley, *Primitive Baptists of the Wiregrass South* (Gainesville:
University Press of Florida, 1998). Crowley has corresponded with this author regarding
Adiel Sherwood. He has made the point that Sherwood's influence did not reach south of
the Ocmulgee River (i.e., the area of old Spanish Florida).

[46] Mathis stressed the role of money in antebellum missionary movements,
supporting the thesis of Kenneth Startup. See James Rhett Mathis, "'Can Two Walk
Together Unless They Be Agreed?': The Origins of the Primitive Baptists, 1800–1840"
(Ph.D. diss., University of Florida, 1997). See also Kenneth Moore Startup, *The Root of
All Evil: The Protestant Clergy and the Economic Mind of the Old South* (Athens GA:
University of Georgia Press, 1997), in which he sees the paranoia of Southern pastors in
the Presbyterian and Baptist denominations over the abundance of money in regard to

Again, the external and internal dimensions of interpreting the identity of Primitive Baptists have not found agreement. The two contested sides of the argument continue to view this denomination in a traditional manner. Therefore, the approach of regional interaction may prove to be more beneficial, especially when opposing sides appeal to particulars. The reaction of Adiel Sherwood to the Primitive Baptists' critique of missionary Baptists and their separation from the advocates of societies can shed more light on the theological perspective of missionary Baptists.

THE KEHUKEE DECLARATION AND
THE STRICTURES BY NEHEMIAH

Sherwood differentiated early reactions to the mission movement from the particular agitation of antimissionism during the 1820s. Although examples can be drawn from earlier rejections of missions and education (such as the Hephzibah Association in 1817), Sherwood saw these periods of dissent as fragmentary and unconcerted.[47] The major beginning of organized discontent occurred when an article, republished by Jordan Smith and written by Joshua Lawrence,[48] came to be circulated in the state.[49] In retrospect, Sherwood asserted that he was forced to answer the charges of a "Reformed Baptist Association" (the circular letter) that led to Kehukee's rejection of all societies having "no warrant

---

slavery. The wealth of the Southern landholding classes (planters and yeoman farmers) drastically increased in the early 1830s, leaving the third class of white society (the landless) adrift.

[47] Boykin, *History of the Baptist Denomination,* 162.

[48] Jordan Smith, moderator of the Hephzibah Association in the early 1820s, separated from the association by 1828. He was the key leader behind the formation of the United Association, later called the Canoochie Association (in order to avoid being confused with the new Arminian/Freewill association with the same name that was formed by Cyrus White and his followers). He died in 1835 and his grave can be found at the Oaky Grove Primitive Baptist Church cemetery in Johnson County, on highway 319, 8 miles northeast of Wrightsville GA. Joshua Lawrence, originally from Georgia, almost moved the *Primitive Baptist* newspaper to Georgia. Instead, he published it in Tarsboro NC.

[49] "Life and Times of Jesse Mercer," *Christian Index,* 4 September 1863, 1.

from the New Testament."[50] Taking Nehemiah as his pseudonym, Sherwood answered these charges of the Kehukee Association by declaring ten "Strictures of the Kehukee Association."[51]

THE DECLARATION OF THE KEHUKEE ASSOCIATION

The Kehukee Association in North Carolina stood as an historic district where Baptists of the Separate and Regular Baptist traditions had ultimately combined into one associational group. Strongly confessional, this association served as a mother association to many others in the eastern regions of North Carolina. In 1826, the pamphlet circulated by Joshua Lawrence agitated the Kehukee Declaration. In 1827, the association passed the first formal declaration of separation and nonfellowship in Baptist life over the issue of extra-ecclesiastical organizations. The declaration stated:

> A paper purporting to be a Declaration of the Reformed Baptists in North Carolina, dated August 26, 1826, which was presented at last Association, and referred to the churches to express in their letters to this Association their views with regard to it, came up for deliberation. Upon examination, it was found that most of the churches had given their opinions; and after an interchange of sentiments among the members of this body, it was agreed that *we discard all Missionary Societies, Bible Societies and Theological Seminaries* [my italics], and the practices heretofore resorted to for their support, in begging money from the public; and if any persons should be among us, as agents of any of said societies, we hereafter discountenance them in those practices; and if under a character of a minister of

---

[50] Sherwood mentioned the irony of associationalism being prevalent in the Primitive movement when there was no explicit call for it in Scripture.

[51] Nehemiah, "Strictures on the Kehukee Association," *Religious Herald,* April–May 1829.

The Southern Baptist Theological Seminary lists these strictures in a pamphlet form, although it could not be found in their holdings. See Nehemiah, *Strictures on the Sentiments of the Kehukee Association, Originally Published in a Series of Essays in the Statesman* (Milledgeville GA: Camak & Ragland, 1829).

the gospel, we will not invite them into our pulpits; *believing these societies and institutions to be the inventions of men, and not warranted from the word of God.* We further do unanimously agree that should any of the members of our churches join the fraternity of Masons, or, being members, continue to visit the lodges and parades, we will not invite them to preach in our pulpits, believing them to be guilty of such practices; and we declare non-fellowship with them and such practices altogether.[52]

Noticing the declaration as an attempt of antimission Baptists to disassociate themselves from the missionary cause and lead others in this direction, Sherwood wrote against their point of view with the tract, "Strictures of the Kehukee Association."[53] Printed originally for the *Federal Union*, a local paper in Milledgeville, Georgia, the tract was reprinted by the *Biblical Recorder* and the *Religious Herald*, the denominational newspapers of North Carolina and Virginia.

NEHEMIAH AND HIS STRICTURES

As Nehemiah (the Rebuilder of Jerusalem's Wall), Sherwood attacked the logic of Kehukee's declaration.[54] In ten strictures, he revealed the

---

[52] W. J. Berry, *The Kehukee Declaration and Black Rock Address, with Other Writings Relative to the Baptist Separation between 1825–1840* (Elon College NC: Primitive Publications, n.d.) 13–14.

[53] The "Strictures of the Kehukee Association" refuted both the actual Kehukee Associational Declaration and the "Declaration of the Reformed Baptist Churches of North Carolina" (a circular present in the 1826 meeting and authored by Joshua Lawrence). The author has been unable to procure a copy of this letter. There are some points in which Sherwood actually answered the letter by Lawrence more than the actual Kehukee declaration. C. B. Hassel described Lawrence as "a man of limited education—was in fact almost destitute of literary attainments; but such were the strength of his genius, his originality of thought, and the force of his native eloquence, that he could move individuals or masses to a wonderful degree" (*History of the Church of God*, 739).

[54] The author discovered the long series of assumed names taken by Sherwood in the papers in two ways. First, Sherwood confessed of a few titles in his memoir. He stated, "I conceived it betrayed a want of modesty to affix my name, or even initials, to pieces; so I assumed a name. So it has always seemed to me—I naturally shrunk from being known

absurdity of the contentions of Kehukee. Nine strictures functioned as a review of each charge, while the last summarized the missionary view of such proceedings. He opened the strictures with his frustration over the circulation of the "Declaration and Circular" (the Kehukee Declaration and the previous letter by Lawrence caused these strictures). These documents had circulated from North Carolina to "us, ignorant Georgians," "battering our wretched condition" and "enlightening our ignorance."[55]

Sherwood first tackled the term *society* used in the Declaration. The Kehukee Association defined a society as an organization such as missionary, tract, and Bible societies as well as theological seminaries. Opposition to an extra-biblical organization came from a strict "Thus saith the Lord" that dictated "every step they take, for every sentiment they adopt, and every measure they recommend."[56] The Kehukee Association held to an inconsistent position; they disliked societies, but the association itself functioned as a society (an entity not specified in Scripture). Nehemiah stated, "Now our Georgia Bibles know nothing about 'Reformed Associations.'" Why would Kehukee oppose societies when it utilized associations with a "meeting on a stated day, a clerk and book for their churches, etc?"[57]

The second and third strictures answered the complaints of missionary work and funding. Nehemiah quoted and answered the Kehukee complaint of twenty years passing with no genuine, local results evident from missionary plans. Discussing terminology,

---

as the author of a paper, as I would from the presence of some lord or king, or some debased and treacherous scoundrel" (Sherwood and Boykin, *Memoir*, 284). Second, in later writings, Sherwood would either admit the authorship of a few articles or the publisher would mistakenly attach his name alongside or below his pseudonym. The latter case occurred frequently in the *Christian Index* in 1862 and 1863 under the pseudonym Testis.

[55] "Strictures on the Kehukee Association," *Religious Herald*, 17 April 1829, 2.

[56] Ibid. Sherwood touched on the different hermeneutic of the missionary Baptists thirty years later. He stated, "We try to obey every direction which is sanctioned by a 'Thus saith the Lord;' but in things of minor importance, in moral duties, we endeavor to imitate the spirit inculcated because there is no letter" ("Life and Times of Jesse Mercer," *Christian Index*, 8 June 1863, 1).

[57] "Strictures on the Kehukee Association," *Religious Herald*, 17 April 1829, 2.

Nehemiah equated being a missionary with being an apostle. Apostles in the Bible proclaimed the word, just like missionaries who distributed Bibles to natives. Missionaries were not beggars who solicited money for personal wealth, as the Kehukee brethren would suppose. They were "the apostles and primitive Christians" who suffered in the early church, were partially awakened in the sixteenth century under the Reformation, and were fully restored in the eighteenth century with the beginnings of the modern missions movement.[58]

Strictures four, five, and six discussed the three objects of missionaries: the slave, the Indian, and the distant heathen. First, the antimission brethren wanted the mission-minded Baptists to "learn their own negroes to read the Bible" (i.e., educate slaves, rather than be concerned with distant lands).[59] Nehemiah answered in the fourth stricture, "We have told the anti-mission party to form a Society for the melioration of the blacks, and we would join them heart and hand—but they have done nothing!"[60] Second, the Kehukee Association considered the money spent educating American Indians as useless and only worsening the savage's behavior. In the fifth stricture, Nehemiah expressed his view that the money spent on Bibles was enlightening, educational, and voluntary in nature. Third, the Kehukee Association believed the local congregation neglected the pastor when missionaries pulled funds from him. Nehemiah countered in the sixth stricture that missionary Baptists did not desire to neglect their pastors. Rather, missionaries suffered neglect as well. He defined a missionary as "any man who is called of the Lord and sent by Him and the church to preach the gospel in various parts."[61]

The next three strictures centering on education concluded Nehemiah's polemic against the remaining aspects of the Kehukee

---

[58] Ibid.

[59] "Strictures on the Kehukee Association," *Religious Herald,* 24 April 1829, 1. This reference hinted at the economic division between the two groups of Baptists (one landless, slaveless, and in constant contact with Indian hostility in Southern society, and the other represented by the wealthy, coastal, landowning class), but this hint can be amplified beyond proportion if one is not careful.

[60] "Strictures on the Kehukee Association," *Religious Herald,* 24 April 1829, 1.

[61] Ibid.

Declaration. The antimission brethren felt that theological seminaries did not produce a "proud, pompous and fashionable ministry."[62] In the seventh stricture, Nehemiah equated the action of utilizing a pastoral mentor's library with attending a school for preachers. Both were centers of learning. The eighth stricture denounced the nonassociation declaration of Kehukee against Bible society members. According to the antimissionists, translators of the Scriptures acted "as a worldly minded Judas betrayed Christ." Yet, Nehemiah questioned their use of the King James Bible because King James paid scholars to translate it.

In the ninth stricture, Nehemiah completed his analysis by answering the charge of ungodliness and disunity that supposedly resulted from the use of societies and seminaries. What did the unregenerate know about salvation and what did the unlearned know about learning? Did not salvation bring organizaton and further learning? Nehemiah saw the lack of practical godliness only in the areas in which it was not inculcated. The Kehukee brethren existed in a "lukewarm, Antinomian state." Only the preaching of the missionary Baptists "can arouse them from their lethargy, and 'provoke them to love and to good works,' and to the use of the means designed to better their own condition."[63]

In his final stricture, Nehemiah outlined five judgments resulting from the spirit of the Kehukee Declaration. First, a spirit of avarice dominated the Kehukee letter. Ministers were simply averse to change and improvement that might shatter their own positions. Second, a spirit "which lords it over God's heritage" existed in the letter. The North Carolina association practiced excommunication and nonfellowship against churches that associated with institutions seeking to spread the gospel. The Bible did not provide an example for such separation. Third,

---

[62] "Strictures on the Kehukee Association," *Religious Herald,* 1 May 1829, 1.

[63] "Strictures on the Kehukee Association," *Religious Herald,* 8 May 1829, 1. Sherwood's strong opinions against the Primitive Baptists became tempered with time. He stated thirty years later, "They hold the truth—they are orthodox, it is readily admitted; but they do not seem to appreciate the truth that orthodoxy cannot flourish, cannot hold its own without effort and sacrifice. So far as they go they are orthodox in doctrine, but in practice they are behind the age and behind Scriptural example and Apostolic zeal" ("Life and Times of Jesse Mercer," *Christian Index,* 8 June 1863, 1).

a spirit of pride dominated the declaration. Ministers feared others who prepared themselves for the ministry. Fourth, the Kehukee document communicated a spirit of popery:[64] "It cries down the means of information, Bible, Mission and Tract societies; so does the Pope, etc. keeps his people and priests as much as possible in ignorance."[65] Fifth, a spirit of infidelity resided in the declaration. Infidels, universalists, cold-hearted professors, and drunken apostates congratulated the antimission movement. If fellowship was the issue, the Kehukeeans should revisit their congratulators.

THE THEOLOGY OF MEANS: A MISSIONARY DOCTRINE

Although Sherwood as Nehemiah functioned as a rebuilder of what he perceived was being torn down, under the pseudonym Melanchthon he established his doctrine of means as a missionary alternative to extremism. On the same newspaper page with Nehemiah, Melanchthon began to set forth a Calvinistic proposal for reaching the lost. For a full twelve months under the title "Essays on Reformation," Melanchthon in the *Religious Herald* expressed his theology of means, concluding with the practical application of urgent preaching. In these writings, he incorporated his soteriological perspectives into practice and he analyzed his opponents' improper deductions between faith and practice.

FAITH AND INABILITY

Faith to Melanchthon must be differentiated from opinion. Following a hermeneutic of recognizing explicit and implicit witnesses, he stated, "There is a difference, I conceive between matters of *faith*, and matters of *opinion*. Matters of faith, are those points on which there is actual testimony presented to us; and as far as that testimony goes, or at least, as far as we understand it, so far may go our faith. Matters of opinion, are those on which there is no testimony—none, I mean, as to their nature."[66] Faith involved what is explicitly stated in the text of Scripture and what

---

[64] Anti-Catholic rhetoric existed in all Protestant circles in the nineteenth century.

[65] "Strictures on the Kehukee Association," *Religious Herald*, 15 May 1829, 1.

[66] Melancthon, "Essays on Reformation.—No. II, *Religious Herald,* 5 December 1828, 1.

is derived from the text. Opinion proceeded from the next stage when speculation moved the interpreter away from the text. The resurrection of the body provided an example for this hermeneutic. The dead's being raised to life eternal represented a fact of faith. However, the speculative details concerning the composition of a resurrected body would be mere "conjectures and opinions."[67] Possessing opinions on the resurrected state could not be considered unbiblical or too speculative as long as they did not contradict the issues of faith. However, opinions should be recognized as opinions and should be differentiated from faith.

Mentioning the two forms of inability, natural and moral, Melanchthon opted for the latter. Inability was not a natural propensity to sin according to the physical nature of the human. Inability, he stated, appeared "shadowed forth in scriptures, under the figures of bodily disease and natural death," but this did not represent its *nature*. Rather, moral inability "consists in an aversion of the heart to godliness" and required the sinner to stand in "his criminality before God and subjects him to divine wrath."[68]

By confusing faith with opinion and not separating moral from natural inability, Melanchthon's opponents have wrapped themselves in "the mantle of false security." They have convinced themselves that they cannot be converted. Salvation could not be a "natural impossibility" and man did not lack "natural faculties." What the sinner lacked was the "moral power" that can only be granted by God's own operation.[69]

DIVINE SOVEREIGNTY AND MORAL AGENCY

Melanchthon continued a balancing act between God's sovereignty and man's free will. Both should be balanced according to duty. In a jovial mood, he declared, "I am aware that there are staunch professors to be found, who would smite me on one cheek, for displacing a fold of Mr. Wesley's prunella gown—and others, who would smite me on the other cheek, for disturbing a curl of Doctor Gill's wig. But I trust there are many who will be disposed to believe, that truth is found between the

---

[67] Ibid.
[68] Ibid.
[69] Ibid.

extremes."[70] Melanchthon appealed to a Calvinist balance, acknowledging that man did have a responsibility to repent and believe. Truth existed between the extremes of hyper-Arminianism and hyper-Calvinism.[71] Sinners deserved "exhortations, injunctions, invitations, etc.," because repentance followed an informative gospel. The saint had the duty to proclaim the gospel and the unconverted had the responsibility to act on what is heard. Melanchton announced, *"Real Christians will perform their duties."*[72]

DUTY AS A CORRECTIVE TO IMPROPER DEDUCTIONS

Melanchton warned his audience of improper deductions in theology. Within his context, this type of religion had been most defective in regard to repentance. No one believed they possessed the duty to repent. He proposed that the problem originated from improper deductions in personal theology. He presented the following argument: "Man is totally depraved; is unable to turn himself to God; and it requires the sovereign agency of divine grace to effect the work: Therefore, our attempts to inculcate religion on the minds of our children, are of little or no consequence. When God undertakes the work it will be effected."[73] To him, propositions A (man is totally depraved) and B (sovereign agency is to effect the work) were viable truths. However, the final statement posing as a biblical truth really came from an improper human deduction. Fortunately, the deduction could be true if qualified. "Therefore, our attempts, etc., *without the blessing of God on our labours,* are of no

---

[70] Ibid.

[71] The proper interpretation of the previous quotation should be that Sherwood saw others brandishing the statements of Wesley and Gill in an extreme fashion.

[72] Melancthon, "Essays on Reformation.—No. 2," *Religious Herald*, 5 December 1828, 1. In the article that followed this one, Melanchthon concluded his theoretical discourse with a practical dilemma: "The spring of human action becomes paralyzed; a pretext is afforded to the ungodly to continue in their sins, and some apology even to Christians, for the indulgence of that indolence to which our nature is too much disposed" ("Essays on Reformation.—No. III," *Religious Herald,* 23 January 1829, 1).

[73] Melancthon, "Essays on Reformation.—No. 2," *Religious Herald*, 5 December 1828, 1.

consequence." Improper deductions proceeded from men who took their Christian duty and the means of salvation lightly.

Melanchthon mentioned another illustration of improper deductions: the argument of divine decrees. "God, in his sovereign pleasure, has decreed the salvation of all [who] are to be saved; the rest, through the sinful propensity of their dispositions, will go on in sin, and of course, will sink to final destruction." With this biblical truth, the following deduction proceeded: "Therefore, all our efforts with a view to the salvation of our children must be useless." Melanchthon assessed the deduction as a "fruit of our *philosophizing* and is owing to our making the decrees of God the rule of conduct."[74]

The Divine Being has revealed a twofold will: *decreeing* and *commanding*.[75] Melanchthon drew these two portions of the divine will from two propositions: divine sovereignty and human accountability. God decreed from eternity what he wills, but he actively commanded according to time and space. His plan operated on the obedience of the servant and should not be neglected. Melanchthon recognized predestination and accountability as irresistibly connected by an unfathomable darkness, which is "impervious" but "adorable." Due to such a mystery, he declared, "Whatever our sentiments may be with respect to divine predestination, let none of us suffer these sentiments to paralyze our efforts.... We use the means, and leave the issue with God."[76]

THE MEANS OF THE GOSPEL AND ITS END IN SALVATION

In May 1833, Adiel Sherwood mounted the pulpit in McDonough, Georgia, to preach to the eleven-year-old Georgia Baptist Convention.[77]

---

[74] Ibid.

[75] Melanchthon stated, "Though Arminians have sometimes ridiculed the idea of a two-fold will in the Divine Being, I must maintain, as undeniable, that there is in God a will decreeing, and that there is from God a will commanding" (ibid.).

[76] Ibid.

[77] The Primitive Baptists in Georgia were still separating from the missionary Baptists in 1833, culminating in the official split of 1837/1838. During the early 1830s, most associations gravitated toward the missions cause. Some associations turned

Since the 1827 Ocmulgee associational meeting, he had seen revival come and go, associations split over missions and education, and the establishment of his own manual labor school. Preaching from the text of Hebrews 2:3, "How shall we escape if we neglect so great salvation," he titled his message "The Doom of those who Neglect the Gospel."[78] Defining the preaching of the gospel as the only means toward salvation, Sherwood saw the terror of God's judgment residing with those who neglected gospel preaching.

In ascending order, Sherwood listed the neglecters of God's salvation: (1) the man who did not frequent God's house and could not hear or respond to the gospel; (2) the person sitting in the sanctuary as one of the "listless and inattentive hearers"; (3) people who heard the word but "neglect[ed] to practice the truths inculcated"; (4) individuals who disregarded their obligation to repent; and (5) the most damnable neglecters, the men and women who professed Christ but "who have not imbibed the Spirit of Christ." These individuals worked counter to the Spirit. Deluded with apathy, they did not care for the lost.

Sherwood closed his sermon by clarifying the problem of preaching without providing the adequate means of repentance in exhortations:

> We have spent too large a portion of our time in edifying professing christians, cheering their hopes and perhaps in cherishing their delusions. Our discourses have not been sufficiently discriminating in their character to make neglecters feel our "hands searching their consciences," and trying to pull them away from the influence of their destroyers. We should detect oftener the various delusions of the devil, to ruin their souls and urge them to flee immediately to Christ without waiting to be better. They are resting in the deceptive hope of being converted in God's good time (i.e. when they get ready)

---

antimissionary according to a majority church vote. The Ocmulgee Association became a Primitive Baptist association and excluded Sherwood from their membership in 1834.

[78] Adiel Sherwood, *The Doom of those who Neglect the Gospel* (Washington GA: News Office, 1833).

and the foundation of this hope must be demolished: it is but a bed of quick-sand—it is frail as the spider's web.[79]

At the Georgia Association meeting in October 1835, Sherwood continued to reiterate this desire to stop the neglect of gospel means. Utilizing the text of Psalm 74:20, he titled his message "The Covenant of Redemption."[80] According to Sherwood, the world without the light of the gospel appeared as a dark silhouette. Only the preaching of God's redemption and the prayers of the saints ensured the conversion of the heathen. According to the Bible, those who go to minister pray before they go. For redemption to be God's goal, God's people must implement the means of his redemption through preparation and action.

The covenant of redemption magnifies God's wisdom, for he has wisely used human instruments to bring the lost to himself. Sherwood reiterated the argument of God's effectual calling without human instrumentality. This unscriptural belief in the lack of means pointed to the actual lack of fruit in the Christian's life. A Christian's inaction "disparage[d] the wisdom of its author." He or she has never known the "pleasure connected with labor," but the "chastisement for inattention to duty."[81]

The covenant of redemption required faithfulness to the means of salvation. Praying and laboring to see the redemption of the lost ensured the intended outcome of God's people.[82] Saints have constantly prayed for God's will and God's work, knowing that the covenant has implied and utilized "human instrumentality." Sherwood concluded this

---

[79] Ibid., 8.

[80] The biblical text states, "Have respect unto the covenant; for the dark places of the earth, are full of the habitations of cruelty." See "The Covenant of Redemption—the true ground of encouragement for Christians to labor for the salvation of the Heathen," *The Georgia Pulpit: or Ministers' Yearly Offering*, ed. Robert Fleming (Richmond: H. K. Ellyson, 1847) 82–90.

[81] "The Covenant of Redemption," 87. Sherwood concluded this point by stating, "The above query was never suggested by a christian heart—it must have been engendered by anti-nomianism and infidelity…. An enlightened child of grace loves to labor for God" ("The Covenant of Redemption," 87).

[82] Sherwood based open invitation of salvation to the lost and open prayers for the lost on the following passsages: 2 Cor 5:20; 1 Tim 2:1; Gal 2:9; Eph 3:6–7; Col 1:27.

perspective and this sermon with a searing twofold pronouncement: neglect and consistency. Those who have neglected the means connected with the covenant of redemption should "reject the covenant itself."[83] It was consistent for those without a theological system to trust in the zeal of their prayers. It was consistent for those who were mere Stoics to believe in the natural outcome of all things. Yet, a "friend of benevolence" represented the greatest consistency. The Spirit accomplished his purposes by working through the believer. "The system which acknowledges God as the *author* of salvation, the Spirit as the *agent*, and christians as the *means*, is the only scriptural system."[84]

MISSIONS AS MEANS AND ITS HISTORIC VALIDITY

From 1836 to 1839, Sherwood disappeared from the Georgia Baptist landscape. He left his church in Eatonton to teach at Columbian College in Washington, DC. Upon his arrival, Luther Rice, the well-known agent of the school, died. For the next three years, the task of saving a Baptist school fell into the hands of Adiel Sherwood. Fund-raising proved to be a trying and sore experience for the Baptist teacher-preacher.[85]

While Sherwood was absent from Georgia, the Primitive Baptists completed their separation from the missionary Baptists. The struggle over missions and means ceased to be an internal issue. Rather, both groups continued to define themselves. The Primitive Baptists claimed the mantle of primitive Christianity and original Baptist principles. Yet,

---

[83] According to time and place, Sherwood had every reason to be stern in his judgment of the opposition. The Ocmulgee Association excluded him and his church. His use of the term *antinomian* accelerated during this era. The lack of fulfilling the duties of one's faith ("duty faith" as coined by the English Baptist Andrew Fuller) became synonymous with antinomianism in his terminology. Of course, he did have reasons for such charges. Thirty years later, he stated, "The 'Primitive Baptist' (Tarsboro, N.C., periodical), for 1837 contains this unscriptural position: 'There is no law which says, Thou shalt believe in the Lord Jesus Christ; nor is there any law which says, Thou shalt repent of thy sins.'...This, when reduced to a single proposition means that the unregenerate are under no obligation to repent and believe the Gospel" (Sherwood, "Life and Times of Jesse Mercer," *Christian Index*, 8 June 1863, 1).

[84] Sherwood, "Covenant of Redemption," 90.

[85] Sherwood stated that he lost money and useful time in this attempt. See Sherwood and Boykin, *Memoir*, 247–53.

the missionary Baptists read their Bibles and history books differently. The Bible and church history in Europe and America taught them that Christianity always spread through the actions of missionaries.

In 1839, Sherwood returned to Georgia as the Professor of Sacred Literature at Mercer University in Penfield. His position instituted the theological department that John Leadley Dagg would chair in 1843. In order to prove the precedent of original Baptists' being missionary, Sherwood delivered a discourse in 1840 to outline missionary Baptist identity. He titled the sermon "The Identity of Primitive and Modern Missions."[86]

Sherwood opened the message by observing the term *missionary* and its etymological equivalent, "to send." He referred to John Gill, who stated, "We should go unto the heathen."[87] If the Bible said to go, were God's people going to those without Christ? Sherwood answered his rhetorical question by proposing a few similar identities between the New Testament and his own time.

Of course, Sherwood qualified each parallel identity according to similarity in principle, not circumstance. The Spirit controlled and sent out his subjects (New Testament missionaries and modern missionaries) in the same fashion. The earliest missionaries such as David Brainerd, William Carey, and Adoniram Judson left their homes to minister to societies lacking a witness. They labored with the same methods and were reviled by the "same kinds of people." They held the same beliefs. Brainerd, Whitefield, Mrs. Judson, and Carey attested remarkably to the doctrines of grace. Primitive and modern missionaries established the same churches, looking to the Savior for the same efficiency and encouragement in his grace. They met similar trials and persecutions, but both were sustained in the same way.[88] As Dr. Gill pointed out, those

---

[86] "The Identity of Primitive and Modern Missions: A Discourse," *The Southern Baptist Preacher* (Washington GA: M. J. Kappel, 1840) 53–66.

[87] Ibid., 54.

[88] Sherwood mentioned the persecution of Georgia Baptists: "Later *missionaries* have been persecuted nearer home. In this State, the friends of missions have been excluded from churches—ministers shut out of houses of worship—threatened with *beating*—meeting-houses have been wrestled from them—been charged with being speculators—preaching false doctrine, and even associations, which were organized as

sustained in the New Testament were sustained *frequently*, enjoying sustenance from a distance.[89] In conclusion, Sherwood saw the missionary Baptists following the example of the Bible as well as Christian history and denominational heritage. They possessed the mantle of historical continuity.

CONCLUSION

Adiel Sherwood provided Georgia Baptists with an activist theology of means. Through his defense of means and his promotion of methods in revival meetings, Sherwood gave Georgia Baptists a distinct alternative to what the Primitive Baptists offered. He believed his view of means promoted biblical and Baptist principles.

Revival meetings mirrored a global view of foreign missions. Both endeavors sought to provide a means for sinners to be converted. Sherwood never saw an inconsistency between devising new methods to reach sinners and the actions of the Holy Spirit. He did not recognize a minimalist view of Scripture, where the means of the gospel had to be stated as a specific action or institution, or else believers were bound to

---

advisory councils merely, have assumed *law-making powers*, in order to eject missionary churches" (ibid., 61).

[89] Sherwood opened and closed his discourse relying upon John Gill. Purposefully, he used Gill along with examples of American mission work. Sherwood referred to Gill more than a dozen times. In regard to giving to missionaries from a distance, Sherwood stated, "Dr. Gill has been quoted largely in proof that the churches sustained their missionaries in primitive times, because he has not, as most modern missionaries and their friends have, been charged with *heresy*; nor can he be considered as being carried away with *new notions*" ("The Identity of Primitive and Modern Missions," 62).

inactivity. His application of missionary theology popularized by Andrew Fuller helped form Georgia Baptist institutions.

4

THE BEGINNINGS OF THE
GEORGIA BAPTIST CONVENTION

Adiel Sherwood's vision for benevolent and missionary institutions culminated in the formation of a state convention. By establishing a state association of correspondence, he redirected the energies of the associations into a more centralized plan while maintaining individual church independence. This shift in emphasis would be vital for associations within a state institution. After Sherwood's relocation to Columbian College and the final separation of Primitive Baptists from missionary Baptists, missionary Baptist associations in Georgia Baptist life continued as organizations of correspondence and fellowship, but they shifted further away from dealing with issues of orthodoxy and practice as the state convention grew. From 1820 to 1836, Sherwood influenced Georgia Baptist associational development and its relationship to the state convention as an initial organizer of a state convention and as an active leader in newly formed missionary Baptist associations.

In 1820, Sherwood returned to Georgia from a visit to New England and began a yearlong work with the Savannah Missionary Society. At the 21–24 October meeting of the Sarepta Baptist Association at Van's Creek Church, near Ruckersville, Elbert County, Georgia, the young preacher wrote a resolution calling for greater means of communication between the associations. Being an outsider from Georgia circles, he gave the resolution to another pastor to present. Julia Sherwood documented this statement in her father's *Memoir*:

At the [Sarepta] session of 1820, I drew up and, through Charles J. Jenkins, the clerk, offered the resolution which led to the formation of the General Association, now called Convention. It was as follows, "Resolved, that we suggest for our own consideration and, respectfully, that of sister associations in this state, the propriety of organizing a general meeting of correspondence." After some discussion the resolution was adopted.[1]

This resolution led to the acceptance of a general meeting in Powelton, Georgia, in 1822. This proposal therefore began the process that culminated in the formation of the Georgia Baptist Convention.

Sherwood's proposal was not original, but it was timely. Previous attempts to form a state organization in the earliest years of the century lasted only momentarily. Led by Henry Holcombe, pastor of First Baptist Church in Savannah, the Baptists of Georgia met for seven consecutive years to fellowship and to build a stronger means of correspondence between the associations. On 1 May 1803, the Georgia Baptists met at Powelton and formed a general committee. As a definition for the purpose of the committee, they adopted the following resolution: "Resolved, that the encouragement of itinerant preaching, the religious instruction of our savage neighbors, and the increase of union among all real Christians, which were the leading objects of the late conference, shall be zealously prosecuted by this committee."[2]

Samuel Boykin pointed out three aspects to this resolution. First, the statement encouraged itinerant preaching. Second, the resolution stated the need for missionary work among Native Americans in Georgia. Third, Georgia Baptists desired greater association or an increased union

---

[1] Julia L. Sherwood and Samuel Boykin, *Memoir of Adiel Sherwood, D.D.* (Philadelphia: Grant and Faires, 1884) 182.

[2] Samuel Boykin, *History of the Baptist Denomination in Georgia: With Biographical Compendium and Portrait Gallery of Baptist Ministers and Other Georgia Baptists* (Atlanta: James P. Harrison and Company, 1881) 44.

among Christian brethren. The first two aspects of the resolution were not debated. The delegates merely lacked the organization to complete them. However, the final portion of the resolution asking for a union of "all real Christians" insinuated aspects of open communion, a possible union of Baptists with their Pedobaptist brethren. Whether or not the threat of losing denominational identity proved to be an actual fear, the lack of participation among Georgia Baptist churches led to the dissolution of the committee in 1810.[3]

Although the Sarepta Baptist Association did not join the Georgia Baptist Convention until two decades later, the Sarepta resolution of 1820 led to the formation of the Georgia Convention. The Georgia and Ocmulgee associations formed the nucleus of a state convention. A writer to the *Columbian Star* announced the purposes of the "General Association" of Georgia Baptists after the meeting in 1822: "to form plans for the revival of religion, to promote uniformity in sentiment, practice and discipline, to augment the number of pious, intelligent and laborious ministers, to act in unison with the Christians of other denominations on the general interests of the Redeemer's kingdom."[4] The statement of purpose of the new *general association* combined elements of the 1803 resolution (i.e., Christian unity) with the traditional goals of local associations (i.e., uniformity in practice and discipline). In fact, within a month, Jesse Mercer defined the constituency of the "general association" as the members of the local associations. Delegates came from the associations, not the churches. Mercer called for three to five delegates from each association.[5]

The General Association of Georgia Baptists changed its name to the Georgia Baptist Convention in 1828, signaling the solidifying aspect of a growing state convention as it moved beyond mere correspondence.

---

[3] Ibid., 55. The committee did accomplish the establishment of Mt. Enon Academy, the first concerted effort to offer Georgia Baptists a means to educate their ministers with a theological education. Yet, this example did not have the full support of the entire denomination. Mt. Enon lasted from 1807 to 1811.

[4] A Baptist, "The General Baptist Association of the State of Georgia," *Columbian Star* (Washington, DC), 17 August 1822, 2.

[5] Jesse Mercer, "The General Baptist Association of the State of Georgia," *Columbian Star*, 7 September 1822, 3.

This could be seen chiefly through the influence of new societies as they attached themselves to a state convention. The formation of societies that corresponded with the state organization became the means for strengthening the general association. The original constitution of the general association of 1822 listed the local associations as the primary source of delegates, with each association given the right to send three to five delegates each.[6] However, the general association in 1826 allowed auxiliary societies to send two delegates each.

The addition of local missionary societies functioned as the means of correspondence for missionary-minded Baptists who could not change the minds of antimissionary Baptists in their local associations. From 1826 to 1838, twenty-six auxiliary missionary societies joined the Georgia Baptist Convention, while the new state convention lost two of its three associations during this period.[7] When the Primitive Baptists completely separated from the missionary Baptists in 1838, societies ceased to appear as correspondents to the state convention. Instead, from 1835 to 1845, the Georgia Baptist Convention received fourteen new associations, replacing the same geographical areas of the previous auxiliary societies.[8] Beginning with the admittance of the Central Association in 1835, Georgia Baptists reconnected their associational framework to the convention. Associations replaced societies due to the elimination of the antimissionary resistance.

THE CHANGING ROLE OF ASSOCIATIONS

The division among the associations in Georgia over missionary causes materialized after the effects of the Georgia Revival of 1827 began to wane. Regardless of doctrinal emphasis, there was an extraordinary increase of baptisms in 1827 and 1828. Yet, when the numerical growth in church membership receded back to the average annual growth before the revival era, revival enthusiasts had to confront traditional interpretations of doctrinal standards.

---

[6] Boykin, *History of the Baptist Denomination*, 105.

[7] Jesse H. Campbell, *Georgia Baptists: Historical and Biographical,* rev. ed. (Macon: J. W. Burke and Company, 1874) 20–26.

[8] Boykin, *History of the Baptist Denomination*, 212.

The two Georgia Baptist histories of the nineteenth century interpreted the rise of antimissionism as godless agitations or as resistance to change. However, a closer look at primary sources shows that the Primitive Baptists merely criticized missionary Baptists' methods for being Arminian and indicative of Arminian doctrine. The emerging Primitive Baptist churches declared non-fellowship with brethren who promoted new methods. By failing to differentiate Fullerite theology from Arminianism, the Primitive Baptists lumped all new methodologies into the category of heresy. With faith and practice being inseparable in their mental framework, any method that urged sinners toward active repentance confirmed the belief of a general atonement. According to their thought, a general atonement necessitated general redemption (i.e., if God intended to save everyone, all will be saved). Primitive Baptists could not visualize the preaching of a universal gospel, while believing in the particular and exclusive acts of God in calling his own to salvation. Any preacher who urged a general appeal for salvation must not believe in a particular atonement.

When the Great Revival of 1827 began within the Ocmulgee Association, the baptismal record for its churches represented a normal sample of a yearly increase in church membership. Thirty-nine churches with 1,918 total membership baptized 164 people representing an approximate growth of 8.5 percent. In 1828, the baptismal record soared: 1,772 people were baptized in the same association with a total membership of 3,455. This represented 51.3 percent growth in one year. In 1829, the association reported 810 baptisms out of a total membership of 3,694. This represented 21.9 percent growth.[9]

From 1827 to 1829, the Ocmulgee Association experienced a soaring number of baptisms within several churches, regardless of their pastors' doctrinal views. In 1827, the Eatonton church with Sherwood as her pastor led the association with twenty-three baptisms. In 1828, Bethlehem church in Jasper County with Cyrus White as her pastor led the association with 179 baptisms. In 1829, Mt. Gilead church of Putnam County led with fifty-three baptisms. By 1836, all three pastors of the

---

[9] *Minutes of the Ocmulgee Baptist Association* (Milledgeville GA: Georgia Journal Office, 1827–1829).

churches that had experienced the blessings of revival stood in three camps: missionary Baptist, Freewill Baptist, and Primitive Baptist. Adiel Sherwood and the Eatonton church, an expelled member of the Ocmulgee and founding member of the new Central Association, belonged to the Georgia Baptist Convention. Cyrus White, the former pastor of the Bethlehem church, served within the United Association, a forerunner of Freewill Baptist associations in Georgia. Rowell Reese and the Mt. Gilead church ministered in the Ocmulgee Association, a newly separated Primitive Baptist association.

CYRUS WHITE AND THE ATONEMENT

In 1830, Cyrus White, pastor of Bethlehem Baptist Church in Jasper County, published a small treatise on the atonement.[10] Prior to this occasion, White served as an itinerant preacher during the Great Revival and as an agent for the *Christian Index*. During the course of the revival movement, he became convinced that the atonement of Christ was not limited to the elect but represented a full atonement for all humanity. While avoiding universalism by applying the atonement in a generic sense to all humans, White viewed God's general provision for sinners as being evident at the moment of conversion. By joining a general atonement to the specific moment of conversion, White promoted an atonement that forgave all who chose to believe at the presentation of the gospel.[11]

Of course, White's position merely stood as an evangelical Arminian position—a normal belief of Methodists. Yet, Georgia Baptist

---

[10] Cyrus White, *A Scriptural View of the Atonement* (Milledgeville GA: Statesman and Patriot, 1830). This small (nineteen-page) but important tract can be found in its original form at the University of Georgia Archives, Athens.

[11] White retained a semblance of Calvinistic terminology. He believed in an ineffectual call. He claimed to believe in the Calvinistic view that God elects individuals, but he inserted the non-Calvinist position that God's call did not reach fulfillment when humans rejected his offer of salvation. He emphasized this dichotomy with the parable of the Lord's Feast: "A rich and costly feast is prepared, or in other words, JESUS has made full satisfaction to law and justice; he has provided every thing which the sinner needs, and he is affectionately urged to the feast; but he makes the most frivolous excuses, and will not come" (*A Scriptural View*, 8).

churches that followed the regular and ordered tradition of Calvinism found this proposal unacceptable. During this time, Baptists in America continued to wrestle with Andrew Fuller's concept of a general provision, a view of the atonement similar to the creedal statement, "sufficient for all, and efficient for the elect." The offer of salvation and Christ's ability to save included all in a general sense, while the application of the atonement through redemption remained particular (i.e., the elect).

In reaction to White's proposal, Jesse Mercer published a series of letters refuting the general atonement view of Cyrus White.[12] Within these letters, Mercer presented Andrew Fuller's distinction between natural ability and moral inability, while retaining a strictly limited view of the atonement.[13] In other words, Mercer refuted White with a view that embraced the older view of John Gill (a strict, limited atonement) and Andrew Fuller's view of human depravity.[14]

---

[12] Jesse Mercer, "Mercer's Letters to White on the Atonement," *Columbian Star*, 28 August–20 November 1830. Jack Tarver Library at Mercer University possesses the original pamphlet. See Jesse Mercer, *Ten Letters Addressed to the Rev. Cyrus White, in Reference to His Scriptural View of the Atonement* (Washington GA: News Office, 1830).

[13] Mercer stated, "It would be well to observe there is a natural and moral ability. The one constitutes us accountable beings; the other consists in well disposedness towards God, our Maker, and fits us for duty. The loss of one destroys responsibility and frees from blame—the loss of the other makes us sinners and subjects us to guilt and condemnation.... A moral inability supposes a natural ability" ("Mercer's Letters to White on the Atonement: Letter VII," *Columbian Star*, 6 November 1830, 293–94).

[14] The first sketch of Cyrus White and his followers is found in S. (possibly Sherwood), "White-ites," *Baptist Memorial and Monthly Chronicle* (March 1842): 77–78. The White-ites (so-called at the time) were an "isolated sect, found principally in Western Georgia and Eastern Alabama. It is composed of the followers of Rev. Cyrus White, who was once a preacher of some reputation amongst the Baptists of Georgia. He embraced Arminian sentiments, and as the Georgia Baptists have ever been noted, (until at least of late years,) for a rigid, adherence to what are termed Calvinistic principles, they soon came into collision with each other" (77). Georgia Baptists withdrew their fellowship from Cyrus White in 1830, and his association, the United Association, withdrew from the Georgia Baptist Convention when their articles of faith did not match those of the convention. In 1839, two associations existed: the United Baptist Association and the Chattahochee United Baptist Association. Correspondence with the Freewill Baptists of North Carolina was attempted. The author stated, "White (who is still living,) and his partisans are undoubtedly Arminians in doctrine. They are also charged by some

Following this debate, the Ocmulgee Association withdrew fellowship from Bethlehem church due to Cyrus White's view on the atonement in 1830. In 1831, White and other supporters of his views formed the United Association. For a few years, this new "Freewill" association corresponded with the Georgia Baptist Convention and contributed in missionary efforts. By 1836, the United Association ceased correspondence. In the 1840s, all records ceased to be published, but one author supposes this group to be one of the forerunners of the Georgia Freewill Baptist movement.[15]

EATONTON AND NEW SALEM CHURCHES

In 1829, the Baptist churches of Eatonton and New Salem began to dispute the claims of their members in the area of church discipline. Pastor Adiel Sherwood of the Eatonton church experienced injury as a moderator within his church as certain members dismissed themselves through illegal procedures. When these members requested the transfer of their letters to the New Salem church, Eatonton would not send them because the applicants were considered disorderly. Although the mismanagement of missionary money (a popular complaint of antimissionary Baptists) was the original reason for leaving Eatonton, their method in leaving the Eatonton church became the divisive issue between the two churches. Later, New Salem appealed to the Ocmulgee Association to settle its claim against the Eatonton church.[16] For three years, the association entangled itself with this dispute, unknowingly

---

with being Socinians, but this charge is certainly not well sustatined. They agree with us in our views of gospel baptism, but practice mixed communion, and are strenuous advocates of camp meetings; appointments for which are usually made at their annual meetings, and published in their minutes" (78).

[15] Damon C. Dodd, *Marching through Georgia: A History of the Free Will Baptists in Georgia* (n.p., 1977) 32–33.

[16] Rowell Reese, pastor of New Salem, later marked himself as a subscriber and contributor to the *Primitive Baptist* newspaper from Tarsboro NC and a central leader among the Ocmulgee Association after the Primitive Baptist split of 1836.

setting a historical precedent in Georgia Baptist life on the role of associational power in Baptist churches.[17]

In 1836, Adiel Sherwood along with other members of a committee in the Central Association provided the account of the Eatonton church's proceedings as part of the Central Association's defense of orthodox polity.

> Between four and five o'clock, P.M. when several members had withdrawn, a motion was made by brother Hill, that all members who wished letters either now, or at the next two conferences should have them. A list was then presented, containing the names of those who desired letters, at the head of which was the name of bro. Armstead Richardson. The motion was put, shall he have a letter? Several members objected, and stated their reasons.
>
> After some discussion, bro. Richardson acknowledged that unanimity in the Church was necessary, in order to the granting of letters of dismission, but that this was an independent Church, and could act as she pleased in the matter. The motion was then made, that a majority should govern in the granting of letters. The Moderator observed, that this was contrary to Gospel order and the practice of all churches, and that he could not, conscientiously, put the motion; begging those who desired letters to wait, and expostulating with them. Bro. Richardson then suggested that the Moderator should leave the Chair and a motion to this effect was made, which was carried—some of the brethren objecting that the Moderator should be removed to effect any particular purpose. The Moderator left the Chair, Brother Clark, one of the deacons, was called to the chair, but refused to go. Brother Hand called to the Chair, and the Clerk having retired, bro. Armstead Richardson, was appointed Clerk, pro tem.

---

[17] Later, the Flint River and Western Associations also divided while the Primitive Baptists gained control of the Ocmulgee and Yellow River Associations.

The motion was then put, shall a majority grant letters to members in fellowship? And decided in the affirmative. Yeas fourteen—Nays seven.

The following members applied for letters of dismission, which was granted, (some of the brethren voting against it) vis: Wittington Wiggins, Waid Hill, and Armstead Richardson.

It was then suggested that bro. A. Richardson could not act as Clerk, as he was dismissed—and on motion, bro. P. T. Richardson was appointed Clerk pro tem.

The Following members then applied for letters of dismission, which was granted by a majority, (some brethren voting against it) viz: Fletcher Lumsden, Joseph Wilkes, Delphia Wilkes, Martha Hill, Martha Whatley, Sally Kendrick, James Bussey for himself and wife Elizabeth Bussey.[18]

Within three days, the faction that voted for its letters of dismission joined New Salem church.[19] When this faction left Eatonton, they accused a Mr. Thomas Head of the Eatonton church with the charges of note-shaving and usury. Apparently, he lent money to church members while he raised financial support for missions.[20] The departing faction left Eatonton due to what they felt was improper church discipline: the church had not excluded Mr. Head. Yet, the irregular and illegal procedures of the departing faction did not justify their charge against missionary mismanagement.

For several weeks, Eatonton excommunicated Brothers Richardson, Hill, and Bussey as well as all other seceding members. When these new applicants of New Salem were denied their letters, Eatonton listed their illegal conduct and departure from the Eatonton meeting as reason enough for a sustained exclusion. In January 1830, the New Salem church requested that Eatonton answer the usury question and restore Brothers Richardson, Hill, and Bussey. In April 1830, New Salem asked

---

[18] *History, Faith, Views, Plans, Etc. of the Central Association; Embracing the Whole Ground of Difference Between Her and Those Associations From Which She Has Separated* (Washington GA: *Christian Index*, 1836) 24–25.

[19] Ibid., 26.

[20] Ibid., 38–39.

the Eatonton congregation for the letters of the seceding members and an apology from Eatonton for excommunicating these members. In September, the New Salem church presented this case to their mutual association, the Ocmulgee.[21]

The associational committee requested Eatonton to restore all seceding members and then release them to New Salem. However, over the following year, some of the returning members, according to the Eatonton church, did not return and fulfill the requirements of restoration. In complying with appropriate steps of restoration, Eatonton also discovered New Salem had admitted some of the excluded as members, thereby frustrating the restoration process. Double crimes confronted the Eatonton church: how members should be properly restored in order to be dismissed, compounded with the problem of restoring members of another church.

For four years, the legitimacy of church independence within a Baptist association became a hotly contested issue. In 1832, the Ocmulgee delegation continued to disregard the internal rights of the Eatonton church, wishing for an admission of guilt and the release of members to New Salem. Unable to reach a solution, the Ocmulgee Association excluded the Eatonton church in September 1833 for the immoral practice of not promising to restore her members. Within a year, Eatonton and likeminded churches of the Ocmulgee and Flint River associations formed the Central Baptist Association, signaling the final stages of the Primitive/missionary split in Georgia. By 1836, the Ocmulgee Association separated from all missionary Baptist organizations, and served as a model for new Baptist associations with the same separatist convictions.

CHURCH AND ASSOCIATION PRINCIPLES NEW AND OLD

Separation among the churches in the Ocmulgee Association did not begin with the Eatonton case. As early as 1830, the Little River church of the Ocmulgee Association attempted to try Cyrus White and his church

---

[21] Ibid., 30–31.

with the charge of heresy (White's view of the atonement).[22] This interaction between the two churches led to the association's intervening and disassociating the Bethlehem church before it resolved the problem between the two churches. With this as the background, three other churches followed Bethlehem in departing from the association.[23]

At the 1829 Ocmulgee Association meeting, two issues were agitated. First, a petition from the 1828 session to withdraw from the state convention was referred to all of the churches. Second, Walnut Creek Church of Jones County inquired, "Did Jesus Christ suffer, bleed and die, on the Cross, for all mankind? Or only, for as many as the Divine Father gave Him in the Covenant of Grace?"[24] In response to the question, the association presented its confession of faith and order as well as its rules of decorum, all standing as their constitution.

Although the Cyrus White case represented a doctrinal issue and the Eatonton case an issue of polity, faith and practice were more closely linked together. Just as a confession of faith defined the beliefs of Baptist bodies, the rules of decorum listed the actions of the assembly in dealing with all problems—doctrinal or practical. The decorum of the Ocmulgee Association contained two rules that became the focus of both sides. Rule four stated, "This Association shall have no power to lord it over

---

[22] It can be inferred from White's preface that he was already excluded after he published his view of the atonement. Apparently, his activities in the Great Revival as a preacher excited the association to take such action.

[23] "Minutes of a Convention of Churches, of the Baptist order who have withdrawn from the Oakmulgee [*sic*] and Flint River Associations; held at Sharon, Henry County, on the 17th, 18th and 19th days of December, 1830. 'Whereas, the Brethren are unacquainted with the conduct of the Oakmulgee Assocation, towards the Churches at Bethlehem, we deem it expedient to state, that the church of Little River had instituted a course of dealings against said church of Bethlehem, which course of dealings was acknowledged to be illegal by many intelligent brethren of the Oakmulgee and other Associations. The Association, nevertheless proceeded to try this church upon her faith in the atonement; and although the delegates from said church declared, that they were not ready for trial for lack of testimony which could be produced, provided a committee were appointed to meet them; yet they proceeded to withdraw from said church, merely because they professed to believe in a full atonement, whereupon the delegates from Hephzibah, New Hope and Mount Pleasant withdrew from the Association'" ("The Secession of Churches from Associations," *Christian Index*, 13 August 1831, 102–103).

[24] *Minutes of the Ocmulgee Baptist Association*, 1829, 2.

God's heritage; nor by which they can infringe upon any of the internal rights of the churches." Rule fifteen, article 3 stated, "If the breach [between churches or church and association] cannot be healed, [the association has the power]...to withdraw from any church or churches, whom they shall look upon to be unsound in principle, or immoral in practice, till they be reclaimed."[25] Between these two principles or rules, the struggle between the Eatonton church and the Ocmulgee Association would continue. Adiel Sherwood insisted on the exclusive rights of the churches and the use of the association as advisory councils. The Ocmulgee Association demanded the power to exclude churches over issues of faith or practice.

In 1831, the Ocmulgee committee appointed the previous year recommended a solution to the associational meeting, claiming the pledges of Eatonton and New Salem in the proposal. The agreement consisted of the following:

> 1st. We recommend to Eatonton church such a modification of the entry on their minutes, on the usury quere, as not to express that "it is consistent with gospel order," and further, that the strong expressions, "discountenanced and put down," be expunged, and some milder terms instituted in lieu thereof.

> 2nd. Being unanimously of opinion that no Baptist church can regularly, according to gospel order and church practice, dismiss a member, unless there is unanimity in the church granting the letter—we therefore advise New Salem church to drop the charge on this point particularly, and all the rest of the charges—and the brethren who have joined New Salem under the letter, obtained by only a majority of Eatonton church, to return to the Eatonton church, and in the spirit of the gospel, acknowledge that their letter was obtained irregularly, and that they regret any hard feelings and irregular conduct, that may have existed in obtaining them.

> 3rd. That upon these brethren so doing, we recommend to Eatonton church to restore them to fellowship, and then, if they

---

[25] Ibid., 4.

wish, to let them depart in peace and brotherly love, by new letters.

4th. We advise that no more should be said between them, on the usury question.[26]

In 1832, the association grew frustrated over the inability of Eatonton to live up to her pledge. In the minutes, the New Salem church claimed to live up to her promise, while Eatonton had not. In 1833, the association admitted to the use of "informal or defective" measures to settle the dispute between the churches but declared that intrusion into church rights was not intentional. During their associational meeting, the two expelled members of Eatonton, Hill and Richardson, met with the Eatonton church behind closed doors. Emerging from a brief meeting, the Eatonton church and Pastor Sherwood announced that reconciliation could not be found between the two men and the church. The church also refused to provide a reason to the association. Consequently, the Ocmulgee Association voted to withdraw fellowship from Eatonton church.

CHURCH AND ASSOCIATION RIGHTS

Following the expulsion of the Eatonton church, Sherwood began to expound in the *Christian Index* the Baptist principles of church discipline. By fall 1833, Jesse Mercer assumed control of the *Index* in Washington, Georgia, moving it from Philadelphia. In September, Sherwood with the pseudonym Melanchthon appeared on the pages of this Baptist weekly. He had not utilized this pen name in several years.[27]

---

[26] *Minutes of the Ocmulgee Baptist Association*, 1831, 2.

[27] Sherwood claimed this right as Melanchthon: "In 1830–2–3 the anti-spirit was somewhat recovering from the castigation inflicted by the strictures [Nehemiah]: they began to persecute the friends of missions and mission churches, and carried their measures in the Flint and Ocmulgee Associations: lording it over God's heritage—making minorities the true church, because they were unfriendly to missions—majorities, heretical and heterodox because they were friendly to them: I began to animadvert on such proceedings in the *Index*, and wrote about one hundred pieces subscribed 'Over West,' 'Melanchthon,' 'Watchman,' etc., showing the errors of the usurpers" (Sherwood, *Memoir*, 283).

In 1829, Sherwood as Nehemiah refuted the Kehukee Association of North Carolina in the *Religious Herald*, the Virginia Baptist newspaper. Alongside this refutation and on the same pages, Melanchthon reviewed the condition of Christendom and proposed a Reformation toward missionary Baptist principles. In 1833, Melanchthon reappeared in the *Christian Index* as the defender of church orthodoxy, the definer of church polity.

On 14 September 1833, Melanchthon announced the core issue at stake with the association: internal rights. He defined these rights as "that which a body possesses within itself, and with which none but the fraternity can meddle."[28] Internal rights were matters of discipline, whether positive or negative. Within the rubric of discipline, three areas of church consent existed: reception, dismission, and exclusion. All but exclusion required unanimity in congregational votes. In reception, "the applicant for membership must obtain the consent of all, else the union will be incomplete; for how can two walk together unless they be agreed!" Dismission also required the consent of all members. Yet, the right to exclude required only a majority vote and only the local church could exclude her members. Melanchthon pointed to scriptural points to justify the right of the church to exclude by stating, "This is clearly taught by the Savior in the 18th of Matthew.... So also in the case of the incestuous member among the Corinthians, the church is directed to deliver him to Satan, to put him from among them, i.e. exclude him. No council, nor helps, nor association, presbytery, nor conference, were necessary; but the church 'gathered together,' was sufficient for this important part of discipline."[29]

In matters of exclusion, Melanchthon noted that unanimity cannot be obtained—someone would always feel sympathetic toward a church member, regardless of biblical fact or principle. If this happened, "unanimity could not be easily obtained, and the unworthy might be retained in the church for years, if only one opposed the exclusion." All three rights belonged to the churches while any intrusion into or

---

[28] Melanchthon, "Is Discipline an Internal Right of the Church?" *Christian Index*, 14 September 1833, 38.

[29] Ibid.

assumption of these rights by the association was to be guilty of "lording it over God's heritage."[30]

Melanchthon further pursued this concept that the association violated the internal rights of the churches. In November 1833, he clarified the case of Eatonton not complying with her pledge due to internal rights. The church would not receive dictated rules from an association on how she would receive her members. The pledge as perceived by Eatonton consisted of restoring excluded members according to Eatonton's own rules of restoration. Yet, the association could not dictate the specific actions to be taken by a church. Melanchthon asserted:

> An Association can not, in the settlement of differences between churches, receive or require a promise involving their internal rights. Why? Because, there is a prior law to wit, the Constitutions of the Associations, which forbid any such infringements on internal rights. The Association which does this, is violating its own Constitution; and should immediately retrace its steps, or it will be justly chargeable with attempting to lord it over God's heritage.[31]

Associations served merely as advisory councils between disputing churches. Melanchthon proposed that beyond basic advice the association cannot intervene between a church and her members. Even in matters of fellowship, for an association to ask a church what her steps in

---

[30] Melanchthon clarified this point further in his next article. The minority must submit to the majority in order for Baptist congregational polity to work. "When a majority decide on exclusion, it is the duty of the minority to submit.... There are few causes of exclusion, but in which some take the part of the offender; but when the majority decide that he is no longer fit for membership, the minority yield, or they become subjects of censure and discipline" ("To 'A Young Member,'" *Christian Index*, 29 October 1833, 63).

[31] Melanchthon, "Can an Association, without violating its own constitution, receive a promise from a church, to perform an act which would prostrate its own internal rights?" *Christian Index*, 12 November 1833, 71).

restoration would be was akin "to intrud[ing] into the private matters of husband and wife."[32]

Associational discipline such as that instituted during the 1829–1834 era in the Ocmulgee Association violated the constitutions of the associations. As those who intervened attempted to maintain a discipline among the churches, they also approached the point of invading church rights. Sherwood made this issue a point of church independence, while never promoting powers of the association. He and his opponents differed on the concepts of church and associational rights. The emerging Primitive Baptist leaders looked at the Georgia Association and others before the modern missions movement as their precedents. Godly discipline in the churches was intimately connected with strong discipline on the associational level. According to this configuration, an association could discipline its churches just as a church disciplined its own members. Yet, Sherwood challenged this tradition on scriptural grounds. Regardless of charges of heterodoxy, the Scriptures did not give associations authority to intervene. In fact, using the same logic of explicit biblicism that Primitive Baptists followed, associations did not exist in the New Testament.

Sherwood as Melanchthon also utilized an older historical fear that predated American or Georgia Baptist past—the tyranny of Roman Catholicism. He noticed a proposition stated by the Ocmulgee Association in its circular of 1833: "When the Union or Communion is broken in that case, the Churches have agreed to put their keys into the hands of the Association." This statement epitomized Melanchthon's contention against the Ocmulgee. They did not possess a clear understanding of an association's relation to the churches. The internal rights of the churches had been redefined by the Ocmulgee as to "build meeting houses, and attend to other unimportant matters." Ambitious men in the association had clouded the true definition of church discipline. Melanchthon warned his readers:

And Constitutions are but cobwebs in the hands of aspiring men when party or self-aggrandizement lead them to action....

---

[32] Ibid.

Think you, that the pioneer preachers, who planted independent churches in the woods of Georgia, ever imagined that before their children should sleep in their graves, that an Association of Churches purely republican in their formation, would be so misled as to adopt such a sentiment as that at the head of this paper? [referring to the title] I object to giving up our keys.

    1st. Because they may never be handed back.

    2nd. Because they may use them to imprison, to stretch and to broil on embers as did their progenitors.[33]

CHURCH AND ASSOCIATION PRINCIPLES

After asserting the rights of the churches, Sherwood through the use of other pseudonyms in the *Christian Index* promoted the principles to accept and reject in church governance. As Watchman, the simple observer of Christendom, the disguised Sherwood delineated the difference between opinion and principle. As he saw it, the opposing party could not draw a line of demarcation between their opinions and their traditional principles. Opinions were matters of polity that do not relate to principle or doctrine. Opinions such as women voting in the church or which day is the Sabbath were points that should not disturb fellowship between churches or between church members. Principles or doctrines were quite different. Watchman declared, "Now if you deny the doctrine of the Saviour's divinity, or that of his resurrection, or of regeneration, this denial destroys my fellowship."[34]

Overwest, Sherwood's pseudonym as commentator on Western civilization in Baptist life, also began to clarify ecclesiastical principles in the dispute.[35] Almost as prolific with Overwest as with Melanchthon,

---

[33] Melanchthon, "St. Peter's Successor, or When the Union or Communion is broken in that case, the Churches have agreed to put their keys into the hands of the Association," *Christian Index*, 3 December 1833, 83.

[34] Watchman, "It is a Contest for Principle," *Christian Index*, 17 December 1833, 90.

[35] The Primitive Baptists had enough of pseudonyms by 1836. Bro. Mosely of the Ocmulgee Association wrote the *Primitive Baptist* to complain, "The fact is, those human invention men are the finest fellows in the world and love you the most and best and whether or not as long as they think there is any hope of winning you over, but let them

Sherwood appeared in 1833 with this new pseudonym to complement the efforts of the Wittenberg reformer. On some occasions, both penmen would respond to each other, but both centered their efforts on defining church independence and associational principles. In 1834, Overwest specifically responded to the 1833 Ocmulgee circular as Sherwood helped form the Central Association.

Overwest recognized that the Ocmulgee Association was claiming that its intention was not to "lord it over God's Heritage" (i.e., the churches) with the practice of exclusion. He distinguished between intention and fact or inference.[36] He also denounced the unfair treatment given even to heretics. Remembering White's expulsion in 1830, Overwest recalled the wide variety of doctrinal positions represented in the Ocmulgee Association. He charged:

> The treatment of Mr. White by the Ocmulgee, far as he may now have wandered, like that towards Mr. Strickland, was designed to drive him at a distance. But they were both Arminians; and were not some others Fatalists? Is Arminianism worse than Fatalism? Why have none been arraigned and tried for that heresy? Or is the majority in the Churches too large for this? The treatment of those two gentlemen was not marked with much fraternal kindness.[37]

Latent behind Overwest's charge of heresy laid the denial of associational enforcement of doctrine. By the use of investigative committees, associations controlled by the antimissionary advocates enforced their confessions through a form of executive power. These

---

lose hope, and take care then if you have any patience you will have a use for it and much prayer—they will belie you in their Bucket letters, published in the Index, I call the Bucketts [sic] because over [sic] ficticious names" (William Moseley, "Report," *Primitive Baptist*, 24 September 1836, 274).

[36] Overwest, "The Eatonton Church was put out of the Ocmulgee Association for not restoring persons whom she had excluded," *Christian Index*, 3 June 1834, 37. In this article, Overwest pointed to the facts rather than declarations of intention. The association went beyond a mere advisory council and expelled Eatonton in the process of making this error.

[37] Overwest, "Strange Proceedings, etc.," *Christian Index*, 17 June 1834, 93.

actions of committees to enforce doctrinal unity violated the constitutions of associations for the sake of promoting the confessions of the associations. From Overwest's perspective, doctrinal uniformity started with the effort of churches to associate, not the association's forcing the churches to be doctrinally orthodox.

In July 1834, another writer, "A Member of the Georgia," wrote the *Christian Index* refuting the three charges attached to the Eatonton church when expelled from the Ocmulgee.[38] With all probability the writer was Sherwood. He served as pastor of a church in the Georgia Association as he served the Eatonton church, before 1833, belonging to both associations. Also, the content of the article conformed to Sherwood's perspective.

After their expulsion, Eatonton and a few sister churches along with seceding churches from the Flint River Association combined their fellowship to establish the Central Association. Yet, three charges confronted this new association as it strove for legitimacy in Georgia Baptist life. The Ocmulgee Association charged the Central churches with being *heretical, immoral* and full of *seceding churches.* "A Member of the Georgia" listed these objections according to the corresponding information behind each charge.

1. Heretical. Those churches which had belonged to the Flint are declared by that body "no longer of our faith and order,"—therefore must be heretical.

2. Those from the Ocmulgee embrace Eatonton, which was dropped for her "immorality" therefore they can not be countenanced.

3. Seceders. This the Association acknowledges in their Minutes and furnishes proof enough: if they have hastily withdrawn from Associations, it is a good reason why they should not be recognized by others till they have acknowledged their errors and been restored.[39]

---

[38] A Member of the Georgia, "Central Association—Objections to Corresponding with her Noticed," *Christian Index*, 29 July 1834, 116.

[39] Ibid.

When the Central Association formed their organization during this year, the specter of Cyrus White followed the reputation (or lack thereof) of the Central Association. First, guilt by association haunted the new body. James Wilson, a pastor in the Flint River Association, participated with White in revivals and in associational endeavors. After White started the United Association, James Wilson helped form the Central Association. With a small effort in deduction, many of Sherwood's opponents attached the same charge of heresy on Wilson's shoulders as well as White's because both shared pulpits. If Wilson was a White-ite, then the Central Association had to be the same. The author, "A Member of the Georgia," separated the Central Association from White on the matter of the atonement by asserting that the members of the Primitive faction in the Flint River Association were reductionists:

> The majority of the Flint folks perceive no difference between *atonement* and *redemption,* and suppose that *general atonement* is the same as *general redemption*; and a man, in their estimation, who believes in a *general provision* limited in its application by the sovereign pleasure of God, is as much a heretic as he who supposes *all are redeemed.* The grand majority of the denomination in the United States and England believe in a general atonement.[40]

Second, opponents charged the Central Association with immorality for associating with Eatonton, even though Eatonton refused to restore unrepentant members. Third, seceders associated with seceders made the entire association evil. The writer countered the entire discussion by questioning the validity of this unbiblical attachment to associations. Where did the Bible command that associations guard and enforce the doctrinal beliefs of individual churches?

Sherwood continued throughout 1834 to drive home the point of orthodoxy based on constitutional principles and explicit biblical example. Melanchthon reappeared in the *Index* but discussed different

---

[40] Ibid.

topics of reformation. Overwest returned in 1835 as the keeper of the
peace between missionary Baptist reactions and Primitive Baptist acts of
separation. Both pseudonyms ceased to speak on direct matters of
associational rights and church freedoms. Actually, Sherwood under his
initials or full name addressed the problems of principle making his ideas
more personal.

In August 1834, Sherwood spoke in a personal manner about New
Salem's pastor, Rowell Reese. Sherwood utilized the Shakespearean
image of Hamlet who smelled treachery near Denmark close to the
rotting flesh of his murdered and betrayed father. "New Salem stated (or
rather the Pastor) that they did write a letter to Eatonton in 1829, to know
the standing of those who were seeking admission, and waited a day and
a half for an answer, but having received none, they were admitted.
Whew!"[41] At this point, the admission of excluded members with church
letters illegally gained "will inevitably draw the inference that something
'rotten' and wicked has been done by that church, of which they are
ashamed." In another article in August, Sherwood noted the concept of
double jeopardy in the relationship between New Salem church and the
Ocmulgee Association. In 1831, the Ocmulgee commanded excluded
members of Eatonton to be restored, but the Eatonton church was
dismissed two years later without the excluded members' being restored.
Now, the association and New Salem claimed that the excluded members
were members of New Salem before the 1831 associational meeting.[42]

In 1835, New Salem confessed to her error of receiving members by
a majority only. She stated at the Ocmulgee Association:

> We, the New Salem Baptist Church, hereby confess that the
> principle to grant letters, or receive members into the churches
> by a majority only, upon which she acted in receiving A.
> Richardson, Waid Hill, James Bussey, and others, is not
> wholesome or commendable, and that she did not design or
> intend to set up said principle, and act as a precedent, and feel

---

[41] A. S., "'Something Rotten' nearer than 'Denmark,'" *Christian Index*, 12 August
1834, 119.

[42] A. S., "The New Salem Case—continued," *Christian Index*, 26 August 1834, 132.

sorry and deeply to regret the afflictions and unhappy difficulties which have grown out of them; and, further, we utterly disavow any intention to act further on the principle.[43]

This admission of error on principle angered Sherwood. The New Salem church accepted expelled members who manufactured their own letters of dismission and accepted them as members with a majority, not a unanimous vote. By admitting to their error in principle, the New Salem congregation should rectify their practice. Sherwood deduced the logical disconnection by way of analogy. "When one man takes away another's property, the law of the land requires it, or its equivalent, to be restored—an acknowledgment that the principle of robbing, is wrong, does not satisfy." This restoration of practice with principle would be made evident by an apology and admission of guilt to the Eatonton church. Sherwood noted that the principle and practice of the Ocmulgee Association and New Salem church continued to be disconnected. His church had not received a resolution or an apology.

Melanchthon wrote his last words concerning this debate and then disappeared from the pages of the *Index* for five years. In this article, he stated his final position on associations in a biblical and historical context: "The Bible furnishes no account how the primitive churches were constituted.... There is no evidence that apostles or ministers were present at their formation.... The Bible knows nothing about a presbytery to attend and see if they are well put together."[44] Churches do not need associations to make them orthodox. Just as Protestants do not believe in apostolic succession, Baptists do not believe in the transfer of holiness from one minister or group of ministers to another. Rather, the association functions as a means of fellowship, not prescribed by Scripture, except in general statements of Christian unity. According to Sherwood, "They [associations] are bodies of expediency and usefulness—can be formed or dissolved at the pleasure of the

---

[43] Adiel Sherwood, "Principle and Practice Disconnected," *Christian Index*, 30 September 1834, 3.

[44] Melanchthon, "Constitution of Churches and Associations," *Christian Index*, 3 November 1835, 2.

constituents,—the churches."[45] Due to the nature of associations' being based on utility, the new associations did not have to be established by an existing presbytery of another association. The foundational history of the Georgia Association and the Philadelphia Association showed this same precedent.

GEORGIA MINISTERS' MEETING

By summer 1836, most associations newly formed were antimissionary or Primitive Baptist. From 1828 to 1836, Georgia Baptist churches torn by factional fighting split over the doctrinal issue of the atonement and the practical issue of missions as well as the benevolent societies that promoted missions. Actually, the doctrinal issue resided in the background of the debate, only to surface when orthodoxy became an issue. The predominant issue when churches and associations finally divided concerned the existence of the true or original church. The term *primitive* proceeded from this argument. The antimissionary Baptists wished for the mantle of being the original Baptists so much that they took great precautions to retain all historical connections to Baptists before the missions movement. When churches split, the antimissionaries attempted to retain the name of the church or ownership of the building. When associations split, the antimissionaries wished for as much connection as possible with the oldest Georgia associations that held to original principles. The Ocmulgee Association's losing all the missionary Baptists through the fallout from the Eatonton case became the highest example of original standing. All other "new" associations of Primitive Baptists drew comfort from being historically connected with the Ocmulgee. This connection strengthened their resolve to continue their separation.

On 7 July 1836, Georgia Baptist ministers met in Forsyth, Georgia, at the Presbyterian Church to reconcile differences among the brethren. The assembly chose Jesse Mercer as moderator and Adiel Sherwood as clerk, just as the earlier Georgia Baptist Convention meetings did. Before proceeding into the business of reconciliation, the assembly adopted the

---

[45] Ibid.

following resolution: "Agreed, that we, as a convention of Ministers, utterly disclaim any intention to dictate to one another, or to the Associations and Churches, but that we aim at nothing more than, by friendly intercourse, and consultation, to encourage fellowship and union."[46]

More than six decades after the resolution passed, S. G. Hillyer, one of Sherwood's students, recalled the words of Sherwood to the gathered host: "Brother Moderator, I propose that we begin right now, and here, to comply with the terms of this resolution; and I am willing to be the first to do it. I know there have been hard feelings between a brother who sits before me and myself. If I ever hurt his feelings, I am sorry for it, and I ask his forgiveness and am willing to give him my hand."[47] With heartfelt gratitude, the brother returned the handshake of fellowship.

With an improved spirit of fellowship, the assembly proposed fourteen questions to be answered. These questions actually served as a defining force of the Georgia Baptist Convention in particular and missionary Baptists in general. The inquiries also centered mostly on the principles Sherwood promoted in the *Christian Index* from 1831 to 1835 (i.e., the rights of churches and associations). The Georgia Minister's Meeting answered the following questions:

1. Do we, as a body on doctrinal points, hold those sentiments, which have characterized Baptist churches from time immemorial, and particularly as embodied and set forth in the Articles of Faith adopted by the Georgia, Flint River, Ocmulgee and Yellow River Associations?

2. Is not a church, constituted on Gospel principles, an independent body in regard to its government, and not subject to any authority but that of Christ, the Great Head of the Church?

3. Have Associations executive or disciplinary power?

---

[46] "Proceedings of the Minister's Meeting at Forsyth, Ga., July, 1836," *Christian Index*, 28 July 1836, 451–53. See also Boykin, *History of the Baptist Denomination*, 186–89.

[47] S. G. Hillyer, *Reminiscences of Georgia Baptists* (Atlanta: Foote and Davies Company, 1902) 26–27.

4. Or, are they merely advisory councils, without authority to enforce their advice?

5. Does the mere secession of a church from an Association effect its character as an orderly body?

6. What are the circumstances connected with the secession of a church from an Association, which impair the standing of that Church?

7. What circumstances connected with the withdrawment of an Association from a church impair the standing of that church?

8. Under what circumstances may a minority of a church be justified in withdrawing or separating from the majority?

9. Is it the sense of this meeting that differences of opinion in the missionary and such like operations should effect [sic] the fellowship of brethren or churches?

10. When a church or churches have seceded from an Association, and produced by such a secession, a division of the church or churches, in what manner consistent with good order and discipline can a union be had?

11. Is it in the opinion of this meeting right, to rebaptize any person who has been baptized on a profession of faith, by a Baptist minister who is held orderly in the estimation of the church to which he belongs?

12. Is the sense of this meeting that the correspondence of Associations should cease on account of differences of opinion between them until all proper means have been exhausted to remove it?

13. Is it the opinion of this meeting, that Baptist Churches should close their doors against ministers without evidence of their unsoundness in faith or immorality in practice?

14. Will this meeting appoint a Committee to whom they will confide the business of drawing up a Circular Address of a conciliary character to the denomination in the State, to be reported to this body for its approval?[48]

---

[48] "Proceedings,"*Christian Index*, 451–53.

The first question concerning the orthodox doctrine of the group asked the assembly to claim the traditional Calvinist doctrine of the Baptists. All agreed as a group, with a few dissenting from the United Association. In response to this lack of a unanimous vote, each member of the meeting was called by name to respond to the confession. All responded in the affirmative, except the United Association delegation. At the next session on the following day, the United Association agreed with the traditional Baptist confessions in Georgia with the exception of the fourth and sixth articles.[49] These two articles asserted election and effectual calling, making the United brethren of a different faith than the Georgia Baptist Convention.[50] Questions two, four, and fourteen received affirmative votes while questions three, five, nine, and twelve were negative. Questions eight and eleven were dropped, while the remaining questions did not receive either an affirmation or negative response.

The Georgia Baptist ministers held another meeting at Covington, in Newton County, on 29, 30, 31 October and 1 November 1836. This conference served two purposes: to reaffirm the ministers' orthodoxy as stated in the first meeting and to accept the Central Baptist Association as a valid, corresponding component of the Georgia Baptist Convention. All new members accepted the traditional Georgia confessions with the exception of James Wilson (Cyrus White's former associate), who said "he could not go so far on election as the others."[51] The ministers

---

[49] "The members of the United Association handed in their answer in writing, touching the Articles of Faith 'Nothing in the Articles of Faith alluded to, presents any difficulty, except a part of the 4th and some connection with it in the 6th,' signed, E. Strickland, John Reeves, Andrew Cumbie, Wm Byars" (ibid.).

[50] One should note that the confessions modeled after the Georgia Association did not address the issue of limited atonement. Article four addressed only particular redemption. Therefore, those Baptists who accepted Andrew Fuller's view of the atonement could still be considered orthodox. The fourth article states, "We believe in the everlasting love of God to His people, and the eternal election of a definite number of the human race, to grace and glory: And that there was a covenant of grace or redemption made between the Father and the Son before the world began, in which their salvation is secure, and that they in particular are redeemed" (Boykin, *History of the Baptist Denomination,* 196).

[51] "Proceedings of the Second Minister's Meeting," *Christian Index,* 24 November 1836, 724; Boykin, *History of the Baptist Denomination* (reprint of proceedings), 192–96. The Jack Tarver Library at Mercer University possesses the original pamphlet edition of the proceedings. See *Ministers' Meeting: Proceedings of the Second Minister's*

reaffirmed the purpose of the meeting to be a forum of fellowship. They did ask, "Is the Central Association, considered as to its constitution, and the circumstances under which it was formed, such a body as should be admitted into the general union?"[52] Stating love as their standard, the ministers at Covington accepted into their fellowship the Central Baptist Association according to the regular standards of associational fellowship. On Tuesday morning, 31 October, Adiel Sherwood vacated his position as clerk, having to return to his new vocation in Washington as professor and agent of Columbian College.

THE PRIMITIVE BAPTIST AND ADIEL SHERWOOD

The Georgia Ministers meetings did not resolve the complaints of the Primitive Baptists, but merely solidified the unity among missionary Baptists. After the first meeting in July, a circular concerning Christian unity issued by the committee was published for the *Christian Index*, the *Sign of the Times*, and the *Primitive Baptist* newspapers.[53]

The Primitive Baptists did not trust the efforts toward unity initiated at Forsyth and continuing at Covington. Rather, they still suspected that these efforts were a disguised attempt to steal their convictions

---

Meeting Held at Covington, Newton County, October 29, 30, 31, and November 1, 1836 (Washington GA: *Christian Index*, 1837).

[52] Earlier in 1836, the Georgia Baptist Association with Sherwood as part of the advisory council accepted correspondence with the Central Association. Five reasons were stated in the minutes: "Reasons for Corresponding with the Central Association: (1) The Central Association is of our faith and order. (2) We believe the Ministers of the Central Association to be pious, evangelical men. (3) The Central Association came together just as our own Association did in 1784. (4) The Central Association is engaged in the same work of faith, and labor of love, in which we are. (5) As far as we have an opportunity of knowing, (and this opportunity with some of us, is by no means limited,) the Central Churches endeavor to maintain a Godly discipline" (*Minutes of the Georgia Baptist Association* [Augusta: W. Lawson, 1836] 8).

[53] Boykin, *History of the Baptist Denomination,* 173. The *Primitive Baptist* began its circulation during summer 1835 in Tarsboro NC, although it almost began in Georgia. Jason Greer, Rowell Reese, and Joel Colley, correspondents with the New York antimission paper the *Signs of the Times*, combined their efforts with other Georgia antimissionary Baptists such as William Mosely and James Henderson to start a paper in Georgia to counteract the impact of the *Christian Index*. For an unknown reason, Tarsboro became a better location for the weekly.

concerning God's providence. Editor Joshua Lawrence of the *Primitive Baptist* continued to react to the declaration of Christian Unity six months after its initial circulation. He charged missionary Baptists with the following tactics under the guise of Unity: "Upon the ground of missions we will unite, nearly or remotely, with Christians or anti-christians, but that we will unite with no others at the expense of missions and that the object of the present movements in these meetings is, to enlarge our ranks and silence opposition; and by soft pretensions to catch craftily some whom we could not openly secure."[54] Rather, the missionary Baptists, if not deceptive, were deceitful. Lawrence claimed, "We of the Old School will not now in so many words, say they are deceitful workers, but if the word of the Lord calls them so, we will not object. Some of them have admitted the want of scripture authority for their 'diversified plans,' and yet they pursue those plans; consequently, they are not to be trusted."[55]

More specific than charges of lying and deceit against all missionary Baptists, many Primitive Baptists had a point of contention against Adiel Sherwood. Within the efforts to raise money for Georgia Baptist missions, Sherwood diverted money from one account to another, leaving the impression of stealing mission money. Jesse Mercer as editor of the *Christian Index* attempted to clarify Sherwood's actions in early December 1836. A Brother Holloway claimed to the *Primitive Baptist* to have proof of Adiel Sherwood's guilt in diverting Georgia Baptist money. This charge coincided with the publication of the July circular of the Georgia Ministers' Meeting on Christian unity. Instead of forgiveness, the charge of dishonesty continued to be attached to the missionary cause by the antimissionary Baptists. Mercer solved the charge with Sherwood's response to him in a former letter: "We have inquired of bro. S. about this matter, and he informed us that the case was not the taking of the Foreign Mission funds and apply them to Domestic Missions; but it was the taking of the mission funds (that is, missionary funds unappropriated) and putting them to the domestic funds because that was low, rather than to the Foreign Mission fund, which was

---

[54] Editor, "The Address," *Primitive Baptist*, 2 February 1837, 42.
[55] Ibid.

more full."[56] Shortly before Christmas, Sherwood sent his own statement to Mercer accounting for the diverted money.

> I was at the meeting of the Putnam Auxiliary, to which allusion has been had, and made statements touching the Convention, but cannot now recollect my precise words. I presume I could not have stated that the Convention had diverted the Georgia Missionary Funds to Domestic use; because this would be unfair. I could not have said they had borrowed, because I find, by Minutes of 1833, that the Domestic Fund is much the largest, and no need of borrowing. I presume the word used, on which those brethren's minds are fixed, was *divide*. I think so, because I find in the Minutes of 1831, this note: "The Treasurer was directed to divide the Mission Fund between Foreign and Domestic Missions, and keep them distinct." Prior to this date, there could be neither diverting nor borrowing; because both Funds were together—i.e. there was no difference: After this period, I find the Domestic is always large, (see Minutes of '33—I have not '32 at hand) and therefore borrowing or diverting would not be needed. I presume it was a misunderstanding of my statement.[57]

CONCLUSION

The associational principle promoted by Sherwood did much to change the function of associations in Georgia Baptist life. Before the General Association of Georgia Baptists in 1822 and the Great Georgia Revival of 1827, associations as the lone enforcers of doctrinal unity remained unchallenged due to the lack of larger organizational structures. When larger means of correspondence and missionary endeavors appeared, associations initially rejected them. This can easily be seen with the early efforts of establishing a correspondence between Georgia Baptist

---

[56] Editor, "Minister's Meeting—'The Address,'" *Christian Index*, 8 December 1836, 753.

[57] A. S., "Much Ado About Nothing," *Christian Index*, 22 December 1836, 789.

associations and the Triennial Convention. Early Georgia Baptist associations functioned as bodies of correspondence, agents of doctrinal unity in a geographical location, and organizations for promoting itinerant preaching. After Sherwood's experience with the Ocmulgee Association and his influence in establishing the Central Association, his view of Baptist associations clarified the already stated view of this body as seen in its articles of decorum. Associations could not "lord it over God's heritage," but they could withdraw fellowship.[58]

A state denomination under the original purpose of establishing closer correspondence did much to unify the associations and really did not threaten them. Yet, the enrollment of auxiliary societies into a general association and changing this general association to a state convention alarmed the Baptists who were not agreeable to missionary work. From their perspective, all extra-ecclesiastical organizations should function as defenders of orthodoxy, not promoters of benevolent causes. Unfortunately, antimissionary Baptists never questioned the validity of associations as scriptural institutions.[59] Under Sherwood's example, the defenders of orthodoxy were not associations, local or state. The churches, as God's local assemblies, were the source of doctrinal conformity.

Unintentionally, Sherwood strengthened polity at the expense of doctrine. When the emerging Primitive Baptists wished for doctrinal

---

[58] In 1854, one of the White-ites, E. Strickland of the United Association, and a Barnabas Strickland protested against unfair treatment in the Tallapoosa Association and its correspondence with the Flint River Association. Barnabas Strickland accused the Flint River Association of the following charge: "To my mind you have trampled underfoot the doctrine of brother Jesse Mercer and other standard ministers of our denomination, viz., Bro. Sherwood, brother Stokes, brother Fleming, and many others in Georgia and other sister States." The Flint River Association did not deny the associational principle of Mercer and Sherwood but overruled the protests of Barnabas Strickland, who illegally represented his association. In one of its subsequent resolutions, the Flint River Association stated, "Resolved, That is our policy to conform strictly to the cardinal doctrines of the Bible, which we believe can be most effectually accomplished by a strict adherence to the principles and practices advocated and maintained by the great body of the Baptist denomination" (J. H. Campbell, "Flint River Association," *Christian Index*, 12 October 1854, 162).

[59] Another term for antimissionary Baptists by the missionary Baptists was *anti-effort* Baptists. The term *primitive* did not become a definite term until the late 1830s.

unity after a massive influx of new members, Sherwood wished for greater organization to achieve his goals of missions and evangelism. By strengthening the independence of the churches, he configured a new dynamic into missionary Baptist polity. The associations retained the disciplinary procedure of exclusion, even in matters of doctrine, but no longer could interfere in the local church to determine its doctrinal stance. Churches could freely relate to any other association or to the state convention itself. By eliminating the traditional role of doctrinal oversight found in eighteenth-century American Baptist associations, Sherwood reorganized the associations into smaller components for promoting societies and mission causes, allowing doctrinal issues to be decided among churches as well as associations as they related to the state convention.

5

MINISTERIAL EDUCATION, MANUAL LABOR, AND MERCER UNIVERSITY

Adiel Sherwood openly advocated the education of Baptist ministers as early as he advocated Sunday schools for children. When he envisioned the formation of the Georgia Baptist Convention in 1822, this larger association of Baptists mirrored the earlier failed attempt of Georgia Baptists in 1803. Not only did Henry Holcombe and Jesse Mercer attempt to establish a state convention at this earlier time, but they also opened Mount Enon College as a result of these early meetings. Both the college and the formation of a general state association met disaster. When Sherwood pushed the same agenda two decades later, he faced a negative precedent. However, his plan proved to be successful. As he helped to initiate the formation of the Georgia Baptist Convention, Sherwood also initiated an early system of ministerial education that answered the need for an educated clergy.

In 1827, Sherwood moved to the Eatonton church to serve as her pastor. He also served as the teacher of Eatonton Academy. In 1828, he began his own private seminary (named "School of the Prophets") with a few students. In 1831, he established a private manual labor school composed of ministerial students on a farm outside of Eatonton. Within a year he demonstrated to the executive committee of the Georgia Baptist Convention the feasibility and success of this new method of education already popular in Germany and New England. Upon the request of the committee, Sherwood released his ministerial students to form the new Mercer Institute in Penfield, Georgia, later known as Mercer University.

Sherwood continued to contribute to early developments in ministerial education. He left Georgia in 1836 to become Professor of Sacred Literature at Columbian College. In 1839, he returned to Penfield, Georgia, as Georgia Baptists reconstituted the Mercer institute into Mercer University. As the first theology professor of the school, Sherwood served as Professor of Sacred Literature for three years. In 1841, he left the state to become the first full-time president of Shurtleff College in Alton, Illinois. He served the school for four years. In 1856, Sherwood returned to Georgia as president of Marshall College in Griffin, Georgia. This school was his last post as an educator. During the Civil War, the college closed, only to reopen briefly during the 1870s.

EARLY CONCEPTS OF MINISTERIAL EDUCATION

The desire for an educated clergy in Georgia epitomized the major efforts of Sherwood in the 1820s. When he entered the state in 1818, he held educational credentials normally found among the Presbyterian clergy, but not the Baptists. Perhaps, from an institutional standpoint, he was the most educated minister in the state, having received a rigorous training at Middlebury College and Andover Seminary. His earliest critique of Georgia Baptist pastors occurred while serving as an evangelist for the Savannah Missionary Society. As early as 1821, Sherwood characterized his pastor as a man whose "notions are different, and he 'wiser in his own conceit, than seven men who can render a reason.'"[1] The knowledge and culture inherent to education appeared to be desirable qualities for Sherwood and other trained ministers in the state. In 1822, at the Powelton conference, the Georgia Baptist ministers who constituted the new general association defined six objects in its foundation. The fifth object stated, "To afford an opportunity to those who may conscientiously think it their duty to form a fund for the

---

[1] Richard Orderly, "My Minister," *Missionary*, 31 December 1821, 1. Orderly was one of Sherwood's first pseudonymns. See Julia Sherwood and Samuel Boykin, *Memoir of Adiel Sherwood, D.D.* (Philadelphia: Grant and Faires, 1884) 283.

education of pious young men who may be called by the Spirit and their churches to the Christian ministry."[2]

In 1825, Sherwood delivered a sermon before the Georgia Association titled "The Careful Minister." Although his speech predated his manual labor school, it did signal his intent to push Georgia Baptists toward desiring ministerial education and refinement. He noted several offences a minister could commit in his delivery, but the major problems attached to preaching were education and the lack of it. Sherwood warned his audience of the two-sided problem of forsaking ministerial learning for expediency or posing as a scholar: "While we maintain it is the minister's duty to descend to the comprehension of his audience; we would throw out a caution against his imitating their low and vulgar manner of speaking, and urge the importance of their rising by degrees to his standard, rather than that he should sink to theirs."[3] While the educated pastor should expect the audience to reach his level of biblical comprehension, he should not pose as something he is not: "But the sacred office is brought into disrepute, not so frequently by ripe and profound scholars, as by those who affect to be such.... From hearing such pretended scholars preach, the idea has got footing, that learning is an injury to ministers, because learned ones cannot be understood."[4]

An educated clergy presented a genuine problem to the Baptist denomination. With uneducated audiences unable to understand their pastors, congregations would inevitably cease to listen to their ministers. However, Sherwood saw the reaction to this problem as an additional dilemma. Uneducated pastors did not fulfill their calling as instructors of God's word. Sherwood noted, "But opposers of science in the ministry, say, 'We do not intend to exclude all learning.' How much then, we ask, would you recommend? You answer, 'Enough to read the Bible.'"[5]

---

[2] Samuel Boykin, *History of the Baptist Denomination in Georgia: With Biographical Compendium and Portrait Gallery of Baptist Ministers and Other Georgia Baptists* (Atlanta: James P. Harrison and Company, 1881) 106.

[3] Adiel Sherwood, "The Careful Minister," in *The Georgia Pulpit: or Ministers' Yearly Offering*, ed. Robert Fleming (Richmond: H. K. Ellyson, 1847) 66.

[4] Ibid.

[5] Ibid., 67.

When Sherwood relocated from Greensboro to Eatonton in 1827, he busied himself with the education of a few ministers. Although he completed extensive journeys throughout Georgia to promote the Great Revival of 1827, he found time to teach at the Eatonton Academy as well as serve as the pastor of the Eatonton church. Sherwood later noted that this year marked the first monetary contribution to ministerial education by the Georgia Baptist Convention.[6] In 1828, the convention allotted money for actual ministerial education rather than mere financial help to buy books. Sherwood opened his private seminary (School of the Prophets) at the Eatonton church with these funds.[7] He stated:

> Rules to regulate the reception of beneficiaries were adopted by the Convention in 1828. One of them is that the applicant must be licensed by his church to furnish instruction, by their pastor, to all young ministers who desired it, with board, &c., for one year, provided the Convention would supply one hundred dollars. This was accepted, and one young man entered immediately, and two the succeeding year, one of who[m] died; the others are now in the field.[8]

Jesse H. Campbell and J. R. Hand were the only two ministerial students recorded by name, although Sherwood taught between eight and ten students from 1828 to 1830.[9] In 1831, he accepted ministerial students in addition to college-bound students as boarders who paid their

---

[6] "In 1827, fifty dollars were voted towards the support of Thomas Walsh, a young licentiate of great promise, then at Athens. He was advised to take a regular college course. The churches, however, called him away; and after a few years of usefulness in South Carolina, 'he fell on sleep.' Fifty dollars were the same year appropriated for standard theological books, such as Buck, Brown, Fuller &c. These were given to ministers who desired to improve their minds. These appropriations were kept up for a number of years" (Adelphos, "Ministerial Education in Georgia," *Christian Index*, 21 December 1837, 821–22).

[7] "This little school of the prophets was the first systematic effort to bestow a theological education among the Baptists of Georgia, and was really the *very beginning* of Mercer University" (Sherwood and Boykin, *Memoir*, 232).

[8] Ibid.

[9] Boykin, *History of the Baptist Denomination,* 144.

expenses through the new manual labor school. In 1832, he released the entire school to the Penfield Institute.

DEFENSE AND DEFINITION OF THEOLOGICAL EDUCATION

During the first three years of the "School of the Prophets" in Eatonton, Sherwood wrote articles for the *Religious Herald* defending ministerial education and refuting the Kehukee Association's attack on theological seminaries. Under the pseudonym Melanchthon, Sherwood wrote a twelve-part series of articles titled "Essays on Reformation." Promoting a reformation in theology and practice, he foresaw the need for an educated ministry that could accurately interpret Scripture and correctly exhort sinners to repent. In fact, Melanchthon believed a pastor's teaching function was connected to his learning mind:

> In the heart of every faithful man, there should be a reigning desire to do what he can, according to his talents and his situation, to promote the cause of God and goodness among men. Now, where this reigning desire is combined with that species of talents which qualifies a disciple of Christ to impart religious instruction, or even exhortation and admonition to others—let him make the attempt, and proceed, as through divine aid he may be enabled.[10]

This assertion countered the prevailing notion Sherwood combated as Nehemiah in his "Strictures of the Kehukee Association." When Jordan Smith of Washington County, Georgia, republished the Kehukee Declaration of North Carolina in Georgia, Nehemiah attacked the emerging Primitive Baptist sect as being inconsistent. He identified the criticism of theological seminaries as "the invention of men, &c., &c., introducing a proud, pompous and fashionable ministry, instead of an humble, pious and self-denying one."[11] Nehemiah noted that any form of theological learning constituted the essence of a seminary. Ministerial mentorship and a theological school basically differed according to

---

[10] Melanchthon, "Essays on Reformation," *Religious Herald,* 6 November 1829, 3.
[11] Nehemiah, "Kehukee Association, No. 7," *Religious Herald,* 1 May 1829, 1.

instructional time and location. When young preachers learned from an experienced pastor, the form of mentorship he received occurred on occasion and without planning. A theological school provided the same sort of learning, except it produced a more consistent and planned type of evaluation.

To Nehemiah, a theological school began when "a poor young man is called of the Lord to preach—his church licenses him,—his brethren desire his improvement, and each throws in his mite to support him."[12] Beginning with a desire for excellence, the new student surrounded himself with books and a few other like-minded students. By conserving the cost of books, a few theological students could improve their minds and save expenses. The communal sharing of ideas and textbooks constituted Nehemiah's definition of a seminary. Of course, Sherwood endeavored to accomplish the same process in Georgia. In Eatonton, Campbell, Hand, and a few other ministerial students shared the books purchased by the Georgia Baptist Convention.[13] Sherwood recalled the texts he utilized in Eatonton: "In 1827, 8, and 9, 31, Books were ordered for some 15 to 20 young ministers: such as Buck & Brown's Dictionary, Edwards and Fuller's works, *Biblical antiquities*, Jameson's *Sacred History*, Maps of Palestine, &c.... In 1828, the Clerk opened a school at Eatonton, where Campbell, Hand, &c., studied."[14]

---

[12] Ibid.

[13] The executive committee reported the following: "(2) Beneficiaries.—Brother Joseph Hand is continued at the Eatonton School another year. Brother Jesse H.Campbell was examined and directed to go there also. (3) Books.—The Clerk was directed to procure Books to the value of $50, which are to be distributed to our ministering brethren as the Committee may deem proper" (*Minutes of the General Association of the Baptist Denomination in Georgia* [Augusta: William J. Bunce, 1829] 5).

[14] Testis, "Reminiscences of Georgia, No. 5, Ministerial Education," *Christian Index*, 18 July 1860, 2. (Testis was revealed as Sherwood when he submitted his fourteenth number in this series on 14 November 1860.) Sherwood may have confused some of these works with texts he utilized in later institutions. He referred to the following textbooks (as discovered in this author's search of original editions): Charles Buck, *A Theological Dictionary* (Philadelphia: W. W. Woodward, 1807); B. B. Edwards, *Encyclopedia of Religious Knowledge: or, Dictionary of the Bible, Theology, Religious Biography, All Religions, Ecclesiastical History, and Missions*, ed. Rev. J. Newton Brown (Brattleboro VT: J. Steen & Co., 1835); Jonathan Edwards, *The Works of President Edwards: With a Memoir of His Life*, 10 vols. (New York: S. Converse,

Earlier in 1829, Sherwood read the circular to the Georgia Baptist Convention, arguing for the use of means in spreading the gospel. Basing his declaration on Mark 14:8, "She hath done what she could," he accentuated the desire for ministerial improvement as it related to the 1827 revival: "Some hundred young men have been called into our churches during the late revival who have gifts promising usefulness, and who, though they feel the need of the assistance which learning profers, are afraid to commence a course of study because it is so unpopular."[15] Sherwood pushed formal ministerial education as the necessary predecessor of an enlightened ministry. Preachers who proclaimed the truths of the Bible boldly for the conversion of sinners needed all the necessary tools for preaching. Although he communicated this to his audience through the circular, he did not convince the executive committee of a new means in educating ministers. Sherwood stated in his *Memoir*, "In that year [1829] I presented to the Executive committee of the Convention a plan for a Manual Labor School for young ministers; but nearly to a man they were opposed to it."[16]

NECESSARY AND DESIRABLE KNOWLEDGE

At the 1830 Georgia Baptist Convention, Sherwood preached an education sermon titled "Knowledge Necessary and Desirable for a Minister of the Gospel," defining his view of ministerial improvement. He first clarified what he meant by the term *knowledge*: "The knowledge derived from experience must of course be very limited."[17] The senses could detect truth, but Sherwood asserted that the Christian religion

1829–1830); Andrew Fuller, *The Works of the Rev. Andrew Fuller*, 8 vols. (Philadelphia: W. Collier, 1820–1825); John Williamson Nevin, *A Summary of Biblical Antiquities; for the Use of Schools, Bible-classes and Families* (Philadelphia: American Sunday-school Union, 1849); Mrs. Jameson, *Sacred and Legendary Art,* 2 vols. (Boston: Houghton Mifflin Company, 1898). Unless there was an earlier edition or a book with the same title, Nevin's work did not exist. An earlier publication of Jameson's work must have existed. She died in 1860.

[15] Georgia Baptist Convention, *Minutes,* 1829, 11.

[16] Sherwood and Boykin, *Memoir*, 234–35.

[17] Adiel Sherwood, *Knowledge Necessary and Desirable for a Minister of the Gospel* (Milledgeville GA: Camak and Ragland, 1830) 4. An extract of this sermon appeared in the *Religious Herald*. See "Desirable Knowledge," *Religious Herald*, 23 July 1830, 1.

dwarfed the human senses. Truly, the experience of the Holy Spirit would be analogous with science (experience required proofs just as experiments needed verification), but the Christian needed certainty based on facts that preceded experience. The objective truth of the Bible provided the factual knowledge that a minister needed at the center of his educational program.

In the body of his discourse, Sherwood divided the educational requirements of a minister into required and optional categories. First, when God called a minister to service and the church recognized his gifts, a *necessary knowledge* existed. The congregation recognized the minister's possession of a call from God, a capacity to teach, good common sense, and an acquaintance with Scripture. Sherwood defined God's call of a minister being "not a vocal one like that addressed to Samuel; but a special impression on the mind of the duty to call sinners to repentance and as anxious solicitude for their eternal salvation."[18] Of course, the call to preach had limitations. The minister's sermons did not contain inspiration equal to the Bible just because God called a man to proclaim his word.[19] Rather, three other aspects of a necessary knowledge would counter any mystical preoccupation with God's calling. A minister should be able to teach, possess good common sense, and hold a basic knowledge of the Scriptures.

Second, Sherwood noticed the need for *desirable knowledge*. At this point, Sherwood recognized a problem that the opponents of education criticized. During this period, the Primitive Baptists developed a theory in which ministers assumed a pastorate with whatever knowledge they already possessed. They did not expect ministers to improve their minds. Rather, ministers merely brought to the ministry whatever God had bestowed upon them. Yet, Sherwood saw a category of mental improvement attached to the ministry. When the elder of the church taught the congregation, he should know the facts related to the text.

---

[18] Ibid.

[19] Within this sermon, Sherwood stated, "The old sentiment that a minister is as certain of his call as of his existence, and inspired to preach, seems now to be classed among the reveries of a distempered imagination" (Sherwood, *Knowledge Necessary and Desirable*, 4). The greatest obstacle Sherwood had to counteract was the theory that preachers delivered inspired sermons, making them infallible.

Last of all, Sherwood outlined six categories of desirable knowledge. The theological student needed to be versed in two historical subjects, the first being the chronology and geography of the Bible and the second being the history of Israel and her customs. The minister also should understand grammar, logic, astronomy, and the learned languages.[20] These six categories accentuated three distinctions: background, interpretation, and proclamation. The minister who was called to teach from the Bible needed a textual, historical, and literary education.[21]

The major obstacle of theological education to Baptists in the South in general and Georgia Baptists in particular was convincing the public of the usefulness of an educated ministry. At the time of the 1830 education sermon, Sherwood had already conducted his private seminary, but he had not launched an effort to convince Georgia Baptists to sponsor a statewide theological school. The emergence of the manual labor education movement opened a door for Sherwood to push for theological education beyond personal mentorship. By being a champion of manual labor, Sherwood convinced Georgia Baptists of its popularity and its utility in producing a trained ministry.

THE EARLY HISTORY OF THE MANUAL LABOR SCHOOL MOVEMENT

From 1832 to 1845, manual labor institutes appeared in Georgia. These institutes combined physical labor with practical learning, dissolving the disparity between educational theory and everyday practicality. The manual labor system attempted either to relate learning to labor or to introduce a means for students to pay their expenses. At first, manual labor institutes began as schools for teenagers (a mixture between a

---

[20] Sherwood, *Knowledge Necessary and Desirable,* 7–9.

[21] "A general acquaintance with the Sciences and whole field of Literature, is desirable. Paul illustrates his subjects and strengthens his arguments by quotations from Heathen Authors and he is a safe pattern for our imitation. It is a well attested that as Science began to decline in the earlier centuries of the Christian era, religion also declined with it. Superstition and extravagance are the legitimate offspring of religion in uncultivated minds.... In New England a great portion of the ministers are men of education: here you can scarcely find a person who can not both read and write" (ibid., 9).

senior high school and a junior college), but advocates of this concept quickly applied it to new colleges. New denominational schools embraced this program early, seeing it as a means to educate their ministers. Protestant denominations connected the concept of masculinity and manual labor with their desire to educate ministers. Within Southern evangelicalism, parishioners desired ministers who sympathized with the same rugged frontier life as their congregations. The manual labor system helped promote this desire and consequently ensured the beginnings of denominational schools.

Within the few studies conducted on the manual labor movement in Georgia, historians have agreed that Adiel Sherwood introduced the manual labor concept into the state.[22] He promoted the idea through his denomination and through the short-lived Teacher's Society of Georgia. Through both avenues, he popularized a concept already popular in Germany and New England as well as a few locations in the South. Sherwood combined the German manual labor system found in the Fellenberg schools with the developing New England model at Andover. He also attached the Southern concern for labor and industry to these two traditions.

THE FELLENBERG MANUAL LABOR CONCEPT

The manual labor concept originated as an educational program under Philip Emanuel von Fellenberg (1771–1844). In the city of Berne,

---

[22] E. Merton Coulter stated, "The Reverend Adiel Sherwood was the pioneer in this movement in Georgia" ("The Ante-Bellum Academy Movement in Georgia," *Georgia Historical Quarterly* [December 1921]: 22). James C. Bonner and Lucien E. Roberts also asserted, "The manual-labor school idea appeared in Georgia about 1830. The leader of the movement was Adiel Sherwood" (*Studies in Georgia History and Government* [Athens: University of Georgia, 1940] 173). Bartow Davis Ragsdale stated, "The system after which Mercer Institute was patterned was that introduced by Fellenburg in the Fellenburg Schools of Germany. The plan seems to have made an early impression on Adiel Sherwood for in 1832 he established a manual labor school on his farm near Eatonton.... The Mercer Institute was founded on principles perfected by Sherwood at Eatonton and the manual labor feature therefore reverted to the Fellenburg idea, which started in Germany" (Ragsdale, "Early History of Baptist Education in Georgia" microfilm [Special Collections, Jack Tarver Library, Mercer University, Macon GA, n.d.] 64).

Switzerland, Fellenberg was born into nobility. His father, a Dutch nobleman, was married to the granddaughter of Van Tromp, a famous Dutch admiral. Schooled at home under private tutors, Fellenberg later received his university training in Germany, including a law course at Tubingen.[23]

Fellenberg began an academy by taking in a few boys into his family. By 1806, this school opened as a separate boarding school in the village of Hofwyl. The children of the socially elite were taught science, agriculture, and manual labor. In a few years, the academy had twenty teachers teaching eighty students. By 1819, over a hundred students attended the school with twenty-five to thirty teachers providing instruction.[24] The course of instruction in the academy included the Greek, Latin, German, and French languages, history, geography, mathematics, natural and mental philosophy, chemistry, music, drawing, gymnastics, natural history in all its branches, and religious instruction.

From the academy, other schools proceeded. To assist financially poor students, Fellenberg took in young people who came to learn a trade through physical labor. The "poor school," or the Farm and Trade school, accomplished two tasks: agricultural labor and mechanical learning. As the students cultivated a farm, they would learn the mechanical repairs of farm tools. The course of study included trades such as blacksmithing and carpentry coincident with the physical labors of the students. Additional schools also sprang from the academy: schools for girls, a school of applied science and a normal (teacher's) school.[25]

Writing the definitive work on the manual labor movement, Charles Bennett noticed the educational theory behind Fellenberg's system:

[Education] must prepare each individual to live a useful, happy, and moral life, but in doing so he believed there should be no attempt to disturb the order of society by confounding the classes. He believed that Divine Wisdom had shaped the order of

---

[23] Charles Alphaeus Bennett, *History of Manual and Industrial Education up to 1870* (Peoria IL: Chas. A. Bennett Co., 1926) 126.

[24] Ibid., 132.

[25] Ibid., 135–43.

things so that some men were born to rule and others to obey, and, therefore, that each should be educated for his own sphere.... The lower should respect and love the higher; the higher should appreciate and have sympathy for the lower.[26]

Fellenberg remained true to his social context as he developed new schools of learning. In an American context, Fellenberg's distinction between social classes would be adapted to the types of students and their curricula. For example, ministerial education combined with manual labor would make the overly mannered New England divines into common laborers for God among the people.

THE MANUAL LABOR SCHOOL MOVEMENT IN AMERICA

In 1819, the Fellenberg plan of manual labor appeared in America as a popular form of education, providing poor students an avenue to receive an education.[27] By 1829, advocates of this fashionable system began to promote it as a remedy for sickness. The secretary of the American Education Society in the thirteenth annual report reported in 1829 that college students exhibited a high rate of mortality and an abundance of ill health.[28] If physical exercise remedied the deleterious effects of cloistered educational life, American educators began to debate the type of exercise that would be proper. A century later, L. F. Anderson claimed the progressive leaders of the Fellenberg schools in America debated two options: the manual labor system and the Gutsmuths-Jahn system of gymnastics.[29] Within a few years, most educators opted for the manual labor concept due to internal and external motivations. The reward of accomplishing an actual task compounded with monetary compensation

---

[26] Ibid., 129.

[27] "An article descriptive of the schools at Hofwyl was reprinted in the *Academician of New York* in 1819. The editor in a postscript recommended the adoption of the Fellenberg system as a means of educating the poor in this country" (L. F. Anderson, "The Manual Labor School Movement," *Educational Review* 46 [June–December 1913]: 375).

[28] Ibid., 370.

[29] Ibid.

or debt relief ensured the "poor school" concept over against any form of gymnastics.[30]

Between the years 1819 and 1830, schools partially modeled after the Fellenberg plan appeared in Connecticut, Florida, Maine, Massachusetts, New Jersey, New York, North Carolina, Ohio, Pennsylvania, and South Carolina.[31] L. F. Anderson divided manual labor schools into two kinds: required and optional. In one form of manual labor, all students had to perform their afternoon duties in cultivating a field. In the other, manual labor served as an option for indebted students.[32]

In 1829, W. T. Brantly, editor of the *Columbian Star*, listed three manual labor schools that served as precedents for future institutes: the manual labor school connected with Andover Seminary in Massachusetts, the Oneida Institute in Whitesboro, New York, and the Maine Wesleyan Seminary. The Oneida Institute followed the required manual labor system while the Andover institute utilized the optional type. Brantly declared, "The most successful experiment is that which has been made at Andover. Indeed it is very much owing to the enterprise and success of the Mechanical Association in the Theological Seminary, in this place, by whose invitation we are now convened, that the mode of exercise which they have adopted is exciting attention widely throughout this country."[33]

At Middlebury College, Vermont, in 1830, John Hough, Sherwood's former professor, delivered an address before the Mechanical Association in which he analyzed the two forms of physical

---

[30] The term *gymnastics* should not be confused with the concept of the German gymnasium, a classical secondary school. The term *gymnastics* in this context means physical exercise used within an educational setting.

[31] Bonner and Roberts, *Studies in Georgia History,* 172–73. Only one school preceded the Fellenberg influence. Dr. John De le Howe in Lethe, near Abbeville SC, founded the first manual labor school in America.

[32] Anderson, "The Manual Labor School Movement," 377.

[33] W. T. Brantly, "Manual Labor and Education," *Columbian Star*, 21 November 1829, 323–24.

exercise: manual labor and gymnastics.[34] He stated, "The exercise of the playground is, in most seminaries at least, usually surrendered, by the more advanced and sedate members, to the younger class of students."[35] Noticing that physical prowess in a learning environment often was relegated to lesser members of the student body, Hough insisted physical work as a better alternative. In 1831, he advocated the manual labor system in the *Christian Index*, reasoning that "Something more vigorous and efficient is demanded by the necessities of our nature, than that nerveless exertion, which never causes perspiration to moisten the brow, unless aided by the sultry ardor of summer's fiercest blaze."[36] Within his discourse, Hough insisted on looking at the body from a medieval and a biblical perspective. Believing in the medieval concept of diverse bodily fluids called humors, he connected the biblical mandate for working by the sweat of one's brow with the expulsion of bodily humors in the form of perspiration.

Theodore D. Weld, an agent of the Association for the Promotion of Physical Education in Literary Institutions, began to tour the southern states in 1831.[37] By 1832, he openly questioned the motivation behind gymnastics. He believed mere exercise to be "fatiguing and uninteresting" as well as "dangerous and unnatural."[38] In a letter from New York to Thomas S. Grimke in South Carolina, Weld inquired into the type of exercise utilized in Grimke's school, attempting to compare gymnastics with manual labor.[39] Grimke responded positively in favor of the manual labor concept, providing five reasons for this preference:

---

[34] John Hough taught Sherwood in 1815. "In 1815, after tidings of the death of Andrew Fuller had reached this country, Prof. Hough, of Middlebury College, mentioned it to me, and expressed great regret" (Sherwood and Boykin, *Memoir*, 54).

[35] Anderson, "The Manual Labor School Movement," 372.

[36] John Hough, "Mechanical Labor Combined with Study," *Christian Index*, 12 March 1831, 164–65.

[37] The American Anti-Slavery Society, formed in Philadelphia in 1833, changed the preaching agenda of Theodore Dwight Weld (1803–1895), a convert under Charles G. Finney. Of course, his advocacy of abolitionism annulled any popularity that he may have gained in the South.

[38] Anderson, "The Manual Labor School Movement," 371.

[39] Thomas S. Grimke, *Correspondence on the Principles of Peace, Manual Labor Schools, &c.* (Charleston SC: Observer Office Press, 1833) 11–16.

1. Agricultural and mechanical employments...are in themselves actually useful and profitable.

2. Such a plan would multiply the associations and sympathies between the best and the least educated classes of our country.

3. On account of the science and knowledge, the skill and ingenuity which they require, they create a more various and permanent interest in themselves, thus combining utility and pleasure in a higher degree than gymnastics.

4. Agricultural and mechanical pursuits are equally adapted to social and solitary employment; and that they furnish a happy variety of in-door and out-door labor.

5. Gymnastics are exercise for the sake of exercise; but agriculture and mechanics are not so.[40]

THE ORIGINS OF THE MANUAL LABOR MOVEMENT IN GEORGIA

Although an American trend in establishing manual labor schools existed, the introduction of the concept within the state of Georgia and Georgia Baptist life came from Adiel Sherwood. He did not introduce a novel concept, but who influenced him has not been discovered. One could connect him to the manual labor schools existing at the two schools he attended: Middlebury and Andover. Likewise, the work of Theodore Weld or Thomas Grimke, as promoters of the system in the South, also could have influenced Sherwood. Yet, only two facts can be

---

[40] Ibid., 14–15. Thomas S. Grimke had two sisters, Angelina and Sarah. Growing up in an Episcopalian home in Charleston, both sisters switched denominational affiliations from the Episcopal Church to the Presbyterian Church and then to the Society of Friends (Quakers). In 1829, the Grimke sisters moved to Philadelphia. In the early 1830s, both sisters joined the abolition movement. In 1836, Angelina Grimke wrote *An Appeal to the Christian Women of the Southern States* demanding that Southern women use their influence in the home to end slavery. Her feminism combined with abolitionism led Angelina Grimke to be banned from Charleston. On 14 May 1838, Theodore Weld and Angelina Grimke were married. See Martin E. Marty, *Pilgrims in Their Own Land: 500 Years of Religion in America* (New York: Penguin Books, 1984) 250–53.

ascertained. Sherwood testified that he knew of the Fellenberg theory.[41] Also, Sherwood experienced physical problems early in his New England school life. Rev. S. P. Whitman claimed, "During his own collegiate course, he [Sherwood] had suffered from want of exercise, and he willingly embraced a plan which rendered out-door employment compulsory."[42] Since the warm climate of Georgia and the physical exertions on his farm helped his health, Sherwood planned for his students to receive the same benefits.

During 1831, Sherwood moved decisively toward establishing his own manual labor school. On 28 January 1831, Thomas Cooper, a Baptist layman, offered Sherwood a tract of land measuring 180 acres near Eatonton for 600 dollars.[43] At the April meeting of the Georgia Baptist Convention, Sherwood resubmitted his proposal to establish a manual labor school and the delegates approved it. The convention adopted the following resolution under article 18 of the minutes:

> *Resolved,* That as soon as the funds will justify it, this convention will establish, in some central part of the State, a *classical and theological school,* which shall unite agricultural labour with study, and be opened for those only preparing for the ministry.
>
> *Resolved further,* That the Executive committee, be requested to devise some plan to raise $1,500, by the 1st day of December next; and if so that a school be opened as soon as practicable. (The committee in session recommend that the agency of *thirty* persons, be secured in various parts of the State, who shall raise by the above time, each $50. About one half the

---

[41] "In making a report to the Teacher's Society on the Fellenberg schools, Sherwood admitted that he did not know much about them at first hand, but said he had ideas of his own on Manual Labor Schools; accordingly he proceeded to report on his own plan" (Elbert W.G. Boogher, *Secondary Education in Georgia, 1732–1858* (Philadelphia: I. F. Huntzinger Co., 1933) 257.

[42] Sherwood and Boykin, *Memoir,* 268.

[43] Boogher, *Secondary Education,* 259.

number is pledged already!! Let such as would become helpers
address the Clerk at Eatonton.)[44]

Throughout 1831, Sherwood, as clerk of the Georgia Baptist
Convention, recorded the monetary pledges of many Georgia Baptists.
Yet, by the fall of 1831, the convention had not purchased land for the
proposed school. Apparently, some prominent leaders in the convention
opposed the plan. Years later, Sherwood claimed: "B. M. Sanders
afterwards so eminently useful, the first teacher and self-denying laborer
in the school, was so fearful that the scheme would not go, that he said
he would take the 30th share, implying that the thing was impossible. J.
E. Dawson knowing of S's remark, exerted himself to procure
subscriptions, declaring Sanders should have no part in the concern,
though he subscribed his fifty."[45] Realizing the Georgia Baptist
leadership could not envision the establishment of a denominational
school, Sherwood purchased the land offered to him by Thomas Cooper
and began his own experiment.[46]

EARLY CONSENSUS IN THE STATE OF GEORGIA

Between Sherwood's original proposal in 1829 and his implementation
of his concept in 1832, a consensus grew within the Baptist
denomination to establish manual labor schools for ministers. As early as
1829, Editor W. T. Brantly of the *Columbian Star* in Philadelphia

---

[44] Georgia Baptist Convention, *Minutes,* 1831, 5.

[45] Testis, "Reminiscences of Georgia, No. 5, Ministerial Education," *Chrisitan Index,* 18 July 1860, 2.

[46] In his memoir, Sherwood recalled, "A school was to have been opened in January of the following year, but in the fall no farm had been purchased, and I discovered that the committee were afraid of putting the plan into practice. I therefore purchased one hundred and sixty acres of land, one and a half miles northwest of Eatonton, from Thomas Cooper, for six hundred dollars, and advertised for eight or ten pupils on the manual labor plan.... The farm upon which I had erected a large and commodious house, a mile and a half northwest of Eatonton, was afterward called 'Sherwood Place.' There Mr. Stanley, a young minister, studied under my direction" (Sherwood and Boykin, *Memoir,* 237–38).

promoted the idea.[47] He noted the relationship between success and hard work.[48] In an 1830 article, he defined a specific plan for establishing a manual labor school, attaching a profit motivation behind it. He instructed his audience to implement the following suggestions:

> 1. Turn a part or the whole of your capital into a farm or plantation, consisting of a suitable quantity of land that shall be unquestionably productive.
> 2. Let the usual implements of husbandry be provided...
> 3. Procure a faithful and prudent man as farmer, or steward
> 4. To procure tuition.... Five hundred individuals who should pay each $5 per annum, would make an amount sufficient to procure instruction for fifty students.[49]

Due to Brantly's paper and the announcement of the Georgia Baptist Convention to establish a manual labor school for ministers, several Georgia Baptists wrote responses to this idea. In 1831, a Baptist layman offered his opinion of the manual labor system to the *Christian Index* (formerly the *Columbian Star*).[50] He applauded the effort in

---

[47] Brantly possessed both an interest in ministerial education and education in Georgia. Before he left Augusta Baptist Church in 1827 to serve as pastor of First Baptist Church of Philadelphia, Brantly taught three ministerial students from 1825 to 1827. Jack Harwell described Brantly's transition in the following manner: "When Brantly moved to the church in Philadelphia, the church could pay him only $1,600 per year, which was less than half what he had earned at Richmond Academy, not to mention what First Baptist Church in Augusta had paid him. So he opened a 'classical school' in Philadelphia to supplement his meager income from the pastorate. To add to this double-load of pastor and schoolmaster, Brantly soon added the title of editor of *The Columbian Star*" (Jack U. Harwell, *An Old Friend with New Credentials: A History of the Christian Index* [Atlanta: *Christian Index*, 1972] 49).

[48] "It is well known that many of the best educated and most useful men of our country have risen to the respectable stations which they occupy, through the hardships incident to labor, poverty, and its attendant, hard work" (W. T. Brantly, "Manual Labor and Education," *Columbian Star*, 21 November 1829, 323).

[49] "The Union of Labor and Study," *Columbian Star*, 20 November 1830, 333–34.

[50] In 1829, Brantly changed the name of the *Columbian Star* to the *Columbian Star and Christian Index*. In 1830, almost one-third of the newspaper agents resided in Georgia. On 1 January 1831, Brantly dropped the title *Columbian Star*, making the paper simply the *Christian Index*. He stated, "We have omitted a part of the title of this paper,

overcoming his prejudices, that if ministers "will labor in order to acquire information, and not set themselves up for gentlemen, too good to take hold of a plough or hoe, or to speak to a poor man like myself. I shall believe they have the cause at heart."[51] E. Battle, an itinerant preacher-missionary in Washington County, Georgia, and a delegate to the 1831 Georgia Baptist Convention, expressed his concern to Brantly:

> It is well known that I am an advocate for the education of young preachers; but I am far from standing alone in my fears of the plan of a manual labor system now recommended. I am pleased with the present arrangement for extending aid to young preachers where it best suits their convenience to study.... [Yet, in regard to the manual labor school, Georgia Baptists should know] what may we expect before every necessary expense can be discharged: and then, perhaps, there may not be Beneficiaries to cultivate the farm.[52]

Battle clarified his position later as a view toward caution, not dissent.[53] By 1832, the proposed plan of the Georgia Baptist Convention to establish a school gained public sentiment.

THE EATONTON MANUAL LABOR SCHOOL

The Baptists of Georgia had already seen one school dissolve quickly. In 1803, Georgia Baptists attempted to unite as a body to support ministerial unity and missions, forming the General Committee of Georgia Baptists. Within four years, three consecutive annual meetings resulted in the establishment of Mt. Enon, a college to educate Georgia Baptist ministers. From 1807 to 1811, Mt. Enon experienced various types of trouble. First, the Georgia state legislature would not grant a

---

viz: *Columbian Star*, having always considered it not suited to the character of a religious paper" (Harwell, *An Old Friend,* 50, 54). In a practical sense, Brantly probably saw the futility of naming a paper after its former location in Washington, DC, and its former aim, the promotion of Columbian College.

[51] Baptist, "Education of Ministers," *Christian Index*, 16 July 1831, 37.

[52] E. Battle, "Education of Ministers," *Christian Index*, 13 August 1831, 107–108.

[53] E. Battle, "Explanation," *Christian Index*, 8 October 1831, 229.

charter to a Baptist school due to the appearance of showing denominational preference. Second, the trustees chose a poor location.[54] Third, the school itself never received adequate funding, dooming its prospects from the beginning.

The specter of Mt. Enon plagued the introduction of a theological education in Georgia Baptist life. Sherwood recalled the reactions of the opposition. He claimed that gloom and doom followed many of his earlier efforts. "Talk of improvements for the ministry, and Mount Enon was named as a certain evidence, that God never designed the Baptists to have a learned ministry, and therefore he blasted the efforts which they had made,—demolished the Babel which they had built!"[55]

Between April and December 1831, the Georgia Baptist Convention failed to acquire the land and make the plans necessary for a manual labor school. Unable to convince the Executive Committee to proceed with the resolution, Sherwood purchased the 180-acre tract offered to him by Thomas Cooper and advertised the beginnings of his school.[56] His 22 December 1831 advertisement in the Milledgeville *Georgia Journal* began with these words:

> The subscriber, having purchased a small plantation near Eatonton, proposes to take six or eight young men of good moral character, between the age of 12 and 17, and to provide for their instruction, in the various branches of education, in agriculture and in the mechanic arts. Apparatus to illustrate the sciences of Chemistry, Astronomy and natural Philosophy, &c. will be procured, and a mechanic shop erected.... Assistance will be

---

[54] Boykin quoted Benjamin J. Tharpe's description of the location: "It appears to me as if, after making the world, the Lord had a bag full of sand left, and, not knowing what else to do with it, he emptied it all out at Mount Enon" (Boykin, *History of the Baptist Denomination,* 61).

[55] Adelphos, "Ministerial Education in Georgia," *Christian Review* (December 1837): 580.

[56] "Sherwood Place" as mentioned earlier no longer exists. The building has long disappeared, but First Baptist Church of Eatonton laid a stone marker commemorating Sherwood Place and Adiel Sherwood at the location of the house in 1938. This marker is located on the west side of highway 441 North, 100 yards north of the northern junction of the 441 bypass and business route to Eatonton.

procured in teaching the mechanic arts, and some of the common branches of education. The object is to make practical men, and qualify them to become good teachers of schools

Sherwood also offered the following plan for instruction as well as the proposed method of study:

> In government, he will endeavour to act the part of a parent, and treat the pupils as his children; but he must be obeyed. He desires no parent to send his son, who is unwilling to have him submit to the regulations of the school. Each student will labour *two or three hours in the day*, or about *one day and a half* in the week. Care will be taken, as the weather grows warm, that they be not exposed to a mid-day sun, till they become inured to athletic exercise, by employing the mornings and evenings. So many hours will not be requisite all the year; but in a busy season, somewhat more.
>
> Each student will provide himself with sheets, towels and blankets; and it will be economical for him to have a coarse suit to wear, during the hours of labour. Books, stationery, oil, &c. will be furnished [to] those who need them, at the lowest price. The times for examinations and vacations cannot now be named. Religious service will be attended every Sabbath in Eatonton, a little more than a mile distant.
>
> Those who wish to enter their sons, must give information and secure places by the 10th January. The school will be opened on the 23d. Letters, post paid, addressed to Eatonton, will receive attention.
>
> REGULATIONS AND TERMS
>
> 1st. The course of instruction will occupy 3 years.
>
> 2nd. Board, lodging, washing, tuition, &c. for the 1st year, will be $90; for the 2d $75, and for the 3d $50. Payments half yearly in advance
>
> ADIEL SHERWOOD. Eatonton, Dec. 16, 1831.[57]

---

[57] Ibid.

How long the school existed remained a mystery for most Georgia historians.[58] Boogher claimed a similar quotation in the *Macon Telegraph* actually represented the second term of the Sherwood school.[59] In his *Memoir*, Sherwood mentioned his reaction to the lethargic attitude of the executive committee occurring in *fall* 1831.[60] In 1837, he mentioned his frustration with the executive committee's failure to act by *December*.[61] However, the above quotation seems to indicate that Sherwood began the school in January 1832.

A week after Sherwood posted his school advertisement, another secular paper in Milledgeville published the same information about the school and applauded Sherwood's efforts. An anonymous author congratulated the proponents of manual labor in educating both ministerial and literary students. Both classes of students would benefit from exercise and would develop an appreciation for mechanical and agricultural labor.[62]

---

[58] Sherwood wrote a brief sketch of Thomas U. Wilkes in Campbell's 1874 *History of Georgia Baptists and* in the *Christian Index*. Boykin cites Campbell in his biographical section, "The project for setting on foot Mercer Institute was then under consideration, but Wilkes had no time to lose. So, at the instance of the writer, Rev. A. Sherwood, at that time residing on a farm near Eatonton, agreed to receive him into his family, and furnish board and tuition, on condition of his working half his time. With this condition he faithfully complied, working at his trade as a carpenter, in the field, or wherever his services were required. This was the origin of Dr. Sherwood's Manual Labor School, which was relinquished as soon as arrangements were completed for the opening of Mercer Institute" (Boykin, *History of the Baptist Denomination,* 584).

[59] Boogher, *Secondary Education,* 258.

[60] Sherwood and Boykin, *Memoir,* 237.

[61] Adelphos, "Ministerial Education in Georgia," *Christian Index,* 21 December 1837, 821.

[62] "Education with Manual Labor," *Federal Union* (Milledgeville GA), 29 December 1831, 3. Two months later, the idea of education with manual labor continued to be praised for the idea of industry. One author asserted, "The many pulmonary complaints, weakly constitutions, and early deaths, which have resulted from a cultivation of the mental and disregard of the physical faculties, strongly demonstrates the dependence of each upon the other, and the propriety of a suitable attention to both. And, while no blessing is more important than health, inasmuch as all others must be more or less deficient, or useless, or joyless, without it, nothing is better calculated to promote it than reasonable exercise.—'Train up a child in the way he should go, and when he is old he will not depart from it'; and a careful observation will shew, that a useful and virtuous

Within a year, Sherwood demonstrated the feasibility of a manual labor school. Sherwood's successful school signified the first effort to establish a manual labor school in the state that worked for students preparing for the ministry or other academic disciplines.[63] This achievement thrust him into several arenas of leadership. In the state convention, his demonstration pushed the executive committee to speed up the plans for a Georgia Baptist school. In the larger realm of Georgia educators, Sherwood promoted his success, thereby inspiring numerous manual labor schools.

On 19 December 1831, several Georgia educators met in Milledgeville, Georgia, to establish a teachers' association called the "Teachers' Society and Board of Education of the State of Georgia."[64]

---

life has been more frequently the consequence of industrious habits, than correct principles" ("Education with Manual Labor," *Federal Union*, 2 February 1832, 2).

[63] Between 1831 and 1845, ten manual labor schools appeared in Georgia. The Baptists sponsored three such institutions: Sherwood's institute, the Penfield Institute (later Mercer University), and Hearn Manual Labor School in Floyd County. The Presbyterians founded three institutes, the surviving institute being the Midway Seminary, now Oglethorpe University. The Methodists established four schools, one of which was the Georgia Conference Manual Labor School. Located near Covington, it became Emory University. The early success of the Baptists in Georgia may have come from their numerical strength. In 1831, almost 32,000 Baptists lived in the state compared to 27,000 Methodists and 3,000 Presbyterians. See Dorothy Orr, *A History of Education in Georgia* (Chapel Hill: University of North Carolina Press, 1950) 146–48.

[64] Orr, *A History of Education,* 104. The James P. Boyce Centennial Library of the Southern Baptist Theological Seminary possesses the two December meetings of 1831 and 1832 and the June meeting of 1833 in the Basil Manly collection. See Teachers' Society in the State of Georgia, *Minutes of the Proceedings of the Teachers' Convention* vol. 7, nos. 5, 10, 25, Basil Manly, Jr., Collection (Milledgeville: Federal Union Office, 1832, 1833). The University of Georgia Library holds a copy of the December 1833 meeting. The Teachers' Society of Georgia held three annual meetings every December (1831–1833) and three semiannual meetings every July (1832–1834). The society discontinued due to lack of support. Apparently, the growth of denominational schools within this period eradicated the need for interdenominational fellowship or secular educational development. One writer in the *Georgia Journal* (Milledgeville GA) expected a grand outcome for the newly formed society: "The convention recently held in Milledgeville, to reinstate the character of the profession in this State. The adoption of some uniform system of instruction will be one of the consequences of this meeting of teachers, and instead of instructing or more properly clogging the youthful mind according to the caprice and humor of every ignorant pedagogue; teaching will become a

Nineteen constituent members founded this organization with Sherwood among them.[65] The stated purpose of the assembly was "to promote the diffusion of knowledge, especially among Teachers, to promote harmony and co-operation in their efforts, and uniformity in their mode of teaching; and thus to render them more useful in their profession."[66] The 1831 meeting centered its discussion on teacher compensation and parental discipline.

A year later (17–19 December 1832), the Teachers' Society met again in Milledgeville. This second annual meeting sponsored a look at manual labor in two respects: as a plan and as a practical issue. Adiel Sherwood addressed the assembly, not on the Fellenberg theory as expected, but on his own proposal. Following his speech, Washington Baird spoke on the utility of the manual labor system.

Dorothy Orr summarized Sherwood's speech on the manual labor system.

He estimated that to run a manual labor school of fifty pupils for the first year would cost $6,178.64, including interest and incidentals. This sum provided $2,000 for the purchase of five hundred acres of land with suitable buildings; $1,200 for the salaries of two teachers; $625 for the purchase of seven horses, a cart, and oxen; $55 for the purchase of ploughs, hoes, axes, spades, and shovels; $678 for twenty cows, corn, and fodder; $600 for wheat, molasses, meat, and salt; [if] food supplies and the land were donated, the expenses would be cut in half. After the school was well under way, the crops produced would help defray the expenses.[67]

---

system, subject to the rules of science, conducted by intelligent and moral professors. Such a reform must be gratifying to all who have the interest of religion, morality and learning at heart" ("Teachers' Convention," *Georgia Journal,* 29 December 1831, 3).

[65] The members included Carlisle P. Beman, Robert C. Brown, Stephen Olin, William L. Mitchell, Francis D. Cummins, Thomas B. Slade, George P. Cooper, B. S. Hardman, E. Weston, Daniel Mahony, Archibald McNeil, Washington Baird, Alexander McDonald, Richard W. Ellis, William Lee, W. Wilde, R. B. Meacham, Adiel Sherwood, and Alonzo Church ("Teachers' Convention," *Georgia Journal,* 29 December 1831, 3).

[66] "Teachers' Convention," *Georgia Journal,* 29 December 1831, 3.

[67] Orr, *A History of Education,* 116.

Sherwood also proposed diversification. Agricultural labor could lead to students making window sashes and Venetian blinds to be imported to cities in the North. This plan would combine the agricultural tradition of the South with a small aspect of mechanical industry. Sherwood also understood that the future intentions to found the Athens Manual Labor School (Presbyterian) in Clarke County and the Penfield Institute in Greene County were already in progress. Sherwood predicted the graduates from these institutes would promulgate future manual labor schools throughout the state.[68]

PENFIELD MANUAL LABOR INSTITUTE

The success of Sherwood's school encouraged the executive committee of the Georgia Baptist Convention to take further steps to establish the Penfield Institute. Earlier in 1829, the estate of Josiah Penfield, a late Baptist layman of Savannah, granted the convention the amount of 2,500 dollars as a fund for education, if the convention could raise a similar amount. Within fifteen minutes, individuals attending the convention pledged the same figure.[69] In 1831, the plan for establishing a school met the convention's approval, but it was not until April 1832 that formal action was taken.

At the 1832 meeting, Georgia Baptists directed the executive committee to buy a tract of land seven miles north of Greensboro with the intention of opening the school at the beginning of 1833. After the 1832 Convention, the committee bought 450 acres from a Mr. Redd and appointed B. M. Sanders as principal.

Ironically, B. M. Sanders, one the primary opponent of the manual labor system, became its chief proponent. Originally, the executive committee offered the office of principal or steward of the Penfield Institute to Sherwood, but he declined it. Later, the committee chose

---

[68] Ibid.

[69] Jesse H. Campbell, *Georgia Baptists: Historical and Biographical,* rev. ed. (Macon GA: J.W. Burke and Company, 1874) 22.

Sanders for the occupation.[70] Sanders proved to be an excellent choice, as he was a Georgia native. Born in Columbia County in 1789, he completed his collegiate training at the University of Georgia in 1809. Ordained in 1825, Sanders served several pastorates in Columbia County until he moved to Penfield in 1833. As principal of the institute, Sanders directed the manual labor aspect of the school as well as its academic initiatives. In 1839, he resigned as principal but retained his residence in Penfield until his death in 1852.

The manual labor plan at the Penfield Institute modeled what Brantly and Sherwood originally had proposed. The core idea of a manual labor institute consisted of physical exercise and monetary efficiency. Before the institute began, Jesse Mercer and the executive committee carefully described to Georgia Baptists the organization and plan of the institute. First, the convention agreed in April 1832 to have a board of trustees composed of five members who were all Baptists to govern the school. These five members would appoint a steward to be responsible for the daily ministration of the student's work. Also, a principal teacher would be elected to teach the students during the morning hours.[71]

By fall 1832, the *Christian Index* announced the opening of Mercer Institute on the second Monday of January with B. M. Sanders as principal of the school. Interestingly, the admission requirements established by the trustees did not limit the school to ministerial students or professed believers:

> The principal object of the Institution is the education of pious young men, who are called to the Gospel Ministry, and have been licensed by the church to which they belong, and have a good report of them that are without,— and particularly to bring their testimonials and avail themselves gratuitously of the advantages of the Institution.—But as we have no reason to

---

[70] "Although requested by Jesse Mercer, James Armstrong, and Judge Stocks, I declined being a candidate for the office" (Sherwood and Boykin, *Memoir*, 243).

[71] "Manual Labor School under the Care of the Ga. Baptist Convention," *Christian Index*, 21 July 1832, 46.

believe that this class of pupils will fill up the school; it will receive, in addition, as many young men of good moral character, as can be provided for, irrespective of religious sentiments.[72]

The circular also stipulated the projected expenses for students: "Board for all over 16 years of age, will be $30 for the scholastic year, and $6 for washing; those under 16, at $5 per month, having a reasonable deduction for their labor.... Tuition will be $9 for the first term, to all engaged in reading, writing, arithmetic, grammar, geography and history."[73] Students were expected to labor in an agricultural setting every afternoon during the week. The circular required three hours of labor a day for "five and a half days in the week."

The executive committee specified the school's schedule. Apparently the plan seemed rigorous, but attainable. Beginning at sunrise, the students followed a specified plan throughout the day. A circular described the proposed system:

> Order of Business—School is opened every morning at sunrise, with the reading of the Scriptures and prayer. The classes are then engaged in school exercises till breakfast, about 1 1/2 hours by the sun. Half an hour's remission is then given, after which they are again summoned to their studies, which are generally continued about two hours—when they all again have a relaxation of half an hour. This is again succeeded by another confinement to study of about two hours more, which approaches generally very near to the time of dining. This arrangement gives between 5 and 5 1/2 hours to study in the forenoon, exclusive of the repeated intervals of relaxation. At dinner the interval of rest extends from an hour to an hour and a half, according to the length of the day. Scholastic exercises are then resumed and continued till within 21/2 hours by the sun, when the School closes by prayer, and teachers and students all

---

[72] "Mercer Institute, Ga.," *Christian Index*, 10 November 1832, 301.
[73] Ibid.

repair to the labors of the farm, except a few whose skill may justify their habitual engagement in mechanical operations.[74]

Mercer Institute in Penfield, Georgia, continued as a preparatory school until 1839, when it was reorganized as a Baptist college. Between 1833 and 1839, Georgia Baptists grew to accept the need for a state Baptist College. Due to the success of Penfield, the decision to open a separate college was discarded in favor of elevating the status of Mercer Institute. B. M. Sanders, though originally elected as principal of the school in 1833, also served as steward of the institute, overseeing both the mental and physical labors of the school. Only two other instructors lent their aid to Sanders during the first six years of the institute: John F. Hillyer and Ira O. McDaniel.[75]

The decision to change the school's curriculum and academic status may have resulted from the shift in the institute's goals. By 1835, the requirements to enter Penfield revolved around three concerns: basic writing ability, good morality, and obedience.[76] By 1838, the need for a Baptist college provided the institute a greater goal in which to implement morality and obedience. The manual labor concept now moved from the preparatory school level to a collegiate status.

MERCER UNIVERSITY

In 1837, the Executive Committee of the Georgia Baptist Convention petitioned the Georgia State Legislature for a charter to establish a college in Washington, Georgia. Although first in establishing a manual labor school, Georgia Baptists were not the first to combine manual labor with collegiate education. In 1835, the Presbyterians in Georgia

---

[74] Edgar W. Knight, ed., "Regulations of Mercer Institute, Georgia, 1832," in vol. 4 of *A Documentary History of Education in the South Before 1860* (Chapel Hill: University of North Carolina Press, 1953) 95.

[75] "Mercer Institute, Greene County, Georgia," *Christian Index*, 10 November 1835, 3.

[76] "Terms of Admission—To be admitted into the Mercer Institute, an applicant must be able to read and spell correctly, and write a legible hand: he must also possess a good moral character, and become subject to the entire control of the authorities of the Institute" (ibid.).

successfully opened a manual labor school in Milledgeville (later named Oglethorpe University). At this time, Jesse Mercer began to agitate the prospect of a Georgia Baptist college to educate ministers. When petitioning the state legislature, Georgia Baptists decided to call their school the Southern Baptist College.

The Georgia State Legislature granted a charter for the school in 1837. However, the executive committee cancelled all plans for such a school due to three factors: the 1837 Depression, the obscure location of the school, and the continual opposition to ministerial education in Baptist churches.[77] The only alternative was to reorganize the existing manual labor school in Penfield into a college. By May 1838, the Executive Committee elected a new board of trustees. In July 1838, the trustees of Mercer University met to elect the faculty and to establish the three schools within the university: the academy, the academic department, and the collegiate department. The faculty consisted of B. M. Sanders as president, Adiel Sherwood as professor of sacred literature and moral philosophy, and J. W. Attaway, S. P. Sanford, and I. O. McDaniel as assistant professors with A. E. Reeves serving as steward of the school.[78]

The collegiate department served more as a theological department than an academic one. The circulars relating to the academic structure of the school specified and divided the school into collegiate and academic departments. James C. Bryant asserted that Mercer University's theological department originated with the election of Adiel Sherwood as professor of sacred literature and moral philosophy.[79] Actually, this was the beginning of a theological department, but it was not specified as one.

---

[77] James C. Bryant, "An Historical Account of Theological Education at Mercer University," *Viewpoints: Georgia Baptist History* 15 (1996): 72–73. The reader should also note that the demography of Georgia changed between 1804 and 1821. The town of Washington contained a larger population at the beginning of the nineteenth century than two decades later. The land lotteries and land grants during these early decades opened the Middle Georgia territory according to the boundaries of the three rivers: Oconee, Ocmulgee, and Altamaha.

[78] "Mercer University," *Christian Index*, 8 November 1838, 694–95.

[79] Bryant, "An Historical Account," 74.

The practice of beneficiaries continued during the early years of Mercer University. The convention continued to provide monetary support to theological students to defray the cost of books and living expenses. Five ministerial students were reported as beneficiaries in 1840, five in 1841, six in 1842, eight in 1843, and nine in 1844.[80]

From secondary sources, it seems apparent that a definitive theological department (if this is an appropriate term) failed to materialize under Sherwood's tenure. He did not formulate a specialized program of instruction. This did not appear until 1845 under John Leadley Dagg. One explanation has been proposed that Sherwood busied himself with preaching engagements and other school matters.[81] During Sherwood's tenure from 1839 to 1841, his teaching duties were not confined to theological students. He recalled, "I commenced my labors in Mercer University, in the month of February, 1839, and heard from eight to eleven recitations every day."[82] However, a specialized program may not have been his intention. Sherwood preferred pragmatism to unrealistic specialization. This can be seen in the early course listings of the school. Notice the requirements of the academic department:

> They shall study English Grammar, Arithmetic, Geography, Ancient, Sacred and modern-Latin Grammar, Historiae Sacrae, Viri Romae, Latin Reader, Caesar's Commentaries, Virgil, Cicero's Select Orations, Mair's Introduction to Latin Syntax, Greek Grammar, and Delectus, the four Gospels and Acts, Graeca Minora, (or Jacob's Greek Reader.) Heathen Mythology, History of the United States, and an easy and short work on Biblical Antiquities.[83]

---

[80] Bartow Davis Ragsdale, vol. 1 of *The Story of Georgia Baptists* (Atlanta: Executive Committee of the Georgia Baptist Convention, 1932) 75.

[81] This has some credibility. Sherwood established the Penfield Baptist Church in 1839 and served for two years as pastor. He also spoke twice a month at Bethesda Baptist Church, the church of his 1820 ordination, from 1840–1841. Although it cannot be proven, he may have helped in the administration of the school. B. M. Sanders retired as president in 1840 and Otis Smith was elected president, serving only two years (1840–1842).

[82] Sherwood and Boykin, *Memoir*, 255–56.

[83] "The Laws of the Mercer University," *Christian Index*, 3 January 1839, 4.

The academic department differed from the collegiate in that the academic specified eight courses within each of the four years of university studies. The collegiate department contained more theological coursework. The collegiate student studied the following courses at the following levels: Evidences of Christianity during the freshman year, Mental Philosophy in the sophomore year, a more difficult Evidences of Christianity and a Natural Theology course in the junior year, and Moral and Mental Philosophy in the senior year.[84]

Apparently, Sherwood's view of a theological curriculum differed from later developments of Southern Baptist education toward a seminary or even a divinity school. Seminaries and divinity schools isolated theological education from secular curricula, as found in literary schools. Sherwood did not follow the later trend of opening theological course work for ministers that excluded literary studies.[85] He injected theological literature into a literary education. The theology student not only gained moral refinement from studying the literature of antiquity, but he received theological training by making the Bible the center of his studies.

On 7 February 1840, Adiel Sherwood addressed the trustees, faculty, and students, defining the purpose of his department chair as it related to the aim of the university.

> A Professorship of Sacred Literature, in an ordinary college, is an unusual appointment; but it will not seem inappropriate when the objects held in contemplation by the Founders of this University shall have been explained. They did not confine their views to an Institution merely Literary—their aim was higher and holier and nobler. The Bible, by way of eminence, the Book of Books, they conceived had been overlooked in the systems of popular education in vogue; had been expelled [from] Schools

---

[84] Ibid.

[85] The Southern Baptist Theological Seminary in Louisville KY became an example of a strictly theological school two decades later.

and Colleges, and they desired to restore it, and introduce such a course of study as would impress its value on every pupil.[86]

As Professor of Sacred Literature, he imparted training to his students comparable and superior to a secular education in classical literature. Considering his ministerial students as prophets, he believed the study of the Hebrew and Greek language combined with the study of antiquity made prophets out of mere preachers. A literary education combined with a theological one strengthened the ministerial student. Not only would an educated preacher communicate well, but he would also exemplify the standard that Baptists were not hostile to education. Sherwood concluded his argument with a simple dictum: "We charge you not to suffer Penfield ever to remind us of the failure of Mount Enon."[87]

In early spring 1841, a shift in Georgia Baptist history occurred. Jesse Mercer died and Sherwood prepared to leave the state. From April to May 1841, Sherwood visited the recently settled states of Illinois and Missouri with J. F. Hillyer. On 7 July Shurtleff College in Alton, Illinois, the school founded by John Mason Peck, elected Sherwood as president. Sherwood vacated his small home in Penfield, Georgia, leaving the state for fifteen years. He exchanged one frontier for another, taking his educational theories with him.[88]

---

[86] Adiel Sherwood, *Address by Prof. Sherwood* (Washington GA: M. J. Kappel, 1840) 3.

[87] Ibid., 12.

[88] Sherwood's connection with Mercer University formally ended in 1841. Earlier in spring 1841, Jesse Mercer died. Sherwood, who seemingly followed greater men (Jesse Mercer and Luther Rice), moved to Illinois under the urging of J. M. Peck. His Penfield residence was advertised to sell for several weeks in the *Christian Index*. The author found the bill of sale in the Patrick Hues Mell, Sr., Collection at the University of Georgia (box 1, file 13): "Receipt of purchase—Received of PH Mell 400 dollars in part of house and lot in Penfield wherein he now resides—January 22, 1845, Adiel Sherwood." P. H. Mell served as professor of ancient languages from 1842 to 1855. Mell completed his career at the University of Georgia (formerly known as Franklin College) from 1856 to 1888 as professor and later vice-chancellor and chancellor.

CONCLUSION

Sherwood's advocacy of ministerial education combined with manual labor exhibited the practical nature of his educational theory. Although he held to this fashionable trend due to his own experiences with bad health, he also foresaw that the image of masculinity being attached to the ministry would prove to be attractive to Baptists of the South. Many Southern communities already prided themselves with military schools where young men lived disciplined lives of learning. By putting ministers behind the plow for three hours a day, ministerial education would provide the common layman a feeling of ease with his newly trained pastor. The student of the manual labor school could graduate with the honor of a proven masculinity, casting off the specter of New England effeminate clergymen, who migrated to the South and West.

Sherwood also contributed in erecting the final distinction between Primitive and missionary Baptists: an educated ministry. With the establishment of Mercer University in 1838, the Georgia Baptist Convention totally represented what the Primitive Baptists protested. In the 1840s and 1850s, Sherwood continued to leave an impact on the Georgia Baptist Convention, but not in its relationship to the Primitive Baptists. That era had ended. Sherwood now turned his attention to polemical writings against Catholicism and Protestants who continued to baptize infants.

6

THE DEVELOPMENT OF
SOUTHERN BAPTIST IDENTITY:
SHERWOOD'S LIFE AND THOUGHT IN THE
ANTEBELLUM OLD WEST

After the antimission controversy in Georgia Baptist life, Adiel
Sherwood began to author more newspaper articles and monographs that
centered on Baptist ecclesiology, or the Baptist doctrine of the church.
His interaction with the national movements of Baptists in the 1830s and
1840s initiated his interest in this subject. In a polemical and interpretive
fashion, Sherwood proposed a biblical model of church polity that
defined the prevalent view of Baptists, and he refuted the theories of
denominations that promoted infant baptism. From 1844 to 1859,
Sherwood produced several writings that represented the views of many
Georgia Baptists, a moderate but logical view of the New Testament
model for Baptist churches. Sherwood maintained denominational
distinctiveness while he avoided the extremes of interdenominational
confusion and sectarian separatism.

In September 1841, Adiel Sherwood and his family moved from the
Penfield campus of Mercer University to assume the presidency of
Shurtleff College in Upper Alton, Illinois. For almost fifteen years,
Sherwood made southwest Illinois and southeast Missouri his area of
ministry, serving several churches and presiding over two educational

institutes. In the West, his close correspondence with men such as John Mason Peck and Isaac McCoy marked him as a pioneer in Baptist ecclesiology. In the Western arena, the growth of non-Baptist denominations threatened the distinct Baptist view of the church. Perceiving a polemical need to defend Baptist principles, Sherwood developed a deep perspective of the scriptural view of the church. In 1857, he returned to Georgia with a well-defined Baptist ecclesiology, formed by this Western experience. Before the Civil War carried many Southern Baptists into battle, Sherwood injected his form of Baptist principles back into Georgia Baptist life through his polemical writings and involvement with the Georgia Baptist Convention and her institutions.

The westward migration of Southern peoples shaped what was originally called the old Southwest (i.e., the states of Indiana, Illinois, and Missouri). As Southerners migrated to the West, they either crossed over the Appalachian Mountains in the corners of Kentucky and Tennessee, or moved around the mountain chain, through the lower South. In the twin-state area of St. Louis, large portions of Southerners from the lower South migrated into the region as either slaveholders or people not hostile to slavery. Dating back to 1818, when Missouri entered the Union as a slaveholding state, the St. Louis region accentuated this social issue due largely to the continual migration of former residents of the Deep South. The westward migration out of Georgia steadily increased after the Creek Wars of 1818–1819 and the Texas War of Independence in 1836. By the 1850 census, this migratory trend became a definite reality.[1] Former residents of Georgia could be found in large quantities in the following states: Alabama contained almost 60,000; Mississippi possessed more than 17,000, Florida with more than 11,000. The largest non-slaveholding state was Illinois with 1,341 former Georgians.

---

[1] William O. Lynch, "The Westward Flow of Southern Colonists before 1861," *Journal of Southern History* 9 (August 1943): 305. Lynch also notes the following figures: "The number of Georgians in Texas in 1850 was 7,639; in Arkansas, 6,367; in Louisiana, 5,917; in Tennessee, 4,863. The Georgia contingent in Missouri was very close to that in Illinois, being 1,254. In Kentucky, there were but 892 Georgians in 1850; in California, the number was 876; in Indiana, 764" ("Westward Flow," 305).

Finding himself in a new location surrounded by Southern traditions (i.e., agrarian lifestyle and slavery), Sherwood struggled with denominational and interdenominational conflicts. His new location represented the crossroads of sectional friction with the westward migration of abolitionists and slaveholders meeting in the St. Louis area. Both groups within their religious denominations represented the fragmentation of Protestantism. Sectionalism drew denominations within a given region together. The Baptists of the South held a greater political affinity with other Southern denominations than with their Baptist brethren in the North.

As important as the issues of sectionalism were, they can easily overshadow the greater theological problems of the day. Sociological concerns did not define Baptist thought and practice. When Baptists grew closer politically with other denominations in their region, they still continued to intensify their efforts to distinguish themselves from the older denominations that practiced infant baptism. The Baptists published more literature on their theological distinctives during this time period than on any other issue, including slavery.[2] Although abolitionism caused division in 1845, slavery did not form the theological objectives of the Baptists of the South. In an accurate manner, the Baptists in the West exhibited a combination of Northern and Southern concerns. As the 1845 split permanently divided the Baptists, the split gradually occurred in the West. Sherwood represented the gradual acculturation to the division. His life before returning to Georgia in 1857 exhibited this quality.

SHERWOOD'S DENOMINATIONAL ACTIVITIES

Sherwood's activity within the national framework of Baptists dated back to his missionary work in Boston and his early activities in Georgia Baptist life. When he submitted a resolution for the formation of a state body among Georgia Baptists, he advocated similar concepts on the

---

[2] Between 1845 and 1860, Southern Baptists published a large number of essays and monographs on strict communion or Baptist polity in general. These authors include Joseph S. Baker, T. F. Curtis, J. L. Dagg, Richard Fuller, J. R. Graves, R. B. C. Howell, R. McDaniel, P. H. Mell, J. M. Pendleton, S. Remington, J. B. Taylor, and J. L. Waller.

national level. In 1823, he attended his first meeting of the Triennial Convention and became a trustee for Columbian College. At this meeting, he submitted a resolution to the convention concerning state conventions. He advocated the formation of such institutions to aid the larger purpose of missions. The convention agreed with his resolution, leaving the process to the states.[3] Sherwood attended almost all of the Triennial meetings from 1829 to 1838 and functioned as a member of the Board of Managers.[4] In 1844, he attended the convention as an independent subscriber from Illinois. In 1845, at the Board of Managers meeting, Sherwood served as one of the committee members chosen to answer the Alabama Resolution, which insisted that slaveholders should be elligible for missionary appointments.[5]

LUTHER RICE AND COLUMBIAN COLLEGE

Sherwood's early acquaintance with Luther Rice thrust him into national denominational work. Within his *Memoirs*, he reminisced of the occasion of his meeting the great missionary of the Triennial Convention. He stated, "About October, 1814, I attended an association at Brandon, and there, for the first time, met Luther Rice, who had been about a year in

---

[3] On 6 May 1823, the minutes noted, "A resolution was offered by Rev. Mer.[?] Sherwood, respecting state conventions, which, after some discussion of its objects, was referred to a committee, consisting of Messrs. Sherwood, Bennet, Bryce, Chase, Rice, Galusha, Willey, and Sharp" ("The Baptist General Convention," *Baptist Missionary Magazine* 3 [July 1823]:141. Two days later, the appointed committee gave the following report: "The committee relative to State Conventions, made a report. They entertain a high sense of the important tendencies of State Conventions. Difficulties have existed, which are now passing away. Brethren in various parts of the country, are convinced of the value of the measure, and in several States, Conventions of this character have been formed. The apprehensions which have been felt, are found to have been ill-founded. Being entirely voluntary, the formation of State Conventions cannot interfere with the rights of the churches; while it will bring together the wisdom, piety, and talent of the denomination, and give a highly desirable concept and energy to their proceedings. The Committee, however, recommend to refer the subject to the wisdom and piety of our brethren in the several states" ("Baptist General Convention," 142).

[4] He missed the 1826 and 1841 meetings.

[5] "American Baptist Board of Foreign Missions: Thirty-first Annual Meeting," *Baptist Missionary Magazine* 25 (July 1845): 147, 150–51.

this country, since his return from India."[6] Through interacting with the Triennial Convention and Luther Rice's involvement with Georgia Baptists, Adiel Sherwood allied himself with the causes Rice promoted.

Luther Rice held a similar connection with Georgia and Baptists of the South as Sherwood did. Born in Worcester County, Massachusetts on 25 March 1783, Luther Rice grew up to exhibit a strong character of independence. At age sixteen, he moved to Georgia for six months, without parental consent, to work for the timber industry. However, he returned to New England and in 1802 experienced a conversion to Christianity. Later, he joined the Congregational Church.[7] In 1812, Rice sailed to India to meet Adoniram and Ann Judson to begin missionary work for the Congregationalists. Upon arriving on the shores of India, Rice became convinced of the Baptist principle of believer's baptism by immersion. Realizing that he and the Judsons had acquired the same conviction, all three missionaries moved their denominational allegiance to the Baptist denomination. In 1814, their change of heart helped spur the foundation of the Triennial Convention, a national effort to support Rice and the Judsons in foreign missions.

As events unfolded, Luther Rice's life developed into one of raising funds for missions, not mission work itself. Rice's earliest journey into Georgia to raise money for missions dated back to 1815–1816. His call for missions giving and organization stimulated the formation of missionary societies in Savannah and in the Sarepta, Ocmulgee, and Hephzibah associations.[8] His earliest efforts consisted of raising money for foreign missions.

By 1821, he also began to promote the founding and support of Columbian College in Washington, DC. Within his plans, the school functioned as a theological institute for ministers who were called into foreign or domestic fields of service. Luther Rice hoped that Columbian

---

[6] Julia L. Sherwood and Samuel Boykin, *Memoir of Adiel Sherwood, D.D.* (Philadelphia: Grant and Faires, 1884) 44.

[7] William Cathcart, ed., "Rev. Luther Rice," in vol. 2 of *The Baptist Encyclopedia* (Philadelphia: Louis H. Everts, 1881) 978–80.

[8] Samuel Boykin, *History of the Baptist Denomination in Georgia: With Biographical Compendium and Portrait Gallery of Baptist Ministers and Other Georgia Baptists* (Atlanta: James P. Harrison and Company, 1881) 76–85.

College would unite the Baptist denomination in America behind the missionary effort. By 1826, Columbian College possessed numerous agents to raise funds within each state. This eased Luther Rice's burden for a school that was continually in debt. Yet, until his death, Rice also functioned as an agent, traveling the eastern seaboard states, raising funds for his school.[9]

On 18 January 1836, Columbian College elected Adiel Sherwood professor of languages and biblical literature and appointed him a general and financial agent of the college.[10] Sometime after this nomination, Luther Rice wrote a letter to Sherwood, encouraging him to accept the position.

You are the individual raised up, fitted and pointed out by Divine Providence, as the very one who can save all, raise up the Institution, and give it character, eminence and very extensive usefulness. The means to do all this, and more that this, are within your power.

And now, my dear brother, what wider field, or more promising sphere of useful exertion can invite the application of your utmost energies?[11]

---

[9] Not many theological and historical studies have been conducted on Luther Rice. His impact on Baptist life in America consisted largely of his establishment of the *Columbian Star* and Columbian College, both in Washington, DC. As an organizational man, he contributed greatly to the development of the Baptists. See L. T. Gibson, "Luther Rice's Contribution to Baptist History" (S.T.D. thesis, Temple University, 1944). James P. Taylor printed a general account of Rice's memoirs shortly after his death, and this monograph was reprinted as a centennial celebration. See Taylor, *Memoir of Rev. Luther Rice, One of the First American Missionaries to the East* (Baltimore: Armstrong and Berry, 1840; reprint, Nashville TN: Broadman Press, 1937). Other substantial monographs include [Elmer Louis Kayser], *Luther Rice, Founder of Columbian College* (Washington, DC.: George Washington University, 1966); Saxon Rowe Carver, *Ropes to Burma: the Story of Luther Rice* (Nashville TN: Broadman Press, 1961); and Evelyn Wingo Thompson, *Luther Rice: Believer in Tomorrow* (Nashville: Broadman Press, 1967).

[10] *Biblical Recorder*, 10 February 1836, 3.

[11] Sherwood and Boykin, *Memoir*, 245.

By summer, a circular appeared in many Baptist newspapers announcing Sherwood's acceptance of the nomination.[12]

Throughout summer 1836, Sherwood began raising funds for Columbian College. The debt of the school, although burdensome, was amendable. In August, he stated in the *Christian Index*, "The financial concerns were not managed with prudence for some years; but it is hoped a lesson has been learned in the school of affliction which will guard against future disasters. The number of students is beginning to increase."[13] In a letter to a friend, Rice bragged, "Since Elder Adiel Sherwood of Georgia has put his shoulders to the wheel with me, confidence is returning; there is a prospect of an increase in the number of students; and I have strong hopes of seeing an eminent College yet before many more years shall have passed away."[14]

On 25 September 25, Luther Rice died, leaving Sherwood a greater burden as Rice's replacement. A Baptist newspaper listed the cause of death as "inflammation of the liver" and noted that Rice had his "horse and sulkey and baggage" sent to Sherwood for the benefit of the college.[15] For two years, Sherwood struggled with easing the debt of Columbian College, traveling the eastern states, concentrating most of his efforts in the South. In a sense, Sherwood functioned as Rice did in

---

[12] [In a circular dated 10 June 1836 but printed in July,] "We take pleasure by saying that the Rev. Adiel Sherwood, of Georgia, has accepted the appointment conferred upon some months ago, and enters upon his duties as General Agent with the prospect of being as successful, as he is energetic" ("Columbian College, D.C., June 10, 1836, Circular," *Biblical Recorder*, 13 July 1836, 2).

[13] Adiel Sherwood, "Columbian College," *Christian Index*, 11 August 1836, 484.

[14] [Elmer Louis Kayser], *Luther Rice, Founder*, 30.

[15] "Death of Rev. Luther Rice," *Biblical Recorder*, 19 October 1836, 3. Sherwood reminisced three decades later, "Never was an instance of more disinterested and benevolent effort exhibited. Day and night, through heat and cold, rain and sunshine, he [Luther Rice] traveled by stage, sulkey, and on horseback and on foot, probably 200,000 miles. He became rich, of course? [*sic*] He was offered the most lucrative and eminent positions as President of College; but he would not abandon his glorious work.—He died Sept., 1836, at Edgefield, S.C., and bequeathed his old horse, sulkey and a few dollars, all he was worth, to the Columbian College!" (Dr. A. Sherwood, "Life and Times of Jesse Mercer," *Christian Index*, 9 March 1863, 4).

his final years, worrying about debt and relying on Southern support of a school for the national denomination.[16]

Sherwood hesitated to begin a public campaign to pay off the debts of Columbian College. Apparently, he first opted for raising funds through the regional agents of the college. Each agent as listed in the Baptist papers would call for support from their local congregations and associations. However, this tactic did not work. The amount of debt became common knowledge, so Sherwood called for public support to dissolve the debt. Owing 15,000 dollars on a 125,000-dollar note, the school needed the support of the Baptists. He wrote:

> Knowing that many persons are tired of the above name [Columbian College], and others indifferent to its interests; it was not deemed proper to bring it again before the public: it was determined to operate in a silent way among its friends and urge to one vigorous effort, lest after all our anxieties and contributions, it should finally sink. But since the papers have named the sum by which it is embarrassed, I think it necessary to make a few remarks, that the friends may know its real condition.... The time is short, to be sure, and let the friends rally at once, and the work is accomplished: they will not sacrifice $125,000 for the paltry sum of $15,000. This is the final effort in regard to debts: if it fail, I shall not trouble them with another plan; if it succeed, there will be no more need.[17]

Throughout 1837 and 1838, Sherwood labored to pay off the remainder of the college debt. In June 1837, he reported, "Last Tuesday, Virginia Baptists came out to save the Columbian College, and in thirty minutes gave pledges for about $3,000,...Prior to this, she was pledged for about $2,900, so that the 'ancient dominion' has now provided for

---

[16] Thompson contended that Georgia and South Carolina deeply mourned the passing of Luther Rice. She also believed Luther Rice could raise more money in the South than in any of the Northeastern regions. See Thompson, *Luther Rice: Believer,* 201–202.

[17] Adiel Sherwood, "Columbian College.—Final Effort," *Christian Index*, 23 March 1837, 186.

over \$5,000 in all."[18] At the close of this year, he noted that he had secured about 13,000 dollars, between 2,000 and 3,000 dollars from debt retirement.[19] By March 1838, Sherwood owed less than 2,000 dollars.[20] Changing his strategy again, he asked for small contributions from individuals, not congregations. On 17 March, Sherwood notified his audience that he would assume the balance of the debt. He mentioned his certainty that "friends of literature" would help him with the "burden," though he was not opposed to making a sacrifice for the cause of the school.[21]

Sherwood returned to Georgia to reorganize Mercer Institute into Mercer University. His experience with fund-raising and administrative work at Columbian College blossomed at Mercer. Yet, before he completed his work for Columbian College, Sherwood experienced the divisive effects of the Bible controversy of the 1830s. The strongest issue binding Protestant denominations in America came unraveled, and Sherwood played an instrumental role in it.

THE BIBLE SOCIETIES CONTROVERSY

The growth of early nineteenth-century missionary work necessitated the translation, publication, and distribution of the Bible. When William Carey, the first modern missionary of the Baptists, began his work in India, he also translated the Bible into the Indian language. In 1833, the British Bible Society refused to print Carey's Bengali version of the Bible due to the term *baptizo* being translated into "immerse." In 1835,

---

[18] Adiel Sherwood, "Letter to the Editor," *Christian Index*, 29 June 1837, 408.

[19] Adiel Sherwood, "To the Editors of the Index," *Christian Index*, 14 December 1837, 802.

[20] "I have raised about \$14,100, and need \$1,900 more, but find that a loan I cannot secure the complement by the time fixed on for payment of the debts. Therefore, I throw out the plan named by Bro. Joshua Key,...let every person or church friendly to the cause, send up each ten dollars. Fair notice is now given to all friends, to lend a helping hand, and they must not charge the agent with blame, if after this, the concern should slip out of our hands" (Adiel Sherwood, "Don't Let the College Be Sold," *Christian Index*, 1 March 1838, 116).

[21] Adiel Sherwood, "Communications," *Biblical Recorder*, 17 March 1838, 3. He stated Georgia and South Carolina combined had contributed \$6,231, Virginia \$5,000, and Baltimore \$1,200.

the American Bible Society rejected the request to print Carey's Bible for the same reason. In 1836, the American Bible Society also refused to print Adoniram Judson's Burman translation of the Scriptures.

The translated meaning of baptism as immersion touched the center of Baptist thought and practice. When translators in foreign lands interpreted *baptizo* as "to immerse," the new converts acted as the Baptists—they plunged new believers under the baptismal waters. Protestant denominations that continued to sprinkle infants obviously saw this action as a threat to their denominational practice. Confronted with this dilemma, both parties had to decide either to transliterate the word *baptizo* "to baptize" or to translate the term to its appropriate meaning of immersion. The Baptists chose the latter.

On 26 April 1837, the Baptists met in Philadelphia to form the American Bible and Foreign Society. The minutes noted at four o'clock P.M., "The Convention was called to order by Spencer H. Cone, of New York, and on motion, Rufus Babcock, Jr., was appointed Chairman, pro tem, and Adiel Sherwood and Baron Stow, Secretaries, pro tem."[22] For the next three days, the convention established the constitution and aims of the new society. Although not explicitly limited to the Baptist denomination, the goals of the society promoted the Baptist cause.[23]

Adiel Sherwood represented the Georgia Baptist Association during the course of the Bible convention. As one of the secretaries of the Bible convention, he helped draft the circular that stated the purpose of the convention. While the delegates debated the aims of the convention, the discussion continued to be quite heated. Although the delegation had already settled the issue of separation from the American Bible Society and planned to form a distinct society, they debated the process of circulating Bibles in foreign fields and at home.

From the beginning, the new society wished to limit their efforts to foreign distribution. Yet, the English version circulated by the American

---

[22] *Proceedings of the Bible Convention* (Philadelphia: Rackliff and Jones, 1837) 3.

[23] Unfortunately, many prominent Baptist historians have not recognized the significance of the Bible Controversy. Historians probably see the Bible Convention of 1837 and later meetings as a New England argument and the Bible Revision movement of the 1850s as a sectional complaint of Southern Baptists. It is apparent that the first controversy drove a decisive wedge in interdenominational cooperation.

Bible Society posed a future dilemma for the ABFS.[24] At one point in the proceedings, the minutes state, "Mr. Sherwood, of Georgia, [one of the Secretaries of the Convention] rose to address the body, amidst the call of 'question.' He said that he was determined to speak, and cared not for the call."[25] The minutes state further:

> Mr. Sherwood said, that he regarded the first amendment— 'In foreign languages,' as the test question—and on this he believed that the Convention would generally agree. He thought that a large majority of it would go for the amendment. He could not go for vesting the Society with the power of distribution at home. To do that, would be to act in direct contradiction of the wishes of his constituents, so far as he understood the object of any meeting in convention.[26]

The convention closed with the decision to restrict its endeavors to foreign fields and foreign translations for the next year.

The ABFS struggled over two issues within the next two decades. First, the American Bible Society briefly became antagonistic toward the new organization. In 1845, William Wyckoff, a leading founder of the ABFS, complained about the issue of sectarianism.[27] The American Bible Society claimed an ecumenical sphere of influence and labeled the ABFS merely a sectarian society for the Baptists.[28] Second, the issue of

---

[24] The American Bible and Foreign Society will be referred to as the ABFS.

[25] *Proceedings of the Bible Convention*, 33.

[26] Ibid. Sherwood preferred to restrict the domestic work of the ABFS to a one-year delay (*Proceedings of the Bible Convention*, 42).

[27] "On the renewal of the application [of the ABFS] in 1845, the American Bible Society threw aside the partial disguise hitherto maintained in its opposition, and openly entered the field against the petitioners. A remonstrance was sent to the Legislature in the name of the Board of Mangers, which assumed as the basis of opposition that the American Bible Society was a catholic, and the American and Foreign, a sectarian Institution, and that, therefore, the latter had no right to the name which its founders had adopted" (William H. Wyckoff, *A Sketch of the Origin and some Particulars of the History of the Most Eminent Bible Societies*, 2d ed. [New York: Lewis Colby and Co., 1847] 78).

[28] One writer for the *Methodist Quarterly Review* complained of Spencer Cone, the president of the ABFS, as representing what Methodists and Presbyterians perceived as

translating the term *baptizo* collapsed on the Baptists in America. When English translations began to appear in the Bible revision movement of the 1850s, the ABFS inconsistently retained the transliterated term *baptize,* proving to some critics that they hoped to keep the denominational name.[29] In 1850, several Baptists formed the American Bible Union, following what they perceived to be the original purpose of the ABFS—baptism should be translated as immersion. However, the debate eventually gravitated toward transliteration, the original position of the American Bible Society.

After the 1845 split between Baptists of the North and South, each denomination settled the problem of Bible translation and distribution differently. Robert Torbet noticed that Baptists of the North finally decided to assign home distribution to the American Baptist Publication Society and foreign distribution to the American Baptist Missionary Union in 1883.[30] Robert Baker asserted that Baptists of the South preferred and gravitated toward forming their own institution for publication and distribution, thereby not dividing their efforts.[31]

---

the Baptists' own self-identity: "The president of the new society endorses the assertion; not aware, perhaps, of the bitter innuendo contained in it, that all who hold to infant sprinkling are popish; or to express it more clearly, and more absurdly, that there are only two religious denominations, to wit, the Baptists on the one hand, and the Roman Catholics on the other" (*An Examination of the Principles and Proceedings of the Bible Society of the Baptist Denomination* [New York: Tract Society of the Methodist Episcopal Church, n.d.]10).

[29] Many non-Baptist groups felt the Baptists should translate their denominational name as a consistent measure. Of course, some Baptists pointed out that if they abandoned their title over the issue of *baptizo,* the Presbyterians and Episcopalians should abandon their titles as they related to *presbeuteros* and *episcopos.* One author listed several leaders who originally opposed the formation of the ABFS over this discernable threat. Among these were "Wayland, Williams, Dowling, Hague, Granger, Westcott, Ide, and Brantly" (Edward P. Brand, *Illinois Baptist, A History* [Bloomington IL: Pantagraph Printing and Sta. Co., 1930] 170).

[30] Robert G. Torbet, *A History of the Baptists,* 3rd ed. (Valley Forge: Judson Press, 1950) 278–79.

[31] "It is evident that Southern Baptists, rather than choosing officially one way or another, preferred to organize their own Bible Board. From that time until the close of the period [1851–1865], the board made reports to the Convention concerning funds raised for the Bible distribution and the work that was done" (Robert A. Baker, *The Southern Baptist Convention and Its People 1607–1972* [Nashville: Broadman Press, 1974] 203).

Although Bible translation and distribution both formed and fractured Baptists in America, it is important to recognize that it shaped the course of Baptist ecclesiology. Being explicitly literal in their interpretation of Scripture, Baptists defended their hermeneutically formed identity. Adiel Sherwood represented this group and followed this course of Baptist development. The definition of baptism formed an ever-growing polemic against infant baptism. As Sherwood played an instrumental role in Baptist life by raising funds for Columbian College or attending numerous Baptist society meetings, his interests in domestic missions increased. Bible distribution and Baptist expansion in the West obviously gained his attention, determining where he would move and what he would write.

JOHN MASON PECK AND HOME MISSIONS

From the first Triennial meeting he attended, Sherwood expressed a desire to reach Native Americans with the gospel. In 1823, the minutes stated, "It is resolved, on motion of Mr. Sherwood, that, under present circumstances, our missionaries should not undertake the translation of the Scriptures into the Indian languages; and that the children be taught, for the present, the English language only."[32] In 1832, Sherwood continued this trend, becoming a constituent member of the American Baptist Home Mission Society in New York. During the 1832 Triennial Convention, the ABHMS was formed. Both Sherwood and Thomas Stocks, a judge from Greensboro, Georgia, attended the Triennial Convention and the first session of the ABHMS. On 27 April 1832, in New York, the ABHMS was formed with Thomas Stocks presiding as chairman over the initial meeting.[33] Rev. Spencer H. Cone of New York proposed the resolution, "That it is expedient to form an American Baptist Home Mission Society."[34] The rest of the meeting concerned the

---

[32] "The Baptist General Convention," *Baptist Missionary Magazine* 3 (July 1823): 142.

[33] From this point onward, the American Baptist Home Mission Society will be called the ABHMS.

[34] *Proceedings of the American Baptist Home Mission Society* (New York: G. F. Bunce, 1832) 4.

election of officers and the scope of the society. Adiel Sherwood made the motion to make North America the arena of the ABHMS, rather than limiting it to the United States.[35]

The ABHMS functioned as a means to promote the preaching of the gospel in North America. Destitute areas of proclamation were largely the aim of the society, although the society did not intend to overlook any particular region. Men such as John Mason Peck advocated the sending of preachers to the pioneer areas of Illinois and Missouri. In fact, one author interpreted that the central reason for forming the ABHMS consisted of J. M. Peck's demand for denominational aid.[36]

John Mason Peck was born in Litchfield, Connecticut, on 31 October 1789. In 1807, he was converted to Christianity and joined the Congregational church in his hometown. Yet, in 1811, he became convinced of the Baptist principles of believer's baptism by immersion and joined a Baptist church. From 1813 to 1816, he served as the pastor of Catskill and Amenia churches in Connecticut. In 1816, he abandoned his pastoral pursuits to study for one year under William Staughton, pastor of Sansom Street Baptist church in Philadelphia. In 1817, he began his service as the first domestic missionary sponsored by the Triennial Convention, moving his family to the Saint Louis area of Illinois and Missouri. In 1822, he made Rock Spring, Illinois, his place of residence. During his earlier years of missionary work, Peck received financial support either from the Massachusetts Baptist Missionary Society or the Triennial Convention. Later, Peck founded his own support through local churches and associations.[37]

---

[35] Charles L. White, *A Century of Faith* (Philadelphia: Judson Press, 1932) 43. Sherwood attended most of the ABHMS meetings from 1832 to 1845. Unlike the Baptist General Convention (i.e., the Triennial Convention), the ABHMS met every year. Sherwood served as a life director from 1832 to 1845. His participation in the committee to answer the Alabama resolution (an inquiry from the Alabama Baptist Convention asking the position of the ABHMS on appointing a slaveholder as a domestic missionary) took place at the Rhode Island meeting in 1845.

[36] Ibid., 42.

[37] William Cathcart, "John Mason Peck, D.D.," in vol. 2 of *The Baptist Encyclopedia*, 892.

J. M. Peck functioned as a pioneer preacher in the Illinois-Missouri frontier.[38] He attempted several means of promoting Baptist missions, as a founder of churches and associations as well as an editor and owner of a Baptist newspaper. Although his opponents ranged from those holding a local antimissionary sentiment to Easterners having an anti-Western bias, J. M. Peck promoted the urgency of Baptist work in the West. He published the newspaper *Pioneer of the Valley of Mississippi* in 1829 and the *Western Baptist* in 1830. In 1831, he merged these two newspapers into the *Pioneer and Western Baptist.*[39] In 1835, the name was changed to the *Pioneer*. In 1836 and 1837, it changed again to the *Western Pioneer and Baptist Standard Bearer* and then the *Western Pioneer*.

Peck also promoted theological education. In 1827, he founded the Rock Spring Seminary at his residence. Yet, for several years, the Illinois

---

[38] Rufus Babcock, a prominent New England pastor, published Peck's memoirs in 1864. Babcock edited the *Baptist Memorials*, a journal to which Peck and Sherwood contributed numerous articles. See John Mason Peck, *Forty Years of Pioneer Life: Memoir of John Mason Peck D.D.*, ed. Rufus Babcock. (Philadelphia: American Baptist Publication Society, 1864; reprint, Carbondale: Southern Illinois University Press, 1965). Several monographs were published in the twentieth century in order to analyze Peck's contributions to Baptist progress or to depict Peck as a rugged frontiersman. See Austen Kennedy De Blois and Lemuel Call Barnes, *John Mason Peck and One Hundred Years of Home Missions, 1817–1917* (New York: American Baptist Home Mission Society, 1917); Coe Hayne, *Vanguard of the Caravans: A Life-Story of John Mason Peck* (Philadelphia: Judson Press, 1931); Kenneth Lee Wilson, *The Man with Twenty Hands: John Mason Peck* (New York: Friendship Press, 1948). One dissertation has taken seriously Peck's efforts toward evangelizing the settlers of the Western frontier, but it utilizes sociological terminology to form a theological analysis. See John Thomas McPherson, "John Mason Peck: A Conversionist Methodology for a Social Transformation on the American Frontier" (Ph.D. diss., Southern Baptist Theological Seminary, 1985). Other research projects preceded McPherson's. See Helen Louise Jennings, "John Mason Peck and the Impact of New England on the Northwest" (Ph. D. diss., University of Southern California, 1961); Matthew Lawrence, "John Mason Peck: a Biographical Sketch ," (M.A. thesis, University of Illinois, 1914). Two recent articles have used Peck, the historical figure, to analyze the Western frontier, providing less information on the man than the sociological setting. See J. Lynn Leavenworth, "John Mason Peck's Ministry and the Flow of History," *Foundations* 17 (July–September 1974): 259–67; Paul M. Harrison, "John Mason Peck: 'American Baptist de Tocqueville,'" *American Baptist Quarterly* 3 (September 1984): 215–24.

[39] H. Louise Jennings, "A First in Religious Journalism," *Foundations* 2 (January 1959): 40–50.

state legislature would not grant him a charter, due primarily to the antieducational feelings of many statesmen.[40] In 1832, he combined his seminary with Alton Seminary, locating both in Upper Alton, Illinois. In 1836, Peck secured a donation of 10,000 dollars from Dr. Benjamin Shurtleff of Boston under the condition that Peck change the school into a literary institute with a theological department. In 1839, the state of Illinois granted a charter due to this provision and the institute became known as Shurtleff College.

The exact occasion when J. M. Peck and Adiel Sherwood became acquaintances remains a mystery. The memoirs of J. M. Peck do not mention his friendship with Sherwood, although Sherwood's *Memoir* does. Julia Sherwood stated, "Dr. J. M. Peck was an intimate friend of Dr. Sherwood, my father, and the two were, for many years, co-laborers in Illinois and Missouri.... Luther Rice was intimate with him [Peck], also, and directed his notice to the barren fields of the West."[41] Possibly, the relationship between Peck and Sherwood existed from their mutual correspondence with William Staughton of Philadelphia or their interaction with the Triennial Convention. Either case would have brought them into close communion with the plans of domestic missions.

However, the offer of Sherwood to preside over Shurtleff College must have come from his connection with J. M. Peck, since Peck continued to serve as one of the trustees of the school. Sherwood had already exhibited great proficiency in raising funds for Columbian College as well as acting as professor and partial administrator of Columbian College and Mercer University. In 1841, Adiel Sherwood became President of Shurtleff College, a school modeled after Mercer University's curriculum, but experiencing fund shortages similar to those of Columbian College.

---

[40] The extreme views of the Parkerite Baptist sect, who held to the "Two-Seed-in-the-Spirit" doctrine, opposed J. M. Peck. See Lamire Holden Moore, *Southern Baptists in Illinois* (Nashville: Benson Printing Company, 1957) 58–59.

[41] Sherwood and Boykin, *Memoir*, 287.

SHURTLEFF COLLEGE AND WESTERN BAPTISTS

On 20 August 1841, the *Christian Index* announced to Georgia Baptists
the election of Adiel Sherwood as President of Shurtleff College:

> This brother has been elected President of Shurtleff College,
> Alton, Illinois, and will probably accept the appointment.
> Georgia Baptists will feel reluctant to give him up, as he has
> been identified with them between twenty and thirty years, but if
> the will of the Lord be so, we must yield. The cause of Christ is
> one, and we shall pray that our dear brother, whose labours have
> been so abundant and so important amongst us, may be highly
> useful to our brethren of the Far West.[42]

On 15 September 1841, Sherwood and his family left the campus of
Mercer University in Penfield, Georgia, to move to Upper Alton,
Illinois.[43] Strangely, the move seemed momentous. Sherwood's close
relationship with the greatest leader in Georgia Baptist life ended as his
work in Georgia came to a close. Just eleven days earlier, Jesse Mercer
died in Washington, Georgia. The loss of Mercer and Sherwood to
Georgia Baptist life signaled a break in Georgia Baptist history. John
Leadley Dagg and Patrick Hues Mell, Sr., would assume instrumental
leadership roles within a few short years.

Sherwood became the first full-time president of Shurtleff College.
The school did not possess much endowment and constantly required
support from the East, preferably the Northeast.[44] A historical account of

---

[42] "Professor Sherwood," *Christian Index*, 20 August 1841, 3.

[43] "This much esteemed brother, left this place on the 15th inst. for Alton, his new
home. He carries with him the regards of the denomination and others, for his welfare.
Our brethren of Illinois will have a valuable acquisition to their ranks, and the College a
faithful and efficient officer. We wish the College and its President abundant success"
("Professor A. Sherwood," *Christian Index*, 24 September 1841, 3).

[44] "Dr. Sherwood was, therefore, the first regular President of Shurtleff College,...a
college charter was granted, in 1835, and the Institution began a prosperous and
successful career as a Baptist Literary and Theological College, although the latter
department was not fully inaugurated until 1841" (Sherwood and Boykin, *Memoir*, 287).

the school described Sherwood's initial entrance into the life of the school:

In the month following Mr. Sherwood's arrival a Sunday school was organized in connection with the institution, and both boarders and day pupils were required to attend this exercise at nine o'clock each Sunday morning in Academic Hall. Attendance on church service, Sunday-school and daily prayers was obligatory, and absences from regular class exercises were punished by the levy of a fine of five cents—in the year following increased to ten cents—for each offence

Sherwood's administration mirrored his past efforts at the Eatonton manual labor school and Mercer University. He expected students to attend to their duties in the classroom and chapel.

The story of Shurtleff College under Sherwood's administration paralleled the events taking place in the Triennial Convention. Cooperation between Baptists of the North and South continued to disintegrate, while Baptists of the West suffered financially from lack of funds. From 1840 to 1845, student enrollment declined at Shurtleff from 101 to 38 students.[45] In 1842, Sherwood took measures to alleviate the financial distress that corresponded with declining enrollment. He eliminated one-half of his salary in order for the school to continue to pay for two professors. In 1845, he agreed to work for an entire year without pay. During this same year, he visited New England to raise support for the school. He wrote his wife from the Board of Managers Meeting in Providence, Rhode Island, reporting his lack of success: "I have not yet received one cent for the College, not even a promise. All say that they have given and are giving so much for their own colleges that they can do nothing for the West. If they accomplish nothing for me at Boston, I shall despair and soon return home."[46] The absence of Southern delegates overshadowed the financial needs of Shurtleff at the Triennial Convention. Within days, Southern delegates formed the

---

[45] Ibid., 103.
[46] Sherwood and Boykin, *Memoir*, 303.

Southern Baptist Convention. Sherwood finished his letter to his wife, "Division between North and South is inevitable. No one from the South here, except Messrs. Campbell, Jeter and Taylor. They all leave for the Southern Convention at Augusta, this afternoon, May 1st."[47] Although he returned with almost 200 volumes of books for the Shurtleff library, he had only raised 338 dollars in cash, with 100 dollars spent on travel expenses.[48]

RELIGIOUS MINORITIES AND SLAVERY

No matter how dismal the picture appeared at Shurtleff, Sherwood's activities in the Illinois-Missouri area actually blossomed in the first years of his Western experience. He acted with incredible energy in the formation of Illinois Baptist institutions. He served as pastor of Alton, Woodburn, and Bunker Hill churches in the 1840s.[49] He reported to his former student in Georgia, J. H. Campbell, his progress in the new country of Illinois:

> The good Lord has preserved us two winters in this climate. Generally our health has been as good or better that when in Georgia. I am sometimes affected with pain in the side or shoulder, but Mrs. S.'s health is better. She is stouter considerably. But remember, I am on the other side of fifty hastening to three score and ten, and must expect ailments. Oh that I may finish my course with joy and usefulness! I have failed to preach only two Sabbaths I think since I have been in the State. Those were in June, when I was indisposed. In Nov. I baptized our daughter Sarah, our son Thomas, Ann, the servant we brought from Georgia, and four others.[50]

---

[47] Ibid., 304.

[48] Ibid., 102–103.

[49] Ibid., 292–93. He also filled pulpits in the St. Louis area on a frequent basis.

[50] Jesse H. Campbell, "Rev. A. Sherwood," *Christian Index*, 12 May 1843, 296. The author of this book is not sure if the reference to "the servant we brought from Georgia" belonged to Sherwood or not.

Religious eccentrics lived in the pioneer regions of Illinois and Missouri. Sherwood encountered at least two religious groups, unknown in Georgia. In 1843, he reported to several Baptist papers his encounter with Joseph Smith, the founder of Mormonism.

I regard the Book of Mormon as an ingenious Romance, designed to prove that the American Indians were descended from the Jews or some oriental nation.... I spent about an hour at the house of the Prophet, as he is called, Joseph Smith. He is about 40, of light complexion, tall, and appears better than I expected. He urged me to stay and preach on the Sabbath, but being engaged, I declined: he then invited me to preach at night in his dwelling, but I suggested the prospect of rain: he answered, you shall have a house full, rain or shine.—He invites ministers to preach, and Methodists, and perhaps others, have accepted the invitation. He began to talk on baptism for remission, and quoted several verses as proof, but I waived the subject as politely as I could.[51]

Sherwood's report obviously predated the escalated violence that attended the Mormon Church later in the year. In 1844, the authorities of Carthage, Illinois, jailed Joseph Smith for burning the building that housed the *Nauvoo Expositor*, a newspaper owned by an antagonistic faction of Mormons who opposed Smith's promotion of polygamy. Later, an angry mob of local citizens stormed the jail, dragged Smith out of the jail, and shot him.

Another religious group that played a more decisive role in Sherwood's Western experience was the Friends of Humanity,[52] a group of Baptists who promoted the gradual emancipation of slaves through legal means (not the abolition of slavery through political means).[53] In a

---

[51] Adiel Sherwood, "The Mormons," *Biblical Recorder*, 26 August 1843, 2.

[52] This term also appears as Friends to Humanity.

[53] "The number of slaves reported by the census of 1800, in Indiana (including Illinois) was 133; in 1810, 237; in 1820, 190; in 1830, none. In 1810, Illinois had 168 slaves; in 1820, 917; in 1830, 746" (James H. Perkins, *Annals of the West*, ed. J. M. Peck, 2d ed. [St. Louis: James R. Albach, 1850] 789).

biographical account of a pioneer preacher, J. M. Peck described the
Friends of Humanity:

> A class of Baptists had commenced organizing churches,
> first in Illinois and then in Missouri, denominated, as a kind of
> distinction from other Baptists, as "Friends of Humanity." They
> were frequently called emancipators by others. They were
> opposed to slavery, and being desirous of operating in a quiet
> and peaceful manner against the commerce in human beings, this
> class adopted rules by which they were to be governed in the
> admission of slaveholders into the churches. The organization
> originated in Kentucky, in 1807, and made division in a small
> association in Illinois in 1809. They would not receive persons to
> membership 'whose practice appeared friendly to perpetual
> slavery;' that is, those who justified the holding of human beings
> as property, on the same grounds of right as they claimed their
> horses or other kinds of property. They did admit to membership
> in the churches of Christ slaveholders under the following
> exceptions.
>   1. Persons holding young slaves, and recording a deed of
> emancipation at such an age as the church should agree to.
>   2. Persons who had purchased slaves in their ignorance, and
> who are willing the church should decide when they shall be
> free.
>   3. Women who have no legal power to liberate slaves.
>   4. Those that held slaves who from age, debility, insanity, or
> idiotcy were unfit for emancipation. And they add, "some other
> cases which we would wish the churches to judge of, agreeable
> to the principles of humanity."[54]

John Mason Peck and his fellow ministers of the Edwardsville
Association in Illinois established correspondence with a Friends of
Humanity association in 1839. Within a decade, the Friends of Humanity

---

[54] An Old Pioneer [John Mason Peck], *"Father Clark," or The Pioneer Preacher*
(New York: Sheldon, Lamport and Blakeman, 1855) 256–57.

dropped their title and became part of the missionary Baptists of Illinois and Missouri. However, their separatist position did serve as an alternative to political abolitionism. Their beliefs easily corresponded with the goals of the American Colonization Society, a plan of Southern emancipators in the Deep South, which encouraged slaveholders to free their slaves by financially supporting their journey back to Africa.[55]

Sherwood's views on slavery would become more evident during and after the Civil War, but he did hold a normative view of the institution of slavery as held by many missionary Baptists of the South. In 1843, he released portions of his manuscript history of Georgia Baptists to the *Christian Index*, in which one extract spoke of the treatment of slaves.[56] Within this article, he assumed the legitimacy of the institution. He acknowledged the contradictory aspects of Georgia Baptist life in which freedoms granted to slaves by the state legislature lessened while the privileges of slaves in Baptist congregations increased. The article concluded, "The owner who treats his slaves cruelly, or feeds and clothes them scantly, is sure to be looked upon with suspicion and contempt."

As the issue of slavery led to the separation of Baptists in the North and South, it did not detract from the progress of domestic missions. At least two attempts had been made to form domestic missionary societies before 1845 to serve Baptists of the South. In 1839, Robert T. Daniel, a Mississippi Baptist pastor, issued the call to form the Southern Baptist Home Missionary Society in Columbus, Mississippi. It only lasted until

---

[55] William Warren Sweet, ed., *Religion of the American Frontier: The Baptists, 1783–1830* (New York: Cooper Square Publishers, 1964) 604–607. Sweet also reported that during this time there were 39 churches with 1,347 members in 4 districts or associations called the North and South Districts in Illinois, the Missouri District, and the Saline district, east of the North and South Districts. During the 1840s, these Baptists slowly abandoned their name and the cause of emancipation as abolitionism became more prominent in Illinois (93–94). In 1847, there were 4,382 antimissionary Baptists in Illinois and 4,336 in Missouri, compared to the 11,603 antimissionary Baptists in Georgia. The Friends of Humanity represented a relatively smaller group as the number of missionary Baptists versus antimissionary Baptists typically represented a 2-to-1 or 3-to-1 ratio before the Civil War (66).

[56] Erasmus, "Extracts from Sherwood's MSS. History of Georgia Baptists, Treatment of Slaves," *Christian Index*, 13 October 1843, 644.

Daniel's death in 1842. Likewise, in 1839, John Mason Peck of Illinois, W. C. Buck of Kentucky, and R. B. C. Howell of Tennessee attempted to form the Western Baptist Home Mission Society but dropped the idea in 1841.[57]

As Sherwood attended the 1844 ABHMS meeting, the threat of denying slaveholders the right to serve as missionaries seemed immanent. On 29 April, Richard Fuller of Beaufort, South Carolina, amended a resolution presented by a delegate from Maine to read:

Whereas, the question has been proposed—whether the Board would or would not employ slave-holders as missionaries of this Society; and whereas, it is important that this question should receive a full and unequivocal answer, therefore

Resolved, That as the Constitution of the Home Mission Society clearly defines its object to be the promotion of the Gospel in North America, and as it is provided by such Constitution that any auxiliary society may designate the object to which the funds contributed by it shall be applied, and may also claim a missionary or missionaries, according to such funds, and select the field where such missionary or missionaries shall reside,

Therefore, 1st: That to introduce the subjects of slavery or anti-slavery into this body, is in direct contravention of the whole letter, and purpose of the said Constitution, and is, moreover, a most unnecessary agitation of topics with which the Society has no concern, over which it has no control, and as to which its operations should not be fettered, or its deliberations disturbed.

2. That the Home Mission Society being only an agency to disburse the funds confided to it, according to the wishes of contributors, therefore, our co-operation in this body does not imply any sympathy either with slavery or anti-slavery, as to

---

[57] Alfred Ronald Tonks, "A History of the Home Mission Board of the Southern Baptist Convention: 1845–1882" (Th.D. diss., Southern Baptist Theological Seminary, 1967) 16–17.

which societies and individuals are left as free and uncommitted as if there were no such cooperation.[58]

At the conclusion of the meeting, a committee of nine members was appointed to decide whether or not the society should be dissolved. The delegates of the ABHMS appointed three delegates each from the North, the South, and the West. These included "Br. H. Lincoln, of Mass., Chairman, J. L. Dagg, of Ga., J. B. Taylor, of Va., W. B. Johnson, of S. C., J. Going, of Ohio, H. Malcom, of Ky., J. [misprint of A.] Sherwood, of Ill., P. Church, of N. Y., H. Jackson, of Mass. And J. Gillpatrick, of Me."[59]

On 2 August 1844, the Executive Committee of the Georgia Baptist Convention submitted the name of James E. Reeve, a Georgia Baptist itinerant minister, to the ABHMS for appointment. The Executive Board of the Baptist General Convention refused to consider the application from Georgia in order to avoid the issue of slavery. Considering the Georgia application a test that the General Convention failed, the Alabama Baptist Convention sent a resolution 25 November to the Baptist General Convention insisting on the equal treatment of slaveholders who wished to be agents and missionaries.

On 30 May 1845, the Board of Managers of the Baptist General Convention met at Providence, Rhode Island, and received a report from the Acting Board committee that formally answered the Alabama Resolution.[60] Committee members consisted of "Messrs. F. Wayland, G. S. Webb, A. Sherwood, J. B. Taylor, E. Tucker, B. Sears, [and] E. B. Smith." Francis Wayland submitted the report of the committee, listing three important points of consensus:

1. The spirit of the Constitution of the General Convention, as well as the history of its proceedings from the beginning, renders it apparent, that all the members of the Baptist

---

[58] *Twelfth Report of the American Baptist Home Mission Society* (New York: John Gray, 1844) 5–6.

[59] Ibid., 6.

[60] "American Baptist Board of Foreign Missions, Thirty-First Annual Meeting," *Baptist Missionary Magazine* 25 (July 1845): 147.

denomination in good standing, whether at the North or the South, are constitutionally eligible to all appointments emanating either from the Convention or the Board.

2. While this is the case, it is possible that contingencies may arise, in which the carrying out of this principle might create the necessity of making appointments by which the brethren of the North would, either in fact, or in the opinion of the Christian community, become responsible for institutions which they could not, with a good conscience, sanction.

3. Were such a case to occur, we could not desire our brethren to violate their convictions of duty by making such appointments, but should consider it incumbent on them to refer the case to the Convention for its decision.

All which is respectfully submitted, in behalf of the Committee.[61]

Important in the committee's answer is that they indirectly violated the neutrality supposedly guaranteed by the Fuller resolution. The committee's response defended the convictions of Northern non-slaveholders as it avoided the question from Alabama. As a member of the committee, Sherwood certainly allied himself with the Baptists of the North who did not want to condone the institution of slavery within the denomination. Conversely, Sherwood as an individual condoned the institution, but not the abuse of slaves. One should recognize the fact that Sherwood did not attend the Southern Baptist Convention in Augusta. In fact, he would not attend a national convention meeting for six years. Until that time, he utilized the support of Northern Baptists in reaching people in the West.

WESTERN BAPTIST PIONEER WORK

Baptist work in the Missouri-Illinois area continued unabated by the events of the Triennial Convention. Sherwood continued to work tirelessly in the fields of Baptist education and ministry, developing

---

[61] Ibid., 150–51.

associations and conventions in Illinois and Missouri. One author asserted that Baptist organization solidified quickly in southern Illinois due to the migratory patterns of Southern people, many from Georgia.[62] This could explain the ease in which Sherwood led the people of his area to form stronger and larger organizations. The new population already possessed a history of solidarity.

On 3–5 October 1844, the Illinois Baptist Convention met at Belleville, Illinois, with Adiel Sherwood serving as moderator. At this meeting, the delegates recommended a union between their convention and the Northwestern Conference (consisting of the states of Michigan, Wisconsin, Minnesota, and Indiana). On 21 November 1844, at Canton, Illinois, both organizations met and decided to form the new "Baptist General Association of Illinois." The week of 18–20 October 1845, at Tremont, Illinois, functioned as the first normal session of the General Association. For many years, the General Association functioned as an auxiliary to the ABHMS and as a society of contributors.[63]

During his last years at Shurtleff College, Adiel Sherwood received an honorary doctorate from Granville College in Ohio.[64] In 1844, the Granville Literary and Theological Institution (as it was formerly called) granted Sherwood the title of Doctor of Divinity.[65] As a normal practice

---

[62] Lamire Holden Moore, *Southern Baptists in Illinois,* 69.

[63] Myron D. Dillow, *Harvesttime on the Prairie* (Franklin TN: Providence House Publishers, 1996) 193–95. This society-based structure would cause problems in funding and administration for several decades.

[64] The school in Granville existed as Granville Literary and Theological Institution from 1832 to 1845, and it embraced the manual labor system. In November 1844, President Jonathan Going, formerly the corresponding secretary of the ABHMS, but then president, died. In 1845, the name of the school was changed to Granville College, and the manual labor system was abandoned. In 1856, the school was renamed Denison University. See William Cathcart, ed., "Denison University," in vol. 1 of *The Baptist Encyclopedia*, 327.

[65] "It was in 1844, while President of Shurtleff College, that the degree of Doctor of Divinity was conferred on Adiel Sherwood by Granville College, Ohio, as he says, 'without my knowledge or expectation;' but, in this instance, at least, it was a degree most worthily bestowed, and one to which he did honor all during life" (Sherwood and Boykin, *Memoir*, 299). Two decades later, Sherwood complained about the impossible responsibility attached to the title of a Doctor of Divinity: "If a D. D. he is supposed to know everything and a little more, on all subjects connected with the Bible—to understand all the original languages in which the scriptures have been written—all the

throughout the United States before the Civil War, many religious leaders received honorary doctorates from friendly institutions. A formal research-oriented doctorate in the field of religion did not exist in America at this time. In the case of Sherwood, most newspaper correspondents and denominational secretaries after 1844 referred to him according to his title.

THE TRUE AND SPURIOUS CHURCHES CONTRASTED

Adiel Sherwood delivered a sermon before the last regular session of the Illinois Baptist Convention in Belleville, Illinois, in 1844 in which he outlined his view of Baptist ecclesiology. Published as a monograph in 1845, this sermon demonstrates Sherwood's conception of the biblical view of the church. Within the setting of a dividing Baptist denomination and a fragmented state of interdenominational cooperation, the outline of a Baptist ecclesiology over against the competing Pedobaptist, or "infant-baptizing," denominations was needed.

Looking toward the unification of the Illinois Baptist Convention with the Northwestern Conference, Moderator Sherwood at the meeting in Belleville, Illinois, seemed to sense the primary problem of churches and church leaders. Immediately, he defined the problem of spurious churches as those who "fix on what they suppose to be the proper course, without inquiring, 'What saith the Scriptures?'—or 'Who readest thou?'" Rather, they are "content to travel the road that runs easiest to their feet, guided by reason, or controlled by expediency."[66] His exhortation to his

---

arguments against infidelity and atheism, and in favor of the genuineness and authenticity of the sacred books. Some conceive he is the most eloquent speaker, the most persuasive orator, ever heard or seen. If he fail to answer expectations, heightened by the opinions entertained by the title: if he preach like ordinary men: if he do not soar into the ethereal regions: if he omit to make a classical allusions Bartow that none of his audience understand: if he do not give rotundity to his well-turned periods: if his sermons are not spiced with Greek and Hebrew, the people conclude that learning is not of much account, and that the titled giant is not stronger than common preachers" (Dr. Sherwood, "Lights and Shadows of Pastoral Life, The Titled Pastor, Number XV," *Christian Index*, 12 August 1862, 3).

[66] Adiel Sherwood, *The True and Spurious Churches Contrasted* (Philadelphia: King and Baird, 1845) 3.

audience contained two parts, one outlining the marks of a true church and the other delineating the six marks of spurious churches.

In part one, section one, Sherwood defined the church in the following manner. A church existed as "a congregation of believers in Christ, who have been baptized on that profession in the name of Father, Son, and Holy Ghost, and who are united together in covenant bonds, to obey the truths, commands, and example of Jesus Christ."[67] The institution of Christ's body on earth did not stand *as* the truth, but *for* the truth. Sherwood carefully expressed the difference between an institution that legislated or embodied truth from an organization that followed the truth. He asserted, "It is not the design of the Apostle…to exalt the church above the truth…The truth to which the church clings must be the inspired truth, else it is no more valuable than the dictates of any fallible man."[68]

Sherwood held to the typical Baptist view of the church. He denied a universal church as existing on earth; instead, it existed in eternity. From an exegetical standpoint, the New Testament did not recognize a visible body larger than the local church.[69] The church did not consist of a national or an international (catholic) character.[70] A national or universal church violated the twofold concept of liberty and discipline. The local church always enjoyed freedom from outside forces and practiced the freedom of disciplining her members. Sherwood acknowledged a mystical body of Christ but denied a visible representation of it in the world. He stated, "If the church were catholic

---

[67] Ibid., 5.

[68] Ibid.

[69] Most Baptists in the South recognized a general body of Christ but denied it could be truly represented beyond the local level. The issues of church discipline and believer's baptism could be administered only on the local level, thereby guaranteeing true representatives of the church. One of the few dissenters of this popular concept was John Leadly Dagg, who insisted on a visible, universal church (see Dagg's *A Treatise on Church Order* [Charleston: Southern Baptist Publication Society; reprint, Harrisonburg VA: Gano Books, 1990] 119).

[70] "The New Testament does not recognize a national church…. It regards all true worshipers as constituting the mystical body of Christ, the sacramental host of God's elect" (Sherwood, *True and Spurious Churches*, 6).

or universal, it would be impossible to execute the discipline enjoined in the New Testament."[71]

Part one, section two of Sherwood's sermon declared that church rights originated from the concept of the primitive church. Sherwood proposed the term *primitive* to mean first or original. Just as scholars identified the first-century Christian Church as the primitive church era, Sherwood followed the same strand of jargon. Earlier, in Georgia, he applied the same term against the Primitive Baptists. Their argument consisted of the identity of the original Baptists, while his assertions centered on the biblical pattern of worship.[72] The essence of wholeness surrounded the early churches: "The primitive churches contained within themselves the elements of completeness for all the duties they were bound to discharge. The members were believers, and such only were knowingly admitted; hence they are addressed as persons capable of understanding, and willing to obey."[73] In the primitive church, the body of Christ functioned as a "voluntary society, organized under the impulse of duty to Jesus Christ," and it possessed the right "to choose officers, receive and expel members, [as] belongs to every voluntary society."[74] As societies composed of voluntary members, the churches held the final right to all matters of ecclesiastical control. No other power on earth has jurisdiction above the local church on matters of faith, order, and discipline.[75]

---

[71] Ibid.

[72] Sherwood's choice of terminology dated back to his *Strictures on the Kehukee Association* in 1828. One recent author noted this chronology in Sherwood's life but failed to connect his purpose of such terminology as he utilized it against the Primitive Baptist movement: "A Georgia writer, Adiel Sherwood, a bitter foe of the Old School Baptists, used 'primitive' to refer to the exemplary pattern of the early church in preaching the gospel everywhere and not to anti-missionary Baptists. 'The apostles and primitive Christians,' he stated, 'obeyed as far as they were able'" (Jerry Newsome, "'Primitive Baptists': A Study in Name Formation or What's in a Word," *Viewpoints* 6 [1978]: 66).

[73] Sherwood, *True and Spurious Churches*, 6–7.

[74] Ibid., 8.

[75] "Churches are independent of all associations, conferences, synods, and prelatical bishops, being the highest ecclesiastical tribunal on earth.... it is plain that from the church there is no appellant jurisdiction" (ibid.,10).

In section three, Sherwood stated that the primitive church or the true church possessed two types of officers: elders and deacons. Sherwood held to the customary distinction of bishops or elders as superintendents of the spiritual functions of the church and the deacons as the officials of the temporal functions. He also equated the term *bishop* with elder and denied bishops were the normative titles for elders in the New Testament. Fellow ministers of New Testament churches utilized the term *brother*, avoiding any form of clerical superiority.

In section four, the ordinances of baptism and the Lord's Supper constituted the only ordained rites required of church members. Again, Sherwood followed traditional Baptist theology in connecting baptism with communion. Only baptized believers could partake of the Lord's Table. Interestingly, he did differ in his view of the primary focus of the Lord's Supper. He stated: "The object [of the Lord's Supper] is the commemoration of his sufferings and death—to show forth the Lord's death till he come…. It is not to show forth our fellowship as Christians to one another, as some have supposed, but to show forth the Lord's death, that we observe this institution."[76] The editor of this printed sermon, J. M. Peck, enhanced Sherwood's statement further in a footnote. He pointed to the objections of non-Baptists against the strict communion practices of Baptists. Many Pedobaptists did not understand this restriction, whereas most polemical writings of Baptists referred to the disconnection between proper baptism and proper communion. The advocates of infant baptism were not properly baptized; therefore, they stood as improper subjects of communion. With only one view of communion, Sherwood eliminated the original complaint of Pedobaptists concerning Christian fellowship. Taking a somewhat divergent view than other Baptist thinkers, Sherwood saw communion, not as a rite of fellowship, but as a rite of worship. The problem was not proper fellowship at the Lord's Table but proper worship. Only baptized believers should worship God through the holy meal.[77]

---

[76] Sherwood, *True and Spurious Churches*, 15.

[77] "Many Christians imagine the Lord's supper is a pledge or a test of Christian fellowship between believers. The Scriptures nowhere teach this notion. Most of the objections to strict communion in our churches are predicated on this mistaken notion about the design of the Lord's supper. As this ordinance is to be observed, not by

In section five of the marks of a true church, Sherwood declared the New Testament model of the church as the pillar and ground of truth. The example of the New Testament anchored the essence, doctrine, and morality of ecclesiological truth. First, the ontological grounding of biblical churches proceeded from the reception of the Bible as "the only authoritative rule and guide of life" and as "the only authoritative directory for Christians."[78] Second, the proper church must maintain the propagation of scriptural truth. Doctrinal grounding in the Scriptures enabled churches to avoid fanaticism. Sherwood assured his audience that they should not equate the task of strictly adhering to Scripture with the beliefs of fanaticism. These two forms of religious expression actually differed widely. Fanaticism "fixes on some vision, theory, or single fact, connected with something marvelous, and adheres to it without investigation."[79] To Sherwood, Joseph Smith and Mormonism provided an excellent example of fanaticism. Third, the morality of a scriptural church carried the greatest proof of evident truth. Although grounded in the Scriptures and holding to scriptural truths, the practice of these truths through holy and consistent living guaranteed the success of true churches.[80]

In his final part of the sermon, Sherwood delineated six marks or evidences of spurious or false churches, providing a polemic against churches that baptized infants and denied the validity of believer's baptism by immersion. The first mark of a spurious church would be the church that "excludes from the favour of God and heaven all not within its pale." Alluding to his earlier discussion on the grounding of truth, false institutions presumed to possess the powers of God, but the powers granted by Scripture made them false organizations. Obviously, Sherwood had in mind the Protestant view of the Roman Catholic Church and her practice of excommunication. Second, he attacked the lack of purity in unscriptural churches. "A spurious church multiplies its members without regard to knowledge and piety," while a true church

---

individual believers, but by churches as bodies politic, of course not only evidence of Christian character, but baptism, are necessary prerequisites" (ibid., note 15).

[78] Sherwood, *True and Spurious Churches*, 16.

[79] Ibid., 17.

[80] Ibid., 18.

"admits to membership those only who give evidence of piety; that is, who are changed in heart."[81] The practice of infant baptism propagated the evil of an unregenerate church membership. Third, the church that attempted "to make laws for its government" provided another example of a wretched institution. "It has been shown that Jesus Christ is the only lawgiver and king in the church, and the inference is irresistible, that all the laws necessary and proper were enacted by Him before the canon of Scripture was closed."[82] Fourth, another type of a spurious church would be the religious opposition to Bible translations and circulation. The Church of Rome opposed the early Protestant reformers, and several Protestant denominations in America have recently done the same. "Even the American Bible Society refuses aid to some who have translated rather than transferred Baptizo and its cognates, preferring to leave the 'missionary at perfect liberty to explain them according to the peculiar views of his particular denomination.'"[83] Fifth, a spurious church persecuted dissenters. Baptists have always been the persecuted; whereas, the advocates of infant baptism have handed out punishment. Sixth, the final mark of a spurious church would be the one "which amalgamates church and state." By combining the identity of the church with the external and natural sphere of human government, advocates of infant baptism have chained the church to a wicked course.

MISSIONARY WORK TO THE INDIANS AND WESTERN CONVENTIONS

Sherwood continued his work in Western home missions functioning as a missionary, pastor, and administrator during the ten years spanning 1846 to 1856. His pastorates were abundant. He served as pastor of several Illinois churches in the late 1840s, but by 1849 he ministered more in Missouri. However, his work from 1846 to 1849 followed a more itinerant schedule. For two years, he journeyed throughout the territorial regions of what had constituted the Northwestern Conference. The conglomeration of states north and west of Illinois not only required

---

[81] Ibid., 19.
[82] Ibid., 22.
[83] Ibid., 26.

itinerant preaching, but large clusters of Native American populations on Indian reservations demanded the most attention in mission work.

During his earliest years out west, Adiel Sherwood came into contact with Isaac McCoy, the pioneer of Native American missions in Baptist life. Born in Fayette County, Pennsylvannia on 13 June 1784, young Isaac moved to Kentucky with his father in 1790. Converted at Buck Creek Baptist Church in 1801, McCoy soon developed an interest in Indian Missions. In 1803, he married Christiana Polk, daughter of an army captain who lost his wife and children to the Ottawa Indians. This same tribe became the subjects of the McCoys' later missionary endeavors. In 1817, the Baptist General Convention appointed Isaac McCoy to the Native American tribes in Indiana and Illinois. His missionary endeavors included Southwest Indiana, Fort Wayne in Indiana, and the Carey Mission he founded in Niles, Michigan, in 1822. From 1826 to 1842, McCoy surveyed new lands west of the Mississippi for the American Indian and submitted his findings to officials in Washington, DC. In 1840, he published *The History of Indian Affairs*, a 600-page history of his missionary work. In 1842, he formed the American Indian Mission Association in Louisville, Kentucky. One night in June 1846, he contracted an illness from a rainstorm while crossing the Ohio River on his way home to Louisville. His last recorded words were, "Tell the brethren, never to let the Indian mission decline."[84]

When Isaac McCoy died in Louisville, Kentucky, his demise brought vacancies as corresponding secretary of the American Indian Mission Board and editor of the *Indian Advocate*.[85] In July, the delegates

---

[84] See William Cathcart ed., "Rev. Isaac McCoy," in vol. 2 of *The Baptist Encyclopedia*, 766–67.

[85] Some of the major works on Isaac McCoy include Robert M. Drury, The Life of Isaac McCoy, Minister, Missionary, Explorer, Surveyor, Lobbyist, Administrator and "Apostle to the Indians," (Kansas City: n.p., 1965); Emory J. Lyons, Isaac McCoy: His Plan of and Work for Indian Colonization (Topeka: Kansas State Printing Plant, 1945). Two dissertations have also included McCoy as a topic. See Edward Roustio, "A History of the Life of Isaac McCoy: in Relationship to Early Indian Migrations and Missions as Revealed in His Unpublished Manuscripts" (Th. D. diss, Central Baptist Theological Seminary, 1954); Albert H. Fauth, "A History of the American Indian Mission Association and its Contributions to Baptist Indian Missions" (Th. D. diss, Central Baptist Theological Seminary, 1953).

to the American Indian Mission Association asked Adiel Sherwood to occupy both positions, which he did for more than twelve months.[86] His family continued to live in Alton, Illinois, during this time, while he was employed with the board. During this time of turmoil, Sherwood traveled the Northwestern territory and corresponded with his constituency through the *Indian Advocate*, providing stability until the board found a more suitable replacement.

In 1848, Sherwood accepted the presidency of the Masonic College in Lexington, Missouri, an institution for the orphans of Masons.[87]

---

[86] "This association had been formed at Cincinnati, in 1843, with the distinct object in view of educating and evangelizing the various Indian tribes of the West, who had been moved from the South by the general government. The particular tribes among the association sent missionaries, were the Cherokees, Creeks, Chickasaws and Choctaws, in the Indian Territory" (Sherwood and Boykin, *Memoir*, 312). Sherwood lived away from his family from 1846 to 1849 (Sherwood and Boykin, *Memoir*, 314–15). In November 1846, he was late to the associational meeting due to his wife's sickness and the distance ("Rev. Adiel Sherwood," *Banner and Pioneer* [Louisville] 12 November 1846, 178). The minutes of AIMA (American Indian Mission Association) acknowledge the temporary appointment of Sherwood. However, much cannot be gleaned from the 1846–1847 issues of the *Indian Advocate*, as it relates to Sherwood. As editor, he never signed his reports, making it difficult to identify them as his literary works or someone else's.

[87] "An educational institution established at Lexington in 1847. Here the orphans of Masons were sent for education, and until 1858 it was an institution known all over the state and throughout the West" ("Masonic College," in vol. 4 of *Encyclopedia of the History of Missouri* [St. Louis: Southern History Company, 1901] 214). As a further note, the buildings of the school lasted throughout the Civil War until a battle between Union and Confederate forces destroyed most of the facility. In 1871, the Grand Lodge of Masons of Missouri donated the property consisting of 7 acres to the Central Female College. See "Central Female College," in vol. 1 of *Encyclopedia of the History of Missouri*, 552–53. It should be noted that the issue of Masonry had lessened in Baptist circles since the final antimission split in 1837. The original Kehukee declaration included a call to separate from Baptists who belonged to a secret society such as the Masons or Odd Fellows. Missionary Baptists avoided the issue frequently. Obviously, Sherwood either condoned the society of Masons or belonged to them. He once compared a secret society to the church by stating, "Would a Mason cry 'bigotry' if denied the privilege of entering a lodge of Odd-fellows? Or because, a mere master in degree, if not allowed to sit with the royal arch masons? By no means. Why then should churches, formed and regulated according to New Testament order, be denominated bigots when their principles accord with the faith once delivered to the saints, and the others differ widely from the pattern exhibited in the record?" (A. S., "Bigotry and Liberalism," *Christian Repository* [April 1875]: 268).

During the school year of 1848–1849, Sherwood boarded with a nearby family and spoke in all the pulpits of the town, except the Episcopal. In 1849, Sherwood left this school in western Missouri and accepted the pastorate of Fee Fee church in St. Louis County, Missouri.[88]

Sherwood's ministerial work continued in Illinois until he moved his family from Alton in 1852. On 28 December 1849, Sherwood gathered with several ministers at a meeting of the "South District Ministerial Conference" in Troy, Illinois, to discuss their dissatisfaction with the General Baptist Association of Illinois. The delegation agreed to reconvene at a later date in order to decide the needs of southern Illinois, such as itinerant preaching. On 24–25 May 1850, a committee of which Sherwood was a member wrote a circular address calling ministers in southern Illinois to meet the following October in order to find a better solution for "the destitution of Southern Illinois and means of supply."[89] On 28 October 1850, at Bethel Church in Saint Clair County, the requested delegation founded the "Baptist Convention of Southern Illinois."[90] J. M. Peck served as moderator and Adiel Sherwood as secretary. They adopted an organizational plan similar to that of the Illinois Baptist Convention (1836–1841).[91] By October 1856, this body voted to dissolve, having acquired the financial support of the ABHMS.

By 1852, Sherwood focused most of his denominational efforts on Missouri. He and his family established their residency in Cape Girardeau, Missouri, where he served as pastor from 1852–1856. At an 1854 meeting with the Franklin Association at Union Church, Sherwood from the New Cape Girardeau Association offered the resolution that led

---

[88] Sherwood and Boykin, *Memoir*, 315. Julia Sherwood listed a future Civil War officer, Colonel A. W. Slayback, as one of Sherwood's students (Sherwood and Boykin, *Memoir*, 316). Col. Slayback "served in the Confederate Army, and rose to the rank of colonel. After the war he went with General Shelby to Mexico, and remained in voluntary exile until 1866." Slayback was shot and killed in 1882 when he confronted a newspaper editor who had personally attacked him in his paper. See "Alonzo William Slayback," in vol. 5 of *Encyclopedia of the History of Missouri*, 606.

[89] Dillow, *Harvesttime on the Prairie*, 288–89.

[90] Moore, *Southern Baptists in Illinois*, 70–71.

[91] Dillow, *Harvesttime on the Prairie*, 289.

to the organization of the Baptist Convention of Southern Missouri.[92] This convention served as an auxiliary to the General Baptist Association of Missouri, since the state association could not supply all the needs of southern Missouri. The life of this organization continued until the beginning of the Civil War, receiving additional support randomly from the American Baptist Home Mission Society and the Southern Home Mission Board.

About 1855, Adiel Sherwood contracted a severe form of rheumatism. While bedridden, he wrote *Notes on the New Testament, Practical and Explanatory*, a synthesis of several prominent commentaries combined with his own. He stated the purpose of the work was to make available to common preachers of the West and South a practical commentary of the New Testament.[93] By early 1857, his doctor advised him to seek a warmer climate for his rheumatism. Sherwood moved to Griffin, Georgia, and assumed the pastorate of the Baptist church and the presidency of a newly formed college.

THE HERMENEUTIC OF BAPTIST ECCLESIOLOGY

Adiel Sherwood never broke his correspondence with Georgia Baptists while in Illinois and Missouri, and he also contributed to the ongoing synthesis of religious literature in the state. In 1847, his brother-in-law Robert Fleming incorporated two of Sherwood's sermons delivered in Georgia in a book he edited titled *The Georgia Pulpit*.[94] In 1849, Robert

---

[92] R. S. Duncan, *A History of the Baptists in Missouri* (St. Louis: Scammell and Company, 1882) 305.

[93] See Adiel Sherwood, *Notes on the New Testament, Practical and Explanatory* (New York: Sheldon, Blakeman and Company, 1857).

[94] The publisher of this monograph labeled it as the first volume, but no subsequent volume ever followed it in later years. Fleming published two of Sherwood's sermons. See Adiel Sherwood, "The Careful Minister," in vol. 1 of *The Georgia Pulpit: or Ministers' Yearly Offering*, ed. Robert Fleming (Richmond: H. K. Ellyson, 1847) 65–81; Adiel Sherwood, "The Covenant of Redemption," in vol. 1 of *The Georgia Pulpit*, 82–90. Fleming married Sherwood's sister, Charlotte D. Sherwood, making her his second wife. See Sherwood and Boykin, *Memoir*, 196. Rev. Robert Fleming was born in Warren County GA 3 August 1797 and died in Navasota TX 29 March 1880. For most of his life, he taught in grammar schools in the counties of Warren, Meriwether, and Talbot. Although Fleming was raised in a Presbyterian home, a Methodist minister led Fleming

Fleming published a polemical writing of his own. He defended Baptist polity through his defense of John the Baptist, a figure who belonged in the New Testament dispensation, not the Old Testament. Sherwood provided a lengthy introduction to Fleming's *An Essay on the Baptism of John*, in which he too defended the position. In 1850, Sherwood published a book elaborating on the same concept and challenging the prevalent hermeneutic of Presbyterians and Methodists. In *The Jewish and Christian Churches; or the Hebrew Theocracy and Christian Church Distinct Organizations*, Sherwood refuted the exegetical and philosophical arguments of Pedobaptists. In this text, he differentiated Baptist ecclesiology from advocates of infant baptism by captivating on one central issue: the Christian Church as having no commonality with the Old Testament dispensation. With both literary pieces, Sherwood outlined the hermeneutical differences between Baptists and their opponents. In this context, he found his niche in the discussion between fellow Baptists and Pedobaptists.[95]

---

to accept the Christian faith. Later, Fleming joined the Baptists due to his examination of the Scriptures. His literary works included *An Essay on the Baptism of John, The Life of Humphrey Posey, The Georgia Pulpit, The Confederate Spelling Book*, and an unpublished English grammar. Living in Georgia most of his life, Fleming moved to Texas as an elderly man and a paralytic. His last words were "I want to go home; take me home!" (Samuel Boykin, *History of the Baptist Denomination in Georgia*, 210–11).

[95] Some of the more prominent monographs among antebellum Southern Baptist discussion of Baptist ecclesiology include James Leadley Dagg, *An Essay in Defence of Strict Communion* (Penfield GA: Benjamin Brantly, 1845); Robert Boyte C. Howell, *The Terms of Communion at the Lord's Table* (Philadelphia: American Baptist Publication Society, 1846); Thomas F. Curtis, *Communion: The Distinction between Christian and Church Fellowship and between Communion and Its Symbols* (Philadelphia: American Baptist Publication Society, 1850); S. Remington, *A Defence of Restricted Communion* (Philadelphia: American Baptist Publication Society, 1852); J. R. Graves, *The Watchman's Reply* (Nashville: Tennessee Publication Society, 1853); J. M. Pendleton, *Three Reasons Why I Am a Baptist with a Fourth Reason Added on Communion* (Louisville: Baptist Book Concern, 1853); Patrick Hues Mell, *Baptism in Its Mode and Subjects* (Charleston: Southern Baptist Publication Society, 1854); Richard Fuller, *Baptism and the Terms of Communion: An Argument* (Charleston: Southern Baptist Publication Society, 1854).

THE BAPTISM OF JOHN

In his introductory essay to Fleming's work, Sherwood outlined the current concern of Baptists with their ecclesiological identity. Most Baptist pastors and theologians interpreted John the Baptist as the institutor of the ordinance of baptism while Jesus Christ confirmed it and gave it a spiritual meaning. Baptist thinkers did not attempt to separate John's baptism from Christian baptism. To do so would be to annul the practice of immersion and its connection with an open testimonial of God's converting grace. Sherwood defined the matter in the following way: "The subject discussed in the following pages has an important bearing in the gospel economy. When the question was proposed to the Savior in the Temple touching his authority to teach, he answered by asking another: 'The baptism of John,—from Heaven or of men?'"[96] Sherwood predicted that the correct identification of John's baptism would be a pivotal issue. He stated, "To admit it was from Heaven,—not from Jewish ceremonies or proselyte washings,—places Pedo-Baptism in as bad a predicament as were the priests."[97] According to Sherwood, John's baptism began during the Christian dispensation. From his perspective, the ministry of Christ inaugurated the new kingdom, and John's baptismal rite was a valid component of this new era.[98]

John the Baptist and his work as an immersionist either belonged to the Jewish or the Christian dispensation. Was Christ's herald the last of the Old Testament prophets or the earliest preacher of the Christian church? Sherwood questioned two primary thoughts of Pedobaptist theology. First, he saw the textual proofs against Acts 19 as a normal exegetical attack on the Baptist form of baptism. In this passage, believers in Ephesus had only received John's baptism of repentance; they had not heard of the complete message of the gospel. Normally, advocates of infant baptism would interpret the passage as stating John's baptism was improper for the Christian dispensation or that John was an

---

[96] Rev. Robert Fleming, *An Essay on the Baptism of John*, with an introduction by Adiel Sherwood, D.D. (Athens GA: W. C. Richards, 1849) ix.

[97] Ibid., x.

[98] "Christ's commands, issued before his death, are as binding upon his disciples as those given after it" (ibid.).

inadequate administrator of the practice. In either case, the ordinance of baptism by immersion was discounted from this textual proof. Second, Sherwood also noticed that scholarship in his day preferred to rob John of his title. For example, individuals such as Leonard Woods, professor at Andover Seminary, called John the Baptist John Baptist.[99]

Sherwood refuted this hermeneutic of implicit example with an explicit exegesis. John's dispensation had to be the beginning of a Christian dispensation for several reasons. First, the prophetic proof as seen in Daniel's seven weeks in Daniel 6 demanded the entrance of a harbinger for Christ's advent. Second, John preached the same message as Christ. Both demanded from their audience the exercise of faith through repentance.[100] Third, Acts 19 actually proved that the ordinance of baptism as instituted by John was not replaced with Christian baptism. John's baptism did not differ from Christian baptism. Fourth, water baptism and the reception of the Holy Spirit were not connected. The baptismal cases in the New Testament differed. On many occasions in the Scriptures, the reception of the Holy Spirit preceded water baptism, proving that the baptism of the Spirit did not hinge on water baptism. Fifth, John's baptism also followed repentance. It did not constitute repentance or ensure it, but it signified a repentant state. In all five aspects, the baptism of John corresponded with the Christian dispensation.

THE JEWISH AND CHRISTIAN CHURCHES

In his monograph, *The Jewish and Christian Churches; or the Hebrew Theocracy and Christian Church Distinct Organization*, Sherwood accurately judged the issue of Baptist ecclesiology to be an issue of authority. He stated, "It is of the greatest importance, that in our church polity we should be guided solely by the Scriptures."[101] Without explicit biblical example, the organization of Christian worship and membership on earth would degenerate into silly superstitions and human traditions.

---

[99] Fleming, *An Essay on the Baptism of John*, xii.

[100] Ibid., xiv.

[101] Adiel Sherwood, *The Jewish and Christian Churches; or the Hebrew Theocracy and Christian Church Distinct Organization* (St. Louis: T.W. Ustick, 1850) 1.

The role of the Bible as an explicit document in establishing external institutions should be followed. Sherwood asserted:

> But it must be conceded, that the Christian world has diverged very far from the unerring standard—that in forming creeds and formulas of doctrine and government, we have mingled with Bible teachings, the commandments and inferences of men. Primitive Christianity, unencumbered by rites and ceremonies, which proud and ambitious dignitaries have introduced for the sake of honor and filthy lucre, was cordial in its obedience and simple in its forms of worship. It inquired, "What saith the Scriptures?" and bowed submissively to its decisions.[102]

Explicit instructions from the Bible should form the issues of faith, practice, and church polity. From Sherwood's perspective, all three are inseparably linked. Practice and polity proceeded from matters of faith, neither being free from biblical example. Sherwood argued this case by dividing his book into two parts, the first part analyzing the inconsistencies of combining the two dispensations, and the second part drawing deductions from such inconsistencies.

Twelve sections outlined the first part of the work. In section one, Sherwood targeted the central problem. He asserted, "The identity of the Church under the Jewish and Christian Dispensations, it is conceived, is a great mistake, and has been the source of serious errors in ecclesiastical matters."[103] The placement of the church in the Old Testament originated from the English version of the Bible. English translators took the Greek word for *assembly* in the Septuagint and translated it as the same term for *assembly* in the New Testament. By equating an assembly of the Old Testament with a body of "the called-out ones" (ecclesia) in the New Testament, religious groups in Western Christianity have confused the same terms with the same institutions. Through this form of equation, the congregations of Israel have assumed the title of the Jewish church, and,

---

[102] Ibid.

[103] Ibid., 2.

consequently, their rites have been transferred to the New Testament church.

In sections two through five, Sherwood argued that in every respect the two assemblies varied and should not be equated. In section two, the members of the Jewish and Christian dispensations differed. Circumcised males, descendants of Abraham, constituted the Jewish congregation of the Old Testament. No exhibition of faith was required for membership. In section three, the ministry and services of the two organizations were distinct. In the Old Testament, the sons of Aaron ministered to the congregation and physical requirements measured their qualifications for entrance. They could not have a physical blight, or deformity, such as leprosy. No physical problem could inhibit their work as priests. However, in the new dispensation, the ministry is a converted one that includes all classes of men. The ministers of the old dispensation followed a hereditary form of administering the rites of the old covenant, while in the new church dispensation ministers preach repentance.[104]

In sections four and five, the ordinances and their recipients vary between the testaments. The symbols of the old dispensation have no substantive reality in the new. The Jewish nation held to circumcision as a distinguishing rite, but other ordinances were included, such as the Passover meal, the feast days, and the types of offerings. However, the New Testament proscribed a simple, primitive form of worship. Two types of officers belonged to the church, and two ordinances were required of the members. The members of the Jewish congregation combined their religion with their national goals, but the members of the New Testament church never combined their spiritual membership with any political institution.

From sections six to nine, Sherwood exposed the inconsistencies that existed in equating circumcision with baptism. First, in section six, he could not visualize the connection of repentance with circumcision. Obviously, repentance preceded baptism in the New Testament, but no

---

[104] "Ministers of the New Dispensation preach the gospel—repentance towards God and faith in His Son—the necessity of regeneration by the Spirit of God—Justification by Faith—a blameless life—the resurrection of the righteous to a blessed immortality, and of the wicked to eternal woe. Frequently they deliver their messages with an earnestness and power that none can gainsay or resist" (ibid., 10–11).

one in the Old Testament had to exhibit any change in the affections when circumcised. In section seven, the kingdom of God inaugurated in the New Testament actually began a "new church," or a new kingdom. None of the institutions of the Old Testament could be transferred into the new. Believers had no spiritual use for a priest, and they did not need the rite of circumcision.[105] In section eight, no New Testament ordinance could be found in the Old Testament. The Hebrews did not practice proselyte baptism (as some scholars suppose), just as Christians did not practice circumcision as a rite. Sherwood also denied that baptism and the Eucharist were seals of the old covenant. He stated, "No intimation is given in the New Testament that God would fulfill to professing parents, who have their children baptized, promises made to the Patriarch."[106] Using the term *seal* is misleading. A seal is a guarantee of a promise. Can baptism guarantee the certainty of a future conversion? The only people who were sealed in the New Testament were men and women who had openly attested the work of grace in their lives through baptism.

In section nine, the connection between circumcision and baptism actually proceeded from the subject of infant membership. Would such membership be transferable from the Old Testament congregation to the New Testament church? If circumcision translated into baptism, would not flesh be confused with spirit? Did the transition between rites only experience a physical transference? Now, Christian parents simply mark off their children to belong to the Christian nation. Yet, where are the conditions for membership? If only one type of child should receive baptism, where is the explicit law requiring it?[107] In section ten, Sherwood questioned the consistency of defining the new ordinances if the two dispensations were the same. Advocates of infant baptism would not admit to the proper definition of baptism because they could not even define the meaning of the rite.

In section eleven, Sherwood gave two summative reasons for rejecting the two dispensations. First, the old dispensation did not require faith and repentance in order to be admitted, while the new dispensation

---

[105] Sherwood, *The Jewish and Christian Churches*, 20–23.
[106] Ibid., 27.
[107] Ibid., 30–33.

did. Therefore, one's ability to satisfy the old rite did not admit one into receiving the new rite. Second, the actual disciples of Christ and converted Jews after Pentecost had to be baptized. If one ordinance replaced the other, then the older one would have satisfied the newer one and would not need a new ministration.[108] In section twelve, he supported these conclusions by analyzing chapters four, nine, and eleven of Romans.

In conclusion, Sherwood proposed five deductions to be drawn from combining the two dispensations as one institution. First, he acknowledged that the most educated men have held to this conviction. Some of the greatest scholars and pious men came from the Presbyterian and Congregationalist denominations. However, they themselves could not decide how to interpret their own ordinance: "Some suppose the ordinance makes children members of the church—others that they are not until they acknowledge the obligations taken by parents on their behalf—others still, that all born in a certain region, where the Christian religion is recognized by the State, become church members by the same right that they become citizens."[109] Second, believing in the solidarity of the Jewish and Christian churches destroyed the purity of the church. The distinction between the church and the world could not be found if no internal requirement qualified the external ordinance. Third, by making Christianity a national and hereditary religion, the power of the Gospel disappeared. No calls for repentance could be extended if the ordinance did not represent the message. Fourth, by connecting circumcision with baptism, the church joined its fate with the state. A logical consistency existed between infant membership in the church and infant membership in a country, especially when the church modeled the nation of Israel. Fifth, and most importantly, by combining the two congregations, human hearts lost their sensitivity to the gospel. Such a system propagated the evils of an unconverted ministry and membership. This would be especially true for the clergy. "Invested with power by the civil government, and bloated with their elevation, they lose—if they had

---

[108] Ibid., 45–46.
[109] Ibid., 58–59.

any—the humility inculcated by the Savior, and act more like demons than human beings."[110]

THE PRAXIS OF BAPTIST ECCLESIOLOGY

From 1841 to 1856, the Georgia Baptist Convention grew into a stronger state convention, while Adiel Sherwood interacted with the westward expansion of Baptists in Illinois and Missouri. Evidence of the improvement in the Georgia Baptist Convention has been measured from the growth of Mercer University, the greater role of the *Christian Index* in Georgia Baptist life, and the additional associations that joined the state organization.[111] When Sherwood returned to Georgia, his new role in the state convention corresponded with the new theme of the day: Baptist ecclesiology. Again, as a pastoral and educational leader, he put into practice the Baptist principles he defended in the West.

MARSHALL COLLEGE AND THE GEORGIA BAPTIST CONVENTION

In 1857, Jesse H. Campbell extended a call to Adiel Sherwood to preside over the new college in Griffin, Georgia. Campbell, one of Sherwood's original students in Eatonton, represented the primary force behind Marshall College. In 1853, the citizens of Griffin, a town on the Atlanta-Macon Railroad, outlined plans to establish a local institution for young men.[112] The trustees intended to establish a nonsectarian, literary institution. As a reflection of this plan, city leaders chose fifteen trustees—eight representing Griffin Baptist Church and seven others, one representing a religious or philanthropic entity, such as the Methodist

---

[110] Ibid., 89.

[111] Samuel Boykin reported that fourteen associations belonged to the Georgia Baptist Convention in 1845 and twenty-two associations in 1861. Most of the new associations petitioned the GBC for membership before 1851. Although twenty-two belonged to the convention in 1850, thirty-five associations did not. However, the nonconvention associations were numerically small. See Boykin, *History of the Baptist Denomination*, 212–21.

[112] "The inception and the promotion of a school at Griffin, aiming at college rank, may be credited chiefly to the Rev. Jesse H. Campbell, then pastor of Griffin. The school was opened in August, 1853, with 40 pupils" (B. D. Ragsdale, vol. 2 of *Story of Georgia Baptists* [Atlanta: Foote and Davies Company, 1935] 330).

Church, Presbyterian Church, and Christian Church as well as the
Masonic and Oddfellow societies.[113]

In 1854, the state legislature incorporated the school, naming it
Marshall College.[114] The trustees chose a 60-acre site and made plans to
subdivide the acreage for fund-raising purposes. For the next two years,
J. W. Attaway functioned as the president of the institution. In 1856, for
an unexplained reason, he withdrew from the school to form another in
Griffin. Under this form of instability, the school once again looked to
Jesse H. Campbell for guidance. Sometime during the 1856–1857 school
year, Campbell was able to regain Attaway's services, but as a teacher.

In early 1857, Attaway and his colleagues at Marshall College
requested that Adiel Sherwood be their new president. The Flint River
Baptist Association reported Sherwood's arrival:

> Early in the Spring, Messrs. Attaway and Brown requested
> us to elect the Rev. Dr. Sherwood, President of the College. This
> was unanimously done. He did not see fit to accept until
> Commencement, 22d July, but with the understanding that some
> endowment be raised to sustain the Faculty. In order to do this,
> we have passed a resolution, promising to secure an amendment
> to our Charter, granting to certain Baptist Associations the right
> to be represented in our Board by two members each, enjoying

---

[113] "The College shall be controlled and governed by a Board of Trustees to be
constituted as follows, as far as practicable: The Baptist Church in Griffin may appoint
eight Trustees, members of the Baptist Church in good standing. The city Council of
Griffin, the Presbyterian Church in Griffin, the society of Episcopal Methodists in
Griffin, the church called the Christian Church in Griffin, Warren Lodge, No. 20, of the
Independent Order of Odd Fellows, in Griffin, and the Meridian San Lodge, of Free and
Accepted Masons, in Griffin, may each appoint one Trustee" (*Minutes of the Flint River
Baptist Association* [Forsyth: Georgia Educational Journal Office, 1853] 10).

[114] Marshall College was named after one of the Georgia Baptist pioneers, Peter
Marshall. Like many antebellum colleges, it began on a large amount of acreage and sold
portions of land to pay building and maintenance expenses. From 1854–1860, Marshall
College fluctuated in attendance from 80 to 100 young men. Marshall College stood on
"a six-acre lot west of Thirteenth street, the building facing the intersection of Broad and
Thirteenth streets." It closed in 1863 because of the severity of the Civil War and
reopened for a few years after the war, only to close again in 1873. See Quimby Melton,
Jr., *History of Griffin* (Griffin GA: Griffin Daily News, 1959) 76–77.

equal privileges with the original Trustees.... There are thousands of students on the west side of the Ocmulgee to whom Griffin is much easier of access than the site of any other College.[115]

Sherwood began his tenure as president with two agendas: create an endowment and attract students in western Georgia. The first agenda proposed the greater problem. Both he and the trustees agreed that 20,000 dollars would make an adequate endowment.[116] Yet, the goal was never reached. The school experienced the effects of a statewide recession in 1857, and confusion still existed over who actually sponsored the school. However, funding shortages diminished when the school dropped the practice of appointing non-Baptist trustees. In 1858, the school moved away from local support to appeal to statewide Baptist sponsorship.[117] In 1859, the Georgia Baptist Convention acquired full control of the school. If not for the advent of the Civil War, Marshall College would have achieved its second goal. The ever-growing use of railroads and the desire for accessibility to colleges placed Marshall in a good location.

---

[115] *Minutes of the Flint River Baptist Association*, 1857, 4.

[116] "Marshall College, at Griffin, renamed after the pioneer Baptist minister in Georgia and his sacerdotal posterity has no endowment; but it has two well-known energetic Teachers—66 to 68 students, constantly augmenting in numbers. They have a good brick edifice, containing a chapel and some six rooms for college purposes. If they had an endowment of only $20,000, to sustain one professor, they would be greatly encouraged; but they will make it go any how. They could enlarge their Faculty—it will have a more College-like appearance, and promise permanence. If some wealthy person does not bestow this sum at once, and could no more worthy object for benevolence be presented? They ought to seek out an agent and make it sure" (A. S., "Baptist Colleges," *Christian Index*, 4 March 1857, 1).

[117] The Flint River Baptist Association passed the following resolution in 1858: "Whereas, it is desirable to put Marshall College entirely under the Baptists, with the hope it will secure a partial endowment, become eminently useful provided it receives proper patronage and especially from the citizens of Griffin. Therefore resolved unanimously, That we will petition the next Legislature to alter the charter as to secure it entirely to Trustees, selected by the Baptists in the present Board" (*Minutes of the Flint River Baptist Association*, 1858, 2).

For three years, Sherwood busied himself with the affairs of a new
Baptist college and the church in Griffin. He held both positions at the
same time. At Marshall College, he moved the school toward statewide
support, but he also found time to include the students in the life of his
church. A small revival of religion took place during the two years
Sherwood served as Griffin's pastor. He reported that as early as March,
Christian laymen began to form prayer meetings and to organize
preaching engagements at meetinghouses. Sherwood also reported:

> Early in August we commenced a morning prayer meeting
> and preaching at night. In the morning, the brethren spoke of
> their feelings, hopes and prospects, relating incidents in their
> experience, which were full of interest, and brought tears in
> every eye. One, two or three, who had frequently desired
> prayers, almost every morning, professed Christ and were
> received for baptism....
>
> Except some six or seven, all are young, from 14 to 22; two
> boys 10 and 12—old enough, however, to express their faith in
> the Savior.... Seven or eight students of Marshall College, where
> are 88 pupils, some in Senior, Junior and Freshman classes have
> also been baptized. It is the fervent prayer of the church that God
> will call some of these young men into the ministry. Total
> number baptized 60, with others received and expected; several
> reclaimed, so that about 70 have been added to our numbers. The
> name of the Lord be praised.[118]

During 1858, the Baptist church in Griffin reported sixty baptisms.
The church under Sherwood's leadership had participated in the 1857
Awakening. The preceding year, only fifteen were baptized and the
following year only three received baptism. However, the marked
increase of baptisms and spiritual awareness in the Griffin church
reflected the course of the nation. Even in Georgia Baptist life,
membership increased by 1,500 people a year from 1853 to 1857. In

---

[118] Adiel Sherwood, "Letter from Griffin," *Christian Index*, 17 September 1858, 2.

1858, Georgia Baptists baptized 8,342 people.[119] In Griffin, Sherwood enjoyed a bountiful harvest during his first full year back. At the end of 1859, he resigned as president of the college and pastor of the church in Griffin. For two years, he resumed his former pastorates of Monticello and Eatonton.

THE TRUE MISSION OF THE BAPTISTS

In 1859, the Southwestern Publishing Company, the printing company of J. R. Graves, published a short work titled *The True Mission of the Baptists*. Within this book, J. M. Pendleton introduced the work of J. B. Jeter, calling for Baptists to stand against the spread of Pedobaptist sentiment. Jeter presented a defense of the Baptists, depicting them as a lowly and persecuted sect of people whom the world reviled due to their adherence to believer's baptism by immersion. Jeter centered most of his argument on the social status of Baptists as a peculiar people.

Sherwood authored a larger portion of the book, claiming to enlarge upon Jeter's defense of Baptist principles. Sherwood saw the task of Baptists from a larger perspective than a persecuted sect. They were not a band of vagabonds but a group of religious reformers.

It is a part of their mission to rectify various mistakes, both historical and theological—to correct errors, expose falsifications of facts, detect fallacies and illogical reasonings, clear up mystifications and false interpretations, make plain many perversions of truth, and contend for the faith and practice of primitive times, endeavoring to bring all God's people into union and action for the propagation of the truth, the whole truth and nothing but the truth.[120]

---

[119] J. Edwin Orr, *The Event of the Century: The 1857–1858 Awakening* (Wheaton IL: International Awakening Press, 1989) 169. Roy Fish also demonstrated that the 1858 Awakening affected the South just as it did the North. See Roy J. Fish, *When Heaven Touched Earth: The Awakening of 1858 and its Effects on Baptists* (Azle TX: Need of the Times Publishers, 1996) 123.

[120] J. B. Jeter, J. M. Pendleton, and A. Sherwood, *The True Mission of Baptists* (Nashville: Southwestern Publishing House, 1859) 31–32.

He saw their mission as including the Bible alone as "the guide in faith and practice," and this involved "the common sense meaning of Scripture as understood by plain men."[121]

Sherwood noticed that Baptists had the task of exposing the prevalent falsifications of their opponents. Advocates of infant baptism falsified the true meaning of Scripture. Often, Pedobaptists would argue several inaccurate statements, such as asserting that proselytes in the Old Testament were sprinkled. Or, John the Baptist actually did not immerse because he did not have enough water near Jerusalem and in most parts of Judea.

Baptists also had the task of clarifying the intentional mystifications of their opponents. Sherwood defined the term *mystify* as "to involve in mystery, to render obscure or difficult to understand, to hide the true meaning in order to deceive."[122] Cases of this included choosing alternate meanings for *baptizo*, such as "to wet" or "to moisten." Of course, the most ludicrous example would be to substitute "to draw" or "to pump" for the verb *to baptize*. If this was so, then the actual ordinance reached absurd proportions. He stated "John iii. 23: John was drawing or pumping near to Salim, and the people came and were drawn or pumped of him! Matt. iii. 5,11: And were all pumped of him in Jordan, confessing their sins. I pump you with water, etc. He shall draw or pump you with the Holy Ghost."[123]

The opponents of Baptists also obscured the commonsense meanings of biblical passages and the logic attached to them. Advocates of infant baptism relied heavily on Romans 4:9–14, but the passage mentioned neither infants nor the baptisms they supposedly received. Rather, the text merely expounded on the faith of the believer and the imputed righteousness that is distinct from the law. What greater logical absurdity can be espoused by connecting circumcision with baptism through a "mere postulation" without definite proof? Sherwood defined

---

[121] Ibid., 32–33.
[122] Ibid., 41.
[123] Ibid., 42.

their logical strategy as confusing the literal meaning of texts with the spiritual as needed.[124]

Pedobaptists also utilized several fallacies. Sherwood defined a fallacy as "a sophism, a logical artifice, [or] a deceitful argument."[125] Pedobaptists confused the order of Christian baptism, making it irrelevant. Instead of repentance preceding baptism, they reversed the order by applying the term *seal* to the ordinance.[126] Both circumcision and baptism were seals of the righteousness of faith, or guaranteed acts of a future dedication. However, the entire construction of seals and the reversals of action and ordinance proved to be fallacious—neither having a basis in reality.

Dogmatisms and subterfuges characterized the hermeneutic of Pedobaptists. To dogmatize was "to assert positively and authoritatively—to pronounce on a subject absolutely, unwilling to listen to plausible objections." Sherwood also judged dogmatists as generally possessing two major traits: "lungs and impudence."[127] They have employed several subterfuges, avoiding the truth by replacing it with a substitute. They have equated immersion with sprinkling, making a measurable practice similar to an inaccurate generalization. Sprinkling connoted the act of pouring or moistening, whereas immersion always meant to plunge into water. Likewise, the time and occasion of the two baptisms, Spirit and water, have been confused. Within the Pedobaptist hermeneutic, the order does not matter.

Sherwood closed his argument by presenting the greatest task of Baptists: to stand against plausible sophisms. Deceptive truth stood as the formidable enemy of Baptists. As proven through his whole discourse, Christian baptism as defined by the Scriptures seemed unimportant to Pedobaptists. They held to human traditions in their baptismal rites, using deceptive means to sustain their practices. Yet, they also wished to separate baptism from communion while pleading with Baptists to share the Lord's table. Sherwood saw the final task of

---

[124] Ibid., 48–49.
[125] Ibid., 50.
[126] Ibid., 53.
[127] Ibid., 62.

Baptists as to refute the beliefs of Pedobaptists by avoiding their table. Until advocates of infant baptism abandoned their unscriptural practice, Baptists could not participate in communion with them. To commune with them, Baptists would be advocating the practice and their hermeneutic that supported their ordinance.

CONCLUSION

The experiences in Illinois and Missouri shaped Sherwood's ecclesiology in a deeper respect than his experience with the Primitive Baptists in Georgia. His earlier debates with antimissionism revolved around the issue of whether methodology defined the theological meaning behind new practices. In the western arena, Sherwood refined his beliefs in the areas of ecclesiastical hermeneutics and polemical defense. He recognized the essential difference between Baptists and older Protestant denominations over the issue of baptism as being an external application of a deeper hermeneutical problem. Baptist ecclesiology demanded a clear break between the two testaments or the two dispensations. Of course, this could have threatened the attachment of Baptists to Reformed doctrine. Pedobaptists intertwined their theology with their practice by connecting God's mysterious act of election with the baptism of infants, the recipients of the Old Testament ordinance of circumcision. Yet, this synthesis of belief and baptismal rite was not as inseparably linked as they may have thought. Sherwood thrust the burden of proof on the shoulders of those who baptized the unregenerate. Baptist ecclesiology did not unravel Reformed theology but consistently supported it. Baptists no longer had to envision themselves as a persecuted sect whose biblical ordinance separated them from the rest of Christendom. They could see their identity as active reformers with a distinct theology.

Organizationally, Sherwood's fifteen-year separation from Georgia only entitled him to greater respect in the late 1850s and early 1860s. He returned as an aged, venerable frontier preacher. No longer did he represent the struggle between missionary and antimissionary Baptists; instead, he stood as a polemicist for Baptist principles and stability. His ecclesiology, although more defined and logical than that of the average

Southern Baptist, represented the same view of the church that Georgia Baptists held. During the early Landmark movement of the 1850s, men such as Sherwood did not accept the form of reductionism that marked later Landmarkism.[128] Rather, Sherwood saw the mission of Baptists in defending truth and attacking error, not separating completely from any Christian organization that did not fully agree with Baptist principles.

Sherwood's ecclesiological views also included his view of religious liberty. His historical view of the progression of Baptist principles involving the Baptist struggle for religious freedoms completed his total view of the church. His historical view of the Baptists also entailed the history of Georgia Baptists. During the Civil War, Sherwood explored the connection between Baptist history and the progress of religious liberty.

---

[128] Conversely, Sherwood could not advocate the doctrine of a visible, universal church that could lessen the view of the local church. The only advocate of this view in Georgia Baptist life would be John Leadley Dagg, and very few Georgia Baptists shared Dagg's opinion. However, Dagg did not confuse visibility with external organization. "The epithet 'invisible,' applied to the true church of Christ is not only incorrect, but it has led into mistake. Men have spoken of this church as a mere mental conception; and they have asked, whether Saul persecuted an invisible church.... He persecuted them as Christian men and women. But the existence of such men and women, like the persecutions which they suffered, was something more than a mere mental conception. Organization is not necessary to visibility; much less is any particular species of it. Rocks and mountains are as visible as plants and animals" (John L. Dagg, *Manual of Church Order* [Charleston: Southern Baptist Publication Society, 1858] 124–25).

7

THE GEORGIA BAPTIST HISTORIAN
DURING THE CIVIL WAR

Adiel Sherwood's last contribution to Georgia Baptist development proceeded from his historical research and interpretation of Georgia Baptist life. As an early compiler of Georgia Baptist documents, he demonstrated that historical certitude was closely related to doctrinal legitimacy. As a historian, Sherwood documented the rise of missionary Baptists and the splintering of antimissionary Baptists within a larger spectrum of religious liberty and historical validity. Georgia Baptist history as he experienced it came out of a historical progression of Baptist principles encased around a broad theme of religious liberty. The dictates of conscience informed by the Scriptures defined the Baptist view of religious liberty. Differing slightly from a strict theory of church succession, Sherwood's theory found examples of religious bodies that held to Baptist principles.

By 1860, Adiel Sherwood had returned to two of his oldest pastorates: Eatonton and Monticello. Both of these churches belonged to the Central Baptist Association, the association formed by Sherwood and his colleagues during the antimissionary split in Georgia Baptist life. After an absence from his two churches and the Central Association since 1836, Sherwood's return marked a time of historical reflection. The *Christian Index* reported his arrival and participation in the 1860 meeting of the Central Baptist Association as moderator and speaker: "Bro. A.

Sherwood preached at 10 o'Clock Sabbath day, from 1st Corinthians, 15 Chapter, and part of the 11th verse. 'So we preach, and so ye believed.' His sermon was worthy of his younger days, and took strong Baptistic ground. He shown [sic] what Baptists generally require their church members to believe.—Though lasting an hour, his sermon appeared only 20 minutes long."[1]

The *Index* later included the text of this message. In a reminiscent spirit, Sherwood addressed the assembly with a historical assessment:

> When first organized we were very zealous in benevolent operations, and inserted in our Decorum our approval of Missions, Sabbath Schools, and kindred objects of Christian effort: But it is feared we have become unmindful of our obligations and the warmth of our zeal has evaporated, not in acts, but in inefficient resolutions. Several huge tracts of country within our bounds are destitute of gospel preaching—fields that would be cultivated are lying waste, and not producing a single blade of virtue for many a square mile.... Associations around us that once groped in the fogs and darkness of anti-ism, are now sustaining missionaries both at home and abroad, while we do neither. Does not this belie our Decorum and early professions? Let us bestir ourselves, and wipe off the reproach which our late apathy has brought upon us, and let us begin to redeem time which we have wasted. If any family altars have been so neglected as to tumble down, let us rebuild them; if our children have forgotten the Sabbath, let us resuscitate the Sabbath School;

---

[1] "Central Association," *Christian Index*, 12 September 1860, 3. Three years later, Sherwood served as the chairman of the revision committee of the Central Association's Articles of Decorum. The major change consisted of the alteration of article four of the 1836 Gospel Order as article one of the 1863 Gospel Order. The original article defined baptism as "dipping," while the new article insisted on the equivalence of the terms *baptism* and *immersion*. This change, although slight, reflected the experiences of Georgia Baptists and Adiel Sherwood with other denominations over the three previous decades. See *Minutes of the Central Baptist Association* (Washington GA: W. A. Mercer, 1861; 1863) 16; 15.

if our prayer-meetings have been thinly attended let us appoint a committee of the whole church and go and inquire the reason.[2]

This sermon challenged the audience to reclaim the historical precedent of Georgia Baptists—obedience to scriptural commands. Within this same framework, Sherwood saw the culmination of history. The liberty of the Christian came with a release from unscriptural, external forces and obedience to the injunctions of the Bible. For the next five years, Sherwood labored to recover this aspect of Georgia Baptist history.

HISTORICAL RESEARCH IN GEORGIA BAPTIST LIFE

During his earlier residence in Georgia, Sherwood worked toward compiling Georgia Baptist materials. While traveling as an agent for Columbian College, he advertised through the *Christian Index* the types of materials needed.[3] One of his frequent announcements requested the following information:

1. Through whose instrumentality was your church gathered; and by whom and when was it constituted?
2. What was its number of members? Who have been Pastors and Deacons since?
3. What ministers have been licensed and ordained in it?
4. What Ministers and distinguished lay-members have been raised up in your vicinity?

---

[2] Adiel Sherwood, "Central Association: Address of Dr. Sherwood," *Christian Index*, 7 November 1860, 1.

[3] "In 1837, I gave notice through the Index that I was collecting materials for a 'History of Georgia Baptists.' Indeed, I began to make collections in 1818, but determined on a work of the kind in 1834. In 1839 I issued proposals—the subscribers were about three hundred and fifty—not enough to justify the undertaking; so when about to remove to this region, I committed the 'History of Associations and Churches,' brought up to 1840, to Jesse H. Campbell. The biographical part I brought with me, intending to furnish matter for the 'Baptist Memorials'" (Julia L. Sherwood, and Samuel Boykin, *Memoir of Adiel Sherwood, D.D.* [Philadelphia: Grant and Faires, 1884] 282).

5. What seasons of revival and trial has your church experienced and endured? What has it done by its substance to promote the cause of Christ?

6. What support does it afford the ministry?

7. Will the churches, in the associations, send up to their annual meetings, the date of their constitutions, if nothing else, and insert it in the minutes?[4]

These advertisements frequented the newspaper during 1837 and 1838, but by 1839 the financial expense of doing a history slowed the process. In 1840, Sherwood abandoned the effort, giving most of his materials to Jesse H. Campbell. While Sherwood lived in Illinois and Missouri, Campbell published a few pieces of the "Sherwood Manuscript" during 1843 in the *Christian Index*. In 1847, Campbell adapted the manuscript into his first edition of *Georgia Baptists: Historical and Biographical*.

THE GAZETTEER AND THE CHRISTIAN INDEX

Sherwood's historical interests were by no means purely religious. As early as 1818, he compiled his own personal reflections on the history and mannerisms of Georgians. He included much of these observations in his *Gazetteer of Georgia*. In 1827, he published a limited number of the first edition in Charleston, South Carolina. In 1829, Sherwood printed his second edition, consisting of 2,000 copies, and they quickly sold. In 1837, the Gazetteer was reprinted and enlarged, but it did not sell very well.[5]

In 1860, Sherwood printed his fourth edition of the *Gazetteer*. He had several reasons for adding additional information. In 1849 and 1854, Reverend George White, a Methodist minister, printed two statistical works of Georgia, claiming both to be pioneer works. The *Statistics of*

---

[4] Adiel Sherwood, "History of Georgia Baptists," *Christian Index*, 2 August 1838, 479.

[5] William Bailey Williford, "The Author" (introduction), in Adiel Sherwood, *A Gazetteer of Georgia; Containing a Particular Description of the State; its Resources, Counties, Towns, Villages, and Whatever is Usual in Statistical Works*, 4th ed (Macon GA: S. Boykin, 1860; reprint, Atlanta: Cherokee Publishing Company, 1970) iv.

Georgia and the *Historical Collections of Georgia* presented lengthy primary source material, but the basic statistical information, such as counties, towns, and bodies of water, were already apparent in the three editions of Sherwood's *Gazetteer*. Sherwood charged White with plagiarism in the preface of his 1860 edition, giving several examples of direct quotations from his 1837 work. White also followed the same format as Sherwood's *Gazetteer*, but omitted any reference to the Baptist minister in both works.[6] The 1860 edition restored legitimacy to Sherwood's previous editions and also accentuated current aspects of Georgia. It outlined the importance and course of Georgia railroads, a vital change in transportation.

Sherwood's numerous historical writings can also be traced to his connection with the *Christian Index*. As early as 1833, when Jesse Mercer bought and moved the paper from Philadelphia, Pennsylvania, to Washington, Georgia, Sherwood wrote several pieces for the periodical. In 1840, Mercer donated the paper to the Georgia Baptist Convention. For the next twenty-one years, the *Index* remained within the convention, although there were attempts to sell it. The 1860 *Minutes* of the Georgia Baptist Convention noted two unsuccessful efforts to sell the paper to private individuals in 1849 and 1856 (25). On the latter date, the convention's executive committee declined to sell on the grounds of losing the paper's allegiance to the Baptist cause and the number of subscribers.

In March 1860, Samuel Boykin, an 1851 graduate of the University of Georgia, assumed the editorship of the *Christian Index*.[7] Born near Milledgeville, Georgia, in 1829, Boykin's family had a religious connection with Adiel Sherwood. Boykin's mother, Narcissa Cooper, was the daughter of Thomas Cooper, an influential layman and deacon in

---

[6] "In his final revision of the *Gazetteer* Dr. Sherwood refers caustically to the Reverend George White's *Statistics of the State of Georgia*, published at Savannah in 1849, whose author quoted liberally from Sherwood's work without permission and often without acknowledgment, who failed to include the noted Baptist divine's name in the list of persons to whom he was indebted for assistance, and who followed the format of the *Gazetteer* while at the same time calling himself a 'Pioneer' in such an enterprise" (ibid.).

[7] William Cathcart, ed. "Rev. Samuel Boykin," in vol. 1 of *The Baptist Encyclopedia* (Philadelphia: Louis E. Everts, 1881) 123–24.

Eatonton.[8] Although Samuel Boykin's family moved to Columbus shortly after his birth, his connection with Sherwood became evident in Boykin's publication of the *Gazetteer of Georgia* in 1860 and Sherwood's numerous articles that began to appear in the *Index* during the same year. In May 1861, the Georgia Baptist Convention sold the impoverished *Christian Index* to Samuel Boykin and C. M. Irwin of Albany.[9] In July, Boykin announced a list of associates. Adiel Sherwood became co-editor, while C. D. Mallary, J. S. Baker, and Sylvanus Landrum served as assistant editors.[10] Sherwood's name appeared as co-editor through most of 1861, but he later dedicated more time to raising money for the paper.[11] Still, from 1861 to 1863, Sherwood contributed numerous historical and ecclesiological articles to the *Index*. Boykin retained the editorship and ownership of the *Index* until 1865, when he sold the newspaper to J. J. Toon of Atlanta.

THE BAPTIST HISTORICAL SOCIETY
OF THE CONFEDERATE STATES OF AMERICA

Sherwood's historical interests also intensified through the organization of a new historical society. From 1845 to 1861, the Southern Baptist Convention existed as a missionary body of Baptists in the South who separated from their Northern brethren over the issue of slavery. Southern Baptists did not wish the act of slaveholding to be an issue of service in foreign and domestic missionary enterprises. When

---

[8] "Brother Cooper was scarcely less distinguished as a lay member, than Mr. Mercer was a minister. In him were joined to a native intellect remarkably clear, discriminating and vigorous, the most excellent qualities of heart; and all was sanctified by fervent and exalted piety.... Long will it be before we shall see in our midst such a *minister* as Jesse Mercer, and perhaps as long before we shall see such a *deacon* as Thomas Cooper. He entered into his rest, July, 1843, in the 73d year of his age" (C. D. Mallary, *Memoirs of Elder Jesse Mercer* [New York: John Gray, 1844] 57–58).

[9] Jack Harwell stated that the two men bought the paper for $2,200, but the subscribers owed the paper $5,500. See Jack U. Harwell, *An Old Friend with New Credentials, A History of the Christian Index* (Atlanta: *Christian Index*, 1972) 88.

[10] Harwell, *An Old Friend,* 93.

[11] The paper began to list Sherwood's preaching itinerary as a means to inform the readers to subscribe. See "Dr. Sherwood's Appointments," *Christian Index*, 25 September 1861, 2.

Southerners seceded from the Union in early 1861, the acts of each state seceding from the United States also affected the Southern Baptist Convention. Apparently, it solidified their identity enough as a Southern denomination to form a historical society.

Several individuals met at Second Baptist Church in Atlanta, Georgia, on 26 July 1861, to establish this society. Upon assembling together, Adiel Sherwood served as chairman of the meeting, and H. C. Hornady as recording secretary. Sherwood appointed a committee of five men—consisting of N. M. Crawford, E. B. Teague, B. F. Tharp, A. Van Hoose, and J. M. Wood—to draft a constitution and bylaws. Upon a motion from the floor, A. T. Holmes, J. J. D. Renfroe, and Adiel Sherwood were added to the committee. Under the articles of the constitution, the assembly called their organization the "Baptist Historical Society of the Confederate States of America." The purpose of the organization would be "to collect, preserve, and diffuse information relating to the history of the Baptists in the Confederate States."[12]

A few items of business followed the presentation of the constitution and bylaws. First, a list of officers was presented and approved. Adiel Sherwood was elected as president of the society along with eleven vice presidents. Second, a library for the society was approved with S. Root as librarian, and agents were appointed to gather information to deposit in this facility. The minutes do not reveal the location of the depository. Third, the meeting closed with the enrollment of fourteen new members and the hearty approval of twenty-two absent individuals.[13]

On 26 July 1862, the Baptist Historical Society reconvened at the First Baptist Church in Atlanta. President Adiel Sherwood was absent, so N. M. Crawford, president of Mercer University, assumed the role as

---

[12] "Proceedings of the Historical Meeting," *Christian Index*, 14 August 1861, 1.

[13] The new members included N. M. Crawford, H. S. Moore, J. T. Clarke, S. Root, B. F. Tharp, W. M. Davis, A. T. Holmes, J. Clarke, E. B. Teague, S. Boykin, A. Van Hoose, J. J. D. Renfroe, J. M. Wood, and H. C. Hornady. The absent advocates of the society included G. T. Wilburn, S. Landrum, D. E. Butler, H. H. Tucker, W. H. Clarke, Thomas Stocks, S. G. Hillyer, G. F. Cooper, Joseph S. Baker, C. D. Mallary, C. M. Irwin, H. H. Bunn, T. J. Burney, R. H. Jackson, A. H. Huntington, T. Rambant, J. R. Graves, W. Newton, Robert Fleming, and A. C. Dayton (ibid.).

moderator. Three members were added to the roll, and officers were elected. Again, the society chose Sherwood as president and added a new slate of vice-presidents. The major thrust of the meeting seemed to be the acquisition of materials. Several members urged each other to send more materials to the librarian. At the conclusion of the meeting, the minutes referred to the Baptist Historical Society of the Confederate States as the Southern Baptist Historical Society.[14] The society adjourned with the intention to meet on the Friday before the first Sabbath in August 1863 at the Second Baptist Church of Atlanta. This meeting never occurred, probably due to the close proximity of Union troops to Chattanooga, Tennessee.[15] The society never reorganized or reappeared after the Civil War.

SHERWOOD'S HISTORICAL WRITINGS AND INTERPRETATION

From 1860 to 1864, Sherwood dedicated numerous articles to the *Christian Index* related to Georgia Baptist history, its relevancy to historiography, and the theme of religious liberty. In May 1860, he began writing a series of essays on Georgia Baptist history that continued for ten months. Under the pseudonym Testis, he shared his reflections on Georgia Baptist life in the 1820s and 1830s. By 14 November 1860, his name appeared with his pseudonym and his assumed title disappeared on 30 January 1861. The total amount of essays numbered twenty-three.

During 1861, Sherwood reappeared under two additional identities, Lexi and Novatian. As Lexi, he published a series of dialogues titled "Religious Liberty" that took place between a father, a son, and the two

---

[14] "Baptist Historical Society," *Christian Index*, 26 August 1862, 1.

[15] One of the last statements of this society appeared in a report from S. Root (Secretary of the Historical Society): "Our collections are not yet very extensive, but we have made a creditable beginning.—Will not all parties interested in the objects of our society forward, me at Atlanta, such donations as may be suitable for our Library. By resolution of the Society, framed likeness of our distinguished living men of our preachers, &c., are especially desired. I hope soon to present a statement of the present condition of our Library" ("Historical Society Library—Recent Contributions," *Christian Index*, 25 November 1862, 4).

historical figures Cotton Mather and Roger Williams.[16] By the sixth issue, he revealed his name and dropped the title of Lexi. On 3 July 1861, Sherwood began another series of writings as Novatian. Titled "The Sect Everywhere Spoken Against," these seven articles accentuated the concept of churches free from the Roman Catholic hierarchy throughout history. Using the biblical phrase that described Christians as the persecuted sect, Sherwood traced the concept of religious liberty through the centuries, identifying religious groups similar to Baptist churches in America. Sherwood printed his name alongside his assumed title on the fifth number, dated 11 September. Novatian must have felt entitled to the revelation after he became president of the Baptist Historical Society of the Confederate States of America.

All of the earlier pieces of Testis, Lexi, and Novatian ceased when Sherwood, under his own name, began publishing a greater project, "The Life and Times of Jesse Mercer." Consisting of about thirty weekly numbers, Sherwood composed a work divided into an introduction and six chapters. Within the introduction, he followed the Baptists from the New Testament to America, avoiding their association with the Anabaptist Munster rebellion and their baptismal succession from Roger Williams in Rhode Island. In chapter one, Sherwood proposed that Georgia Baptists and the issue of religious liberty formed the foundations of the convention. In chapter two, he applied the missionary example of the Bible and the British Baptists to the early formation of Baptist associations in Georgia. In chapter three, Sherwood traced the reaction of antimissionary elements in Georgia associations. In chapter four, he analyzed the injection of new measures into Georgia Baptist life, including the Georgia Revival of 1827 and earlier cases of revival movements. In chapter five, he described the growth of the Georgia Baptist Convention and Mercer University. In chapter six, he showed that several religious newspapers shaped Baptist growth in Georgia.

---

[16] Lexi, "Religious Liberty: Family conversations, embracing the important part taken by Baptists, in the History of the past, in regard to the great principle of Soul-liberty," *Christian Index*, 9 January–13 February 1861. Three other articles were published consecutively after these numbers under Sherwood's own name.

Under four successive articles, Adiel Sherwood as Lexi formulated his view of Georgia Baptist history. The dominant theme of religious liberty encapsulated his historiography. Liberty of conscience freed from external political and religious restraint but dedicated to biblical instruction epitomized his view of history. He first defined religious liberty as it related to conscience: "It is the right to worship God according to the dictates of our own consciences—freedom from restraint in religious matters: that is, we are said to enjoy this freedom when we attend on whatever ministry we please and are not obliged to obey laws enacted by government that oppress the conscience."[17] However, he also recognized that an authoritative base informed the conscience. The Scriptures instructed the saint to follow the proper inclination. The right to possess the freedom of conscience proceeded from the Scriptures:

> The New Testament is their Text book, the only guide for Christians in faith and practice. They try to follow its teachings in all matters that relate to liberty, churches and members.... This people need no Rubric—no Confession of Faith—no Discipline; for all is plain in the N.T. Every one is a priest qualified to offer spiritual sacrifice. Math. 18th and Cor. Afford all instructions for the management and remedy for both private and public offences.[18]

Any religious sect before the Reformation that followed this model exemplified a type of Baptist group. In America, religious liberty characterized American Baptists in the American Revolution and in the formation of the United States. It also formed the identity of missionary Baptists in Georgia. Their compulsion to follow the commands of Scripture forced missionary Baptists in Georgia to cast off associational tyranny.

---

[17] Lexi, "Religious Liberty," *Christian Index*, 9 January 1861, 1.
[18] Lexi, "Religious Liberty: Its Origin," *Christian Index*, 13 February 1861, 1.

RELIGIOUS LIBERTY AND CHURCH SUCCESSION

As a historian and theologian, Adiel Sherwood first perceived that the key to understanding Baptist origins flowed from the concept of religious liberty. Under the pseudonym Novatian, he advocated the need for purity as provided under the example of the New Testament. Ecclesiastical genuineness ensured doctrinal purity. He claimed a New Testament church was a body of God's believers who suffered for ecclesiastical purity. They were "the sect always spoken against" in the book of Acts.

This sect meant the followers of Christ in Apostolic times and in later days those who have "kept the faith once delivered to the saints," in contradiction to those that loved a showy pompous religion, with unscriptural forms and ceremonies, borrowed from heathen rites and idolatrous customs—that introduced new orders and ranks into the clergy—that framed laws to suit the taste and circumstances of the age, and so heathenized Christianity that neither Paul nor Peter would have known it in its new dress and dull formality.[19]

Following a trend evident in Southern Baptist life of his era, Sherwood associated organizational purity with doctrinal legitimacy.[20] In other words, the outward forms of ecclesiastical institutions did not make Baptists orthodox, but they did reflect doctrinal integrity. The outer reflection modified inner conviction.

As Novatian, Sherwood outlined the external marks of a genuine body of believers. Apparently, his conceptual image of dissenters throughout church history included individuals who advocated simplicity and dissented over extravagant forms of worship. This form of positive reductionism epitomized Novatian's vision of church and state. Ecclesiastical forms in contradiction to scriptural precedent combined

---

[19] Novatian, "The Sect Everywhere Spoken Against: Number I," *Christian Index*, 3 July 1861, 1.

[20] This trend characterized the interpretive starting point of the early Landmark movement in Southern Baptist life, although this Baptist form of high ecclesiology did not interact much with soteriological and christological concerns.

primitive church life with human excess. Seven aspects of simplicity marked true churches throughout history:

1. They insisted more upon faith than upon rites and forms.
2. Never would acknowledge the ordinances of corrupt Rome. They disowned the Pope, the anti-Christ foretold in the New Testament, and all his descendants, that derived authority from him.
3. The personality of religion. That is, that religion is not a national nor family matter, but one that concerns each and every human being, capable of understanding and performing what the Bible enjoins.
4. Great sticklers for rights of conscience and religious liberty—hence never persecute.
5. Repudiate the union of Church and State.
6. Maintains the spirituality of the Churches.
7. Acknowledge Christ as the only Lawgiver in Zion

Novatian next claimed that the above requirements did not belong to some sects. Certainly, Roman Catholicism violated scriptural separation from the world. The Episcopal church, "the eldest daughter of Rome," did not possess legitimacy due to being formed according to the political expediency of Henry VIII. Presbyterians and Independents could not be a persecuted sect; both combined church and state either in Scotland or New England. Methodists and the Disciples of Christ were not old enough. All prominent religious groups did not possess doctrinal purity and worldly separation.[21]

The mantle of historical continuity belonged to the sect or sects that followed the New Testament. Novatian quoted Moshiem's *Ecclesiastical History*: "The true origin of this sect, is hid in the remote depths of antiquity."[22] However, he did not name this sect, but analyzed the

---

[21] Novatian, "The Sect Everywhere Spoken Against: What Sect is This? Number III," *Christian Index*, 17 July 1861, 1.
[22] Novatian, "The Sect Everywhere Spoken Against: Characteristics of this Sect, Number 4," *Christian Index*, 24 July 1861, 1. He also stated, "History may mislead you,

scriptural hermeneutic that an ancient sect had to follow. If religious groups holding to scriptural exactitude existed before the Protestant Reformation, how did they really interpret the Bible? First, the basis of their faith and practice proceeded from the Bible alone.[23] Second, any other authoritative bases were considered nonessentials. External religion based on human tradition carried no weight.[24] Finally, when it came to biblical interpretation, the sects that held to the Bible alone interpreted the Bible through the use of plain common sense.[25]

In his 1863 series, "Life and Times of Jesse Mercer," Sherwood identified the ancient sects who followed a New Testament example in their church polity. First, he denied the charge that Baptists came from Munster and American Baptists came from Roger Williams. Comparing two historians, Moshiem and D'Aubigne, on the charge of the Munster rebellion, Sherwood preferred D'Aubigne's denial that the men of Munster were Anabaptists. Also, Sherwood rejected the baptismal connection of Roger Williams to American Baptist life. He opted for the Newport congregation in Rhode Island as the first Baptist congregation because it could be connected with a Welsh Baptist past and an American Baptist future.[26]

Second, Sherwood presented a lineage of Baptists leading to the Reformation. He did not choose a direct path through the centuries. Beginning with Claudia of Briton mentioned in Philippians 4:2 and 2 Timothy 4:21, Sherwood placed her in the historical line of King Lucius of Wales, a convert in AD 189 when Faganus and Domicanus served as missionaries to the Welsh people. In AD 600, the Welsh refused to convert to Roman Catholicism, choosing to suffer persecution and promote their own form of missions. Through this line of Welsh dissent,

---

but the Acts, the only true ecclesiastical History cannot mislead" ("Sect Everywhere Spoken Against," 1).

[23] Dr. Sherwood, "The Sect Everywhere Spoken Against: Number 5, Peculiarities," *Christian Index*, 11 September 1861, 1.

[24] Dr. Sherwood, "The Sect Everywhere Spoken Against: Number 6, Peculiarities," *Christian Index*, 18 September 1861, 1.

[25] Dr. Sherwood, "The Sect Everywhere Spoken Against: Number 7, Peculiarities," *Christian Index*, 25 September 1861, 1.

[26] Dr. A. Sherwood, "Life and Times of Jesse Mercer: Introduction," *Christian Index*, 19 January 1863, 1.

the Baptist presence could be seen in England and the United States. Sherwood also listed other groups who suffered persecution for the sake of purity: Novatians, Donatists, Paulicians, Petrobusians, Lollards, Albigenses, Waldenses, and Berengacians.[27]

Third, Sherwood connected the sects of the past with his present denomination over the issue of biblical authority. His criteria followed his earlier example as Novatian. The Bible had to be a church's sole authority. Separated from the control of political governments and independent as local bodies, believing churches involved the cooperation of autonomous individuals. With this sort of equation, Sherwood made the following deduction: "If the reader of history in those books which describe a people existing in the early ages of the Christian era, professing such and such sentiments; and discover in later times, those that possessed the same;—would not the inference be logical that, although living in different and distant periods, they were identical?"[28] However, Sherwood did not bind himself to a strict view of church succession. He chose to believe in the succession of church principles. In fact, he spoke quite adamantly against the first perspective that attempted to find a Baptist church in every century.

> True succession does not consist in names but in principles; for the Apostles left no successors in men, either bishops or elders; but their writings show the materials of the churches, its officers, ordinances, polity and discipline. If we find in any age, pious people embodied in churches, bearing the distinctive marks of the models left in the New Testament, we may regard them as having an indisputable title to be the descendants of the Apostles. This is all for which the Baptists are claimants. They do not pretend to name any church and minister and try to show regular succession through them, but rely on their agreement with the New Testament pattern in every important point that

---

[27] Dr. A. Sherwood, "Life and Times of Jesse Mercer: Introduction," *Christian Index*, 26 January 1863, 1. Sherwood relied more heavily upon a popular history of his day. See J. Davis, *History of the Welsh Baptists* (Pittsburgh: D. M. Hogan, 1835).

[28] Dr. A. Sherwood, "Life and Times of Jesse Mercer: Introduction," *CI,* 2 February 1863, 1.

relates to ecclesiastical matters. This is more safe and certain than to follow down through the muddy streams, pursued by learned Hierarchists and Historians, men that could discover no pious people—none worthy the name of Christians except such as were connected with the State, holding both the purse and sword of the nations under their sway and drunk with the blood of the saints for a dozen centuries.[29]

RELIGIOUS LIBERTY AND AMERICAN BAPTISTS

If religious liberty could be seen in ancient religious groups, the concept appeared to be more evident in Sherwood's view of American Baptists. In 1838, shortly before he assumed his work as professor at Mercer University, Sherwood presented an argument for religious liberty in the Baptist denomination of America. In an article of the *Christian Review*, he presented Baptists as a persecuted sect who stood for liberty of conscience. Persecution began in Massachusetts as early as 1644 when anyone belonging to the Anabaptists was banished from the colony. In 1658, the Quakers suffered the same fate. During this time, from 1657 to 1662, the Puritans passed numerous laws against both the Baptists and the Quakers. In subsequent years, other waves of persecution followed the Baptists as they traveled further south, especially in New York, Virginia, South Carolina, and Georgia.[30]

Baptists in America not only suffered persecution, but they stood for liberty of conscience. In Rhode Island, Roger Williams presented the idea of denying the government the right to interfere in religious duties. Isaac Backus later strengthened this belief. In Virginia, Baptists prayed for their legislators, but they refused to preach in the locations specified

---

[29]Dr. A. Sherwood, "Life and Times of Jesse Mercer: Introduction," *Christian Index*, 9 February 1863, 1. "What did Christ and the inspired Apostles command, and what are the examples on record for our guide? Neither expediency nor tradition would satisfy the sincere and conscientious enquirer after truth: how does the record read? This alone would guide his steps and quiet his conscience" ("Life and Times of Jesse Mercer," 1).

[30] Adelphos, "The Influence of the Baptist Denomination on Religious Liberty," *Christian Review* (September 1838): 333–42.

by the legislature.[31] In Georgia, Baptists after the Revolution refused the equal allocation of tax money to every denomination. They believed tax money given even to their cause controlled their religion.[32]

Religious liberty grew out of Baptist polity. Sherwood noticed that Congregational and Baptist churches held the same form of government but possessed a different type of membership. Instead of infants initiated by baptism, the Baptists only allowed individuals convinced of their position with God to become members. This insistence of conversion also resulted in an intimate individualism. By standing for one's position with God, a man or woman held to the correctness of his or her own views, basing their belief on their relationship with God. Under this formula, religious liberty became "a Baptist watchword, a kind of talisman, which operates like a charm, and nerves every man for action."[33]

Religious liberty resulted in civil liberty. These two terms were not coterminous in Sherwood's thought. One proceeded from the other. As Baptists stood for the expulsion of religious persecution, they also applied this principle to other sects. Sherwood pointed to the problem of persecuted sects becoming the persecutors after religious liberty was entrusted to them. In a short piece relating religious liberty to the history of Georgia Baptists, Sherwood noted that the change in religious status never changed the Baptist view of religious liberty and civil liberty: "This paragraph in the history of the Baptists, as well all furnished by Rhode Island, puts the seal of silence on the general opinion that all sects will persecute, only give them the power. The Baptists never did persecute, and would never admit the doctrine of the union of church and state."[34] As advocates of religious and civil liberty (freedoms for the Baptists and any other religious group), Baptists possessed the greatest

---

[31] Ibid., 338.

[32] Ibid., 339. Silas Mercer and Peter Smith opposed the Georgia legislature over this matter in 1785. See Dr. A. Sherwood, "Life and Times of Jesse Mercer: Chapter I," *Christian Index*, 16 February 1863, 1.

[33] Adelphos, "The Influence of the Baptist Denomination on Religious Liberty," *Christian Review* (September 1838): 341.

[34] Rev. A. Sherwood, "A Day's Ride in Georgia," *American Baptist Memorial* (Richmond: H. K. Elyson, 1855) 11.

means of expressing patriotism. They could defend their own principles and support the freedoms of others in a free state.[35]

RELIGIOUS LIBERTY AND THE CIVIL WAR

Sherwood also envisioned the role of religious liberty being active as the Civil War progressed. In an unusual manner, he busied himself in a reminiscent task of recounting the twin concepts of religious and civil liberty in the American Revolution and then applying them to the Civil War. Both military encounters epitomized the struggle of Baptists to ensure religious liberty for their constituents and other religious groups.

In 1862, Sherwood attended the Georgia Baptist Convention as a delegate from the Central Association, serving on a committee to look into Sabbath violations. The entire assembly voted to print tracts for Confederate soldiers, reminding them of their religious duties and devotions.[36] The Georgia Baptist Bible and Colporteur Society published several tracts, one of them authored by Sherwood. Titled "Conversation in a Tent," the author exhorted his audience to be faithful to God and man, delineating the difference between patriotism and salvation:

> I address you as soldiers, as men that have not sought office—as men that will fight, but never run from the enemy—as those that love their country, and will contend for its rights to the death, though you wear no lace or gold on your uniform: you are privates, but men of strong arms and courageous hearts, and in the language of Burns' song, "a poor but honest sojer." Home and friends are dear to you, and rights and interests are precious to be watched with sleepless vigilance: but all these are not of so much importance as the soul. Have you thought of this? Have

---

[35] "If we hold in respectful remembrance the patriots and soldiers of the Revolution, whose efforts and sufferings, under God, made us an independent nation, and secured for us civil and political liberty—much more are we under obligations to those by whose toils and troubles we now enjoy the rights of conscience, for these are more valuable, dearer than the other" (Dr. A. Sherwood, "Jesse Mercer and His Times," *Christian Index*, 11 November 1864, 4).

[36] *Minutes of the Baptist Convention of Georgia* (Augusta: Georgia Advertiser's Office, 1862) 7.

you cared for the interests of your undying spirit? Have you ever been concerned about your future condition, whether it will be happy or miserable? Your love of country, your patriotism, is not questioned. If the invader comes, he will pass your threshold only over your lifeless corpse. This is right and praiseworthy; but patriotism cannot be substituted for religion, nor save the soul.[37]

Sherwood also recounted a deathbed experience he noticed as a volunteer chaplain to a hospital unit, picturing it as the missing element in the Southern fight for freedom:

I saw a soldier on his dying bed. He was tenderly nursed by mother, sisters and other friends; but their efforts were in vain to save his valuable life. A few days prior to dissolution, delirium seized his brain. What a sad sight! He muttered incoherent sentences about the camps, the battle-field, and cars in which he came home; but not a word about Jesus or his soul. As he had given that no concern in life, as his friends understood, it is feared all is lost. He was brave amidst the showers of bullets and grape, and escaped death. But disease, soon after a mighty contest, accomplished what the weapons of the enemy could not. Such may be your end, and such the instrument used to stop your pulse and chill the warm current of your life. Believe in Jesus, repent of sin, become a soldier of the cross; then you will be prepared to live usefully and die happily.[38]

Beginning in 1863, Sherwood added the Greenville church in Meriwether County to his ministerial charge.[39] Already living on his 200-acre farm near Indian Springs, in Butts County, Sherwood drove his horse and buggy to this distant church in West Georgia, but he retained the churches in Eatonton and Monticello. In February 1864, he

---

[37] A. Sherwood, *Conversation in a Tent* (Macon: Georgia Bible and Colporteur Society, n.d.) 1–2.

[38] Ibid., 4.

[39] "Dr. A. Sherwood has been called to the Greenville church for this year" ("Personal," *Christian Index*, 6 January 1863, 2).

experienced a horse accident, but later he was able to attend the Georgia Baptist Convention in April.[40] This marked the last meeting of the Georgia Baptists before the demise of the Confederacy and great emotion was attached to it. Sherwood delivered the concluding prayer.[41]

SHERMAN'S MARCH TO THE SEA AND THE TEST OATH

Beginning November 1864, Sherwood experienced a yearlong struggle for survival. Finishing with the burning of Atlanta, General William T. Sherman began a sweep through Central Georgia on the way to the Atlantic Ocean, disabling railroads and burning houses and farms. Sherwood's farm in Indian Springs met the same fate as all other houses in Sherman's "March to the Sea." The invading army burned most of his possessions, including many of his writings. Sherwood's daughter recounted: "His memorialist recalls distinctly a visit made to him at his plantation in the year 1865, after the army of invasion had ravaged his premises; the learned Doctor of Divinity and President, coat off, was plowing his cornfield on the summer day, with the same cheerfulness and willingness that he worked on his father's farm sixty years before."[42] However, the unusually hot and dry winter that attended Sherman's destruction of Georgia did not help the crops of 1865. Sherwood suffered a bad harvest. He also experienced the death of his youngest son, William Early, a sixteen-year-old child who died during this turbulent time.

In early 1866, the *Christian Index* published Sherwood's letter from Missouri. With all his losses in Georgia, the aged Baptist minister returned to a portion of property he possessed in Missouri. He wrote to his Georgia audience a few words of comfort and warning:

Sherman's raid injured me so much that I could not make a crop. I sold my furniture; rented my farm, and returned to this

---

[40] "Dr. Adiel Sherwood met with an accident lately from his horse taking fright and dashing him against a well. But he is happily recovering, and it is hoped, will soon be restored to his usual health" ("Personal," *Christian Index*, 26 February 1864, 1).

[41] Georgia Baptist Convention, *Minutes*, 1864, 12.

[42] Sherwood and Boykin, *Memoir*, 335.

region the last of September. I have a little left here and all my
children around me, except one married daughter in Charleston.
The climate is not so pleasant nor healthy as that of Georgia.
More money may perhaps be made by the young, but I advise all
who can get bread, to remain in the South.

A new Constitution for Missouri was ratified by the people,
in June, requiring an oath from ministers, lawyers, doctors, etc;
but prescribes that even sympathizers with the rebellion may not
vote. Most of Baptists, Presbyterians and Catholics, refuse to
take it. It is hoped the Legislature, now in session, will modify or
afford relief in some way.

The churches have been torn up both in this State and
Illinois by parties; i.e., some approved and some opposed the
war; some ministers preaching Jesus, and some _____ and the
war! It is sad to name such things.[43]

He also recounted his final days in Georgia:

We had some blessed meetings in Butts county, Georgia, in
July and August. I preached nearly every day at Towaliga,
Liberty, etc. At the latter, twenty were baptized.

Alton College, where I labored for years, has now over two
hundred students—fifty looking towards the ministry.

Truly as ever your brother in hope of a better country.

Adiel Sherwood.[44]

Difficulties did not end for Sherwood when he moved to Missouri.
He moved into an era and location of intense political struggle. Under
Reconstruction, the Republicans in the US Congress imposed upon all
seceding states the requirement of swearing allegiance to the Union and
recanting any loyalty to the Confederacy. Of course, the nature and
extent of the oath became a troublesome issue. Most Southern men either

---

[43] Adiel Sherwood, "Letter from Rev. A. Sherwood, D.D.," *Christian Index*, 6
January 1866, 5.

[44] Ibid.

did not want to break a previous oath, or they felt that they never actually rebelled against any country. They simply had been defending their view of liberty. As far as the extent of the oath, legislators insisted that all professional people swear allegiance to the Union, including ministers. To Southern clergy, this was equal to swearing loyalty to Caesar. Sherwood stood as one of the dissenting clergy. By not taking the oath, he was barred from preaching in Missouri. The *Christian Index* reported: "This venerable brother is now residing in St. Louis. Not being able to preach on the Western bank of the river, he crosses over to the East. The loss of Missouri is a gain to Illinois. So much for the test oath which would be supremely ridiculous if it were not superlatively wicked."[45]

However, Sherwood also claimed he never stopped to "speak for Jesus" on the Missouri side of the river.[46] On 12 October 1866, Sherwood preached the introductory sermon to the Saint Louis Baptist Association from Jeremiah 6:16, "Stand ye in the ways, and see, and ask for the old paths, where is the good way, and walk therein, and ye shall find rest for your souls."[47] As a member of Third Baptist Church in Saint Louis, Sherwood functioned as a temporary home missionary for several years, preaching to country churches and former slaves. In 1867, he reported spending a year preaching to five separate congregations.[48]

RELIGIOUS LIBERTY, SLAVERY, AND THE COLONIZATION OF AFRICA

As early as the beginning of the Civil War, Sherwood's view of religious liberty included the advocacy of the institution of Afro-American slavery. From Sherwood's perspective, the Bible supported both the

---

[45] "Rev. Adiel Sherwood, D.D.," *Christian Index*, 19 April 1866, 4. The Methodists created a greater stir than the Baptists. See W. M. Leftwich, *Matryrdom in Missouri* (St. Louis: S. W. Book and Publishing Company, 1870), one of the earliest monographs concerning this struggle.

[46] Sherwood and Boykin, *Memoirs*, 345.

[47] *Minutes of the Forty-seventh Meeting of the St. Louis Baptist Association* (St. Louis: Clayton & Babington, 1866) 3.

[48] "Brother Sherwood is now preaching at Mount Olive, and at Smith's School House, 1st and 2nd Sabbaths; allowed him $21.75 for traveling expenses in visiting Concord, Brush Creek, and Indian Prairie Churches; in all $28.75" (St. Louis Baptist Associaton, *Minutes*, 1867, 9).

institution of slavery and the concept of religious liberty, called *soul liberty*. First, he stated his opinion of the institution:

> Nor would I own one, yet I cannot see sin in the institution itself, if the slaves be properly treated. Neither the Savior nor the Apostles condemn the relation of Master and slave: Paul teaches both their duty—the former to treat the subordinate properly, and the latter to obey for conscience sake. The lawgiver of the universe and the church shuts the gates of heaven against drunkards, adulterers, and other wicked classes but never censures slaveholders. Tens of thousands were in bondage in apostolic times, but if the relation were criminal, would the New Testament not condemn it?[49]

Second, Sherwood judged the threat of abolitionism to be a threat to biblical authority. According to his opinion, advocates of the abolition of slavery in America merely followed the earlier abolitionist movement in England.[50] Yet, abolitionists did not receive their authority from the Bible. The major evil of slavery consisted of the enslavement of the soul. With fair treatment of slaves and proper biblical instruction, the owner of slaves guaranteed his servants the right of soul liberty:

> But then the slaves enjoy soul liberty, a much higher privilege than mere bodily freedom; the slave of a good master is better off, with the usual enjoyment of hearing a pure gospel, and

---

[49] Adiel Sherwood, "Religious Liberty and Slavery," *Christian Index*, 20 February 1861, 1.

[50] "I am under no obligation to shape my views of right by what England chooses to call just and proper, when she forced the institution upon us in our colonial state. I am independent and old-fashioned enough to go by the decisions of the Bible in questions of morals, caring very little about any which have not this Book as guide and criterion. Give up the Scriptures—appeal to the opinions of the age for light and direction, and you are like the mariner, without chart or compass, exposed to every rock and quicksand, on which the storms of life may dash your vessel. Show that the Bible condemns or censures the relation of master and slave, and my tongue is silent; but I am not to be driven from my position, impregnable as the everlasting hills, by fashion, fanaticism or ridicule" (ibid.).

trusting in a complete salvation, than he, whose mind has been blinded by the traditions and mummeries of popery, and taught to rely on priestly efficacy. If I must have an enslaved body or mental vassalage, and a fettered conscience, give me the former, for it will soon cease.[51]

Third, Sherwood saw abolitionism as a perversion of Scripture and its advocates as demagogues. He recounted:

About forty years ago, some very sanctimonious persons whose fathers had become rich by the slave trade, began to groan over the guilt of slavery, repudiating all connection with the hated thing, and dis-fellowshipping all involved in the institution or sympathizing with it. It has become a profession to inculcate hatred against the sinfulness of slavery in Books, schools and families: more than two Presidential campaigns have been conducted on this plank in the platform: "No more slave territory;" and the South which did most to acquire land from Mexico, was to be shut out from its enjoyment.—Others have taught the same erroneous interpretation, and the consequences are before us. Where men are so wedded to cherished theories, so prejudiced against obvious truth as to pervert the plain meaning of words; there is no safety in their interpretations.[52]

---

[51] Sherwood, "Religious Liberty and Slavery," *Christian Index*, 20 February 1861, 1. "No master pretends to control the conscience of his slave only by the Bible and evangelical preaching: he is free to confess Christ and unite with God's people, and attend on the means of grace; thousands belong to the various religious persuasions and are traveling to the promised land, better off than the free in many lands…. I regard abolitionism as the 2d or 3d edition of the Salem Witchcraft" ("Religious Liberty and Slavery," 1).

[52] Dr. A. Sherwood, "Perversions of Scripture: Doulos and Kindred Words," *Christian Index*, 5 August1862, 1. Earlier, he noted the problem of sectionalism: "I have witnessed the passions of our people excited in Boston to a furious storm, on an evil which was a thousand miles off, and with which they had no concern; it was however under the speeches of political agitators that coveted notoriety and office" ("Religious Liberty and Infant Baptism," *Christian Index*, 27 February 1861, 1).

In reality, Sherwood represented a typical view of Southern Baptists in regard to the institution of slavery, but he did make a unique connection between it and the Baptist view of soul liberty. Like other Baptists in the South, he insisted African Americans had a soul that needed salvation. As noted in chapter six, when the Southern Baptist Convention was founded in 1845, Sherwood advocated African colonization as a means to rectify the problem of the institution of slavery. This conviction reflected two concerns: a legal dissolution of the institution and the propagation of missionary efforts in Africa.

After the Civil War, Sherwood also expressed his view of the racial constitution of African Americans and their mixture into a white society. In an article for the *Missouri Baptist* in Palmyra, Missouri, he advocated the removal of Africans from America because the process would produce several advantages:

1st. Reconstruction of the Southern States would be accomplished much easier, if they were not connected with the question.

2d. All fear of conflict, riots, assassinations, et. cet., would be dispelled.

3d. The expense of removal and support for one year, would be less than the millions now expended in sustaining them here.

4th. The great end of Providence in allowing them to be brought to this country, would be accomplished.... God could have prevented their enslavement, if it had so pleased Him; but saw fit to allow it in order to christianize that whole country, by restoring their posterity to it.

5th. The civilization of Africa would open an immense field to commerce, which our own country would easily control.[53]

---

[53] A. S., "The Freedman, No. 2," *Missouri Baptist Journal*, 14 January 1867, 1. Sherwood politely qualified his views in the following manner: "These views, in regard to the colored race, though suggested with diffidence, because of the magnitude of the subject, have been turned over in my mind for several years, and are now published in sincerity and strong confidence that they will, if adopted, be a blessing to the country and the freedmen. I belong to no political party. I speak from long observation and experience of the character of the colored people, and hope they will inwardly digest the issues

Sherwood's conviction of African removal cannot be viewed as a simplistic version of Southern racism. A genuine financial problem plagued Southern states, even in Georgia. During the early years of Reconstruction, Sherwood raised money from Missouri and sent it to the depressed regions of Georgia. On 18 April 1867, the *Christian Index* stated, "Rev. A. Sherwood, D.D., writes, in a private letter from St. Louis, April 11th: 'I secured last week, an appropriation of $1,200 for the poor of Spaulding, Pike, and Monroe counties, from the Southern Relief Society of this place, which will be forwarded in provisions.'"[54] In June, Sherwood addressed the subscribers of the Missouri Baptist to send money to Georgia: "Dear Brother—Sir: I receive letters every week from Georgia, begging for food; two from my old neighborhood, saying starvation must be the fate of some, unless friends from abroad furnish relief. I have sent some, but nothing commensurate with their necessities."[55]

In 1868, Sherwood continued to express his views of the black race as the effects of Reconstruction intensified them. First, he saw that legal equality posed a threat to racial distinction.

If we give them civil and political equality, the result will be social equality; just as certain as the laws of gravitation. This is the evil against which I would warn my countrymen, one of the fellest curses that ever befell a nation. It is presumed that many are not aware of the fatal consequences of the amalgamation of the races. Over thirty years ago Massachusetts passed stringent Laws against the union of the white and colored races in

---

presented: for they are designed to be communicated in great kindness of spirit. These thoughts have been maturing in my own mind for a quarter of a century, and hence are not crude suggestions, developed without reflection and prayer. They are the result of careful study and examination of what will contribute most to the usefulness and happiness of the colored people" ("The Freedman, No. 2," 1).

[54] "Southern Relief," *Christian Index*, 18 April 1867, 2.

[55] "Note from Rev. A. Sherwood, D.D.," *Missouri Baptist Journal,* 3 June 1867, 2.

matrimony. It corrupts and degrades both, and renders them unfit for a free government. [The primary example being Mexico.][56]

The crossbreeding of the races threatened the genetic outcome of both races. Sherwood's view did not denigrate the black race, but the mulatto race. Holding to a common theory of his era, Sherwood perceived the races to hold genetic advantages common to their own race but deleterious to a hybrid individual: "The man of pure blood, white or black, in this country frequently reaches the age of one hundred years; while it is very rare to find a mulatto over sixty: the mixture deteriorates the constitution; it loses its robustness and is more subject to disease. God seems to set his work of disapprobation upon this hybrid, this commingling of the races."[57] Second, he promoted the colonization of Africa for the betterment of the black race and the relief of congressional spending. Apparently, he equated the presence of a free slave population in the United States with a continual financial burden on the federal government.

As Reconstruction began to recede in 1871, Sherwood wrote another article advocating the colonization of Africa, without a heightened racial overtone. His evangelical reasons for the endeavor appeared to be more evident.

A quarter of a century ago, the writer urged the purposes of the Society in several articles, in a weekly, pleading the usefulness of colored men of education and intelligence in that dark land. They could teach them in agriculture, the arts, as well as the great truths of the Bible. One such colored man could do more good than half a dozen white men. Race, color, has a magic power over an ignorant and superstitious people. He would be listened to and gain their confidence. My convictions have not been changed on this subject. One hundred educated, pious colored men, in twenty years, under God's blessing, would

---

[56] A. S., "The Freedman," *Missouri Baptist Journal*, 17 July 1868, 1.
[57] Ibid.

enlighten large portions of that dark land and make it blossom as the rose. Hence I go for the education of the colored man.[58]

Sherwood also stated a historical apology for slavery. In retrospect, he saw the hand of Providence at work preparing African Americans for service in their homeland.

It is possible that God permitted them to be bondmen in the South that they might be instructed in useful arts and then go back to enlighten their brethren in that dark land. Joseph informs his brothers that in his bondage, God had great designs of mercy; why may not this be the case in regard to Africa? True, some were harshly treated and oppressed; yet over 250,000 were members of Evangelical churches in the South, and humble followers of Christ. Let us encourage their education, that they may be qualified to be eminently useful in their father-land. This may compensate in some measure for their hardships in years gone bye.[59]

Sherwood's view of slavery and race within the framework of religious liberty changed over time. During the Civil War, he defended the institution according to the Baptist principle of soul-liberty. The spiritual world was more important than the physical. Yet, after the Civil War, he utilized a different hermeneutic. One could say that Sherwood used a consistent interpretation in both instances. The institution of slavery could be defended from a scriptural standpoint. Yet, the racial distinction in American slavery could not. When the institution of slavery was removed from Southern society, racial equality had to be reinterpreted. Sherwood represented the type of Southern Baptist who wished for the salvation of all African Americans without granting them social equality. In Sherwood's case, the only alternative that would reconcile his conviction of soul-liberty with racial inequality was to remove blacks from his society and place them into a homogeneous

---

[58] A. S., "African Colonization," *Christian Repository* (October 1871): 273.
[59] Ibid., 274.

population. The colonization of Africa began in Sherwood's thought in the 1840s as a means of emancipating slaves without imposing legal and racial problems on Southern society.

POLITICS AND CIVIL LIBERTY

Sherwood believed that the separation of church and state guaranteed civil liberty. According to his perspective, the role of abolitionism before and during the Civil War did much to combine the church with the state, thereby annulling the effects of evangelical religion. Before the Civil War, revivals of religion were flourishing, but after the Civil War the house of God was forsaken. Political involvement in religion destroyed the spiritual functions of the church.

The Civil War contributed toward the demoralization of American religion. Just as Northern abolitionism divorced religious moralism from scriptural injunctions, the political activism of the North injected a foreign element into religious services. As a result, the desire to see the conversion of souls was exchanged for the enthusiasm of victory. Sherwood noted, "During the late contest and since its termination, hundreds of men that used to attend on the means of grace and some that professed piety, have declared openly their disbelief in religion. Why? Their answer is, because all our sacred services are clothed in political robes, and our sermons, prayers and hymns are mingled with the speech of Ashdod."[60] Sherwood charged the North with desecrating the Sabbath for political gain. By engaging in this process, the North robbed congregations of their object of worship. The religion of an individual's standing before a holy God became a religion of the state. He observed, "They [the North] used on the Sabbath to have political discourses, prayers, songs, to be found in no book for the sanctuary, flags over the pulpit, martial music, verses that praised and idolized John Brown and glorified the lamented President."[61]

In a positive sense, civil liberty proceeded from the proper type of religious liberty. Religious liberty as a form of religious separatism originated from the example of following God rather than men.

---

[60] A. S., "Politics and Religion," *Missouri Baptist Journal*, 23 December 1867, 1.
[61] Ibid.

It was the first announcement of soul-freedom the people had ever heard; that is, that men entrusted with the blessed gospel should obey any authority prior to the behests of Caesar. It filled the people with wonder; they had no proper idea of the Supreme Being, and supposed secular rulers were supreme. Civil rights have never been enjoyed in their full extent where religious liberty has been ignored or suppressed; for this is the true foundation of civil rights. The New Testament furnishes the true knowledge of religious prerogatives; it designates the character of those who are rightful members of the churches, the disciples of the Savior, and places them all on the platform of equality.[62]

Difficulties existed in confusing civil liberty with civil religion. Civil liberty relied upon an a priori conviction of biblical truth. Civil religion replaced the truth with the importance of the state. Lacking a genuine relationship with God damaged one's relation to the state. Patriotic and moral duties came from knowing the Creator.[63]

The Last Years of the Historian

Adiel Sherwood lived his final days in Missouri. From 1865 to 1879, the aged Baptist preacher busied himself with several country pastorates including Concord, Sulphur Springs, Kirkwood, Antioch, Mt. Olive, and Fee Fee, as well as frequently preaching to African American congregations in Saint Louis.[64] He wrote frequently for the *Missouri Baptist* in Palmyra, the *Central Baptist* and Ford's *Christian Repository*, both in Saint Louis, and the *Religious Herald* in Virginia. Many of the

---

[62] Rev. A. Sherwood, "Religious Liberty the Precursor of Civil Reform," *Christian Repository* (October 1872): 267.

[63] "We recur again to the basis of our proposition that our obligations to our Maker are first to be understood and discharged. Among these are obedience, the rights of conscience, soul-freedom. If ignorant of our relations to our final Judge we shall fail to perform our duties to our country, nor shall we know how to treat our fellow-citizens, nor allow them the same privileges we claim for ourselves" (ibid., 268).

[64] Sherwood and Boykin, *Memoir*, 345.

same topics about which he wrote for forty years in the *Christian Index* reappeared in these western papers.

His historical work continued in Missouri. He corresponded with Georgians who wished to form the Georgia Historical Society, excited about their endeavors. He worked with Missouri Baptists to compile short church and ministerial sketches.[65] Sherwood also made a historical gesture through raising an endowment for William Jewell College, the Baptist school in Missouri. Due to this effort, a departmental chair was named after him.[66]

In the two sessions of 1870–1871, Sherwood served as one of the vice presidents of the Southern Baptist Convention. In 1870, the convention met in Louisville, Kentucky, and abandoned any attempt to join the convention to the American Baptist Home Mission Society. In 1871, the convention met in Saint Louis, Missouri. This marked Sherwood's final attendance of a national meeting.

On 22 May 1879, Jesse H. Campbell, Sherwood's oldest living student, published an excerpt of a letter he received from his mentor. It read, "I did hope to attend the meeting in Atlanta, but the state of my health prevented me from doing so. I see the Lord is reviving His work in the dear old State, for which no day passes but that I remember you all in my prayers. I try to talk a little occasionally, not preach, for my breath is so short. I try to write a little for the papers and for Ford's *Repository*, etc. Don't forget me in your petitions."[67] Campbell reflected on the impact of this aged minister.

---

[65] Sherwood played an active role as the receiver of historical materials. See A. S., "History of Missouri Baptists," *Central Baptist*, 3 May 1869, 2; A. S., "History of Missouri Baptists," *Central Baptist*, 5 June 1869, 2. His Georgia correspondence is noted in Sherwood and Boykin, *Memoir*, 347.

[66] "At the meeting of the Missouri Baptist General Association, held in Columbia, in 1869, Dr. Sherwood was the first to propose the endowment of the President's Chair in William Jewell College, and made a liberal subscription for the purpose. In forty minutes a sufficient sum to complete the endowment was subscribed by others, and as an expression of their esteem and veneration the Chair was called 'The Sherwood School of Moral Philosophy.'" See James G. Clark, *History of William Jewell College, Liberty, Clay County, Missouri* (St. Louis: Central Baptist Print, 1893) 180n.

[67] J. H. Campbell, "Rev. A. Sherwood, D.D." *Christian Index*, 22 May 1879, 2.

Dr. Sherwood is now in the eighty-eighth year of his age. No man of my acquaintance has been more laborious and self-sacrificing in the cause of Christ. The Georgia Baptist Convention originated with him, as did also Mercer University, indirectly if not directly. No man of his day did more for the cause of literary and theological education in this state than he, especially among the Baptists. I thank God that He has lived to see somewhat of the fruit of his labors.[68]

In August, Adiel Sherwood contracted a form of fever that included symptoms of typhoid and malaria.[69] Within a week, on 19 August 1979, he died. Two days later, Dr. W. Pope Yeaman conducted the funeral at Third Baptist Church in Saint Louis, Missouri. Adiel Sherwood was buried in Bellefontaine Cemetery in the Baptist Lot, a lot of Missouri Baptist preachers. The Sherwood family buried him close to the grave of John Mason Peck. Two months later, Dr. George A. Lofton, Sherwood's pastor who was absent from his funeral, preached a memorial sermon of the deceased minister.[70]

CONCLUSION

Adiel Sherwood's role as a Georgia Baptist historian helped define the perception of Georgia Baptists within the larger Southern Baptist world. Due to his longevity, Sherwood was able to remember events as an eyewitness and initiator, which other men were unable to do. From his perspective, the division of Baptists over missions, the issue of slavery, and the Civil War were historical examples of the Baptist struggle for religious liberty. The succession of Baptist principles consisted of men

---

[68] Ibid.

[69] In 2000, the management of the Bellefontaine Cemetery, under the care of Manuel Garcia, provided the writer with the following information. Adiel Sherwood of 1219 Missouri Avenue, St. Louis, died 18 August 1879 and was interred 20 August 1879. Fever of the typhoid and malaria forms were the causes of death.

[70] George A. Lofton, "Memorial Sermon of Dr. Adiel Sherwood, Delivered at Third Baptist Church, St. Louis, Mo., Oct. 12, 1879," typed manuscript (photocopy), Special Collections, Jack Tarver Library, Mercer University, Macon GA. An extract of this sermon is partially located in Sherwood and Boykin, *Memoirs*, 370–78.

and women who throughout history grappled with the issue of the soul's competency before God. Believing in the dictates of Scripture and being free from the restraint of unbiblical moral crusades, Baptists had the right to claim a historical connection with biblical orthodoxy.

Although Sherwood posited several claims that seem antiquated to contemporary historians, he did accomplish much in preserving the denominational identity of Georgia Baptists. The historical writings of Adiel Sherwood outlined the view that became popular in subsequent histories. The story of Southern missionary Baptists in the state of Georgia was seen as a victory of biblical principles. Missionary Baptists stood for following the explicit commands of Scripture in sending missionaries. Southern Baptists held to a biblical view of the institution of slavery as well as a scriptural concern for the souls of their slaves. Within both contexts, Georgia Baptists who belonged to the Georgia Baptist Convention represented these victories.

8

THE LEGACY OF ADIEL SHERWOOD

When Georgia Baptist churches admit new members into their fellowship, or when new messengers attend the Southern Baptist Convention, the strong connection between the churches to the convention becomes apparent. Conventional Baptists have a completely different mind-set than those who never developed networks beyond a local association. Not only have churches developed a strong national system of correspondence and missionary work, but they have grown to support auxiliary agencies that define and support what Baptists believe. In a strong sense, the institutions, societies, and ideas that Adiel Sherwood promoted have continued to the present day.

Adiel Sherwood, an all-but-forgotten Southern Baptist minister, was a leading figure in his era. Twentieth-century scholarship neglected many organizers within the Southern Baptist matrix, only giving a few leaders acclaim. The theological thought and demonstrative actions of many Southern Baptist founders normally did not become subjects of historical research. If they proved to be highly instrumental in organizing the first session of the convention in 1845 or if they acted as a destructive force in the growth of the denomination, historians dedicated attention to them.[1]

Adiel Sherwood, a prolific author of contemporary thought, offers a better picture of Baptist life in the South as it occurred. Through the pen

---

[1] W. B. Johnson and J. R. Graves are notable examples of founders who were given positive and negative credit for Southern Baptist beginnings.

of Sherwood, the historian can trace the concerns of Georgia Baptists. This source of history represented the immediate thought of nineteenth-century Baptists; they were common men and women who read their weekly newspapers. Adiel Sherwood initiated many organizations and injected many thoughts into Georgia Baptist life through this source. Subsequently, his formative influence in a state denomination left a historical and theological impression on the development of the Southern Baptist Convention.

HIS CONTRIBUTIONS

As his writings and actions indicate, Sherwood promoted revivalism and a theological perspective to justify his methods. His use of aggressive preaching and early polemical writings changed the evangelical thoughts of Georgia Baptists. By utilizing several societies within churches and communities, he attempted to lead Georgia men and women toward active evangelism. He initiated the formation of Sunday schools as adjunct organizations to churches and organized temperance societies as a solidifying force in changing public opinion. His establishment of the first Baptist Sunday school and the first temperance society in the state served as indicators for future efforts. Both types of organizations prepared people's hearts for revival.

Sherwood changed Georgia Baptist life after his involvement in the Great Georgia Revival of 1827. Within his struggle with the antimissionary element, he correctly advocated the supremacy of the church to determine its own doctrine and practice. Yet, his actions did help move Georgia Baptists further away from the traditional role of associational oversight. During this period, the introduction of ministerial education occupied Sherwood's time. He introduced the manual labor system into Georgia as a remedy to satisfy Georgia Baptists' aversion to a dignified and lettered clergy.

After the Southern Baptist Convention was formed, Sherwood served as a practitioner of Baptist principles and a historian of Baptist life. His writings on ecclesiology reflected and confirmed the opinions of Georgia Baptists. Georgia Baptists, like other Baptist bodies in the South, argued their case for believer's baptism by immersion against the other advancing Protestant denominations. They also embraced an ecclesiology that allowed interdenominational cooperation. Through his polemical writings and his works with national societies, Sherwood left an imprint on Georgia Baptists by insisting that Baptist distinctives define their associations and convention. As historian, Sherwood was responsible for successfully compiling the earliest materials in Georgia Baptist life.[2] Not only did his attention to Georgia Baptist history establish necessary documentation, but it also gave legitimacy to the works of missionary Baptists. The Georgia Baptist Convention and its agencies grew because they followed the example of Scripture.

In summary, Sherwood was responsible for numerous organizations and events in Georgia. In 1819, he established the first Baptist Sunday school. In 1820, he wrote a resolution that led to the formation of the Georgia Baptist Convention. In 1827, he formed the first temperance society in Eatonton, Georgia. During the same year, he delivered numerous sermons that promoted the Georgia Revival while he began to instruct ministerial students. In 1831, he promoted the founding of a Baptist school for ministers by starting his own manual labor school. This led to the formation of Mercer Institute in Penfield, Georgia. In 1836, he led in the formation of new Baptist associations in Georgia, gathering up churches expelled from associations controlled by the antimissionary Baptists. In 1839, he established the first theological department at Mercer University. In 1857, he presided over Marshall College in Griffin. During the Civil War, as co-editor of the *Christian Index*, he delivered his version of Baptist history to the subscribers of the newspaper.

HIS EFFECT ON THE GEORGIA BAPTIST CONVENTION

Sherwood's intervention into Georgia Baptist life helped mold the state convention into an influential member of the Southern Baptist Convention. This strategy assumed that state conventions were vital to the health of the national one. Pictured in this manner, a state convention

---

[2] Morgan Edwards and David Benedict accumulated materials in Georgia, but it was under Sherwood's concerted efforts that a manuscript became available for Jesse H. Campbell, Thomas Armitage, and Samuel Boykin.

included delegates from churches and local associations who achieved their goals through diverse societies that were attached to the convention. These delegates worked through societies that promoted the religious objectives of Bible and tract distribution, the organization of Sunday schools, and the promotion of temperance causes. Sherwood's idea of forming a state convention by incorporating diverse societies deposited a viable method into a state convention that was later adopted at the national level.

The historiography of W. W. Barnes and Robert A. Baker originally noted the influence of state conventions on the larger national convention. In a bibliographic essay, William H. Brackney outlined several historiographical landmarks in Baptist studies. According to his analysis, the first two works to change recent Baptist historiography were W. W. Sweet's *Religion on the American Frontier: The Baptists 1783–1830* and W. W. Barnes's *The Southern Baptist Convention, 1845–1953*.[3] The first monograph challenged an earlier view of Baptists as mainstream, urban, and middle-class people by picturing Baptists as a frontier people. Sweet gave credibility to his thesis with a heavy emphasis upon primary materials coming from the frontier regions of Kentucky, Illinois, and Missouri. Sweet demonstrated that the issues of antimissionism and slavery formed Baptists as a frontier people. However, he may have erred in allying the issues with the type of people involved. The issues formed both urban and frontier Baptists. W. W. Barnes followed Sweet's thesis further with the introduction of a similar but somewhat different thesis. He developed the theory that Southern Baptists were formed not exclusively out of their stand on slavery, but out of their regional and ecclesiological differences with the North.

Robert A. Baker followed Barnes's distinctions further with his work, *The Southern Baptist Convention and Its People, 1607–1972*.[4] In this monograph, Baker introduced the role of state conventions in

---

[3] William H. Brackney, *The Baptists* (Westport CT: Praeger Publishers, 1994) 134. See also William Warren Sweet, *Religion on the American Frontier: the Baptists 1783–1830* (New York: H. Holt, 1931); William Wright Barnes, *The Southern Baptist Convention, 1845–1953* (Nashville: Broadman Press, 1954).

[4] See Robert A. Baker, *The Southern Baptist Convention and Its People, 1607–1972* (Nashville: Broadman Press, 1974).

forming the success of the national convention.[5] Yet, at this point, Baker departed from his predecessor. Barnes stressed the role of associations and the formation of mission societies, but he did not lay any importance on the next Baptist development, the formation of state conventions. However, Baker noticed the historical link between missions and associational connectionalism resulting in state organizations. State conventions appearing between 1821 and 1845 served as a solution to the problem of societies.

Baker noted the trend before 1845 toward forming state organizations in the South. Many Southern states united behind missionary and benevolent societies through the organization of larger statewide associations. By 1845, the measurement of success differed in each state. In Virginia, the General Association did not maintain the interests of Baptists in the state due to too many competing societies. The North Carolina Baptist Convention derived its original existence from the formation of a broad benevolent society that reorganized as a state convention. In Kentucky and Alabama, state conventions appeared shortly before the 1845 schism, barely embracing a conventional system. In Mississippi, the state convention dissolved under the pressure of antimissionism, while Tennessee's state convention fractured according to regional issues. In Texas, the early entrance of antimissionary Baptists suppressed any movement toward a state organization. However, South Carolina and Georgia shared a greater heritage of stronger centralization. In 1821, South Carolina Baptists formed the first state convention in the

---

[5] John T. Christian served as an earlier example of a Baptist historian who recognized the value of state conventions as a needful tool for the Triennial convention, but he did not connect this factor with the future success of the Southern Baptist Convention. He stated, "It was apparent to all Baptists who had studied the situation that something was lacking in their organization. The association had been the unit of their counsel and missionary operations. The Triennial Convention was made up of missionary societies and such other bodies as cared to cooperate. To remedy this manifest defect State Conventions, or General Associations, were formed in various states. These gave a medium of communication, a rallying place for all of the interests in the bounds of the state, and a method of coordinating the work of the several states. These conventions brought compactness and unity of purpose to the churches of the denomination" (John T. Christian, *A History of the Baptists of the United States From the First Settlement of the Country to the Year 1845* [Nashville: Sunday School Board, 1926] 453).

South to promote missions and an educated ministry. In 1822, Georgia Baptists formed a state convention that progressively embraced diverse missionary emphases under one organization.[6]

Although Baker's argument was persuasive, the importance of state conventions as formative to the Southern Baptist Convention suffered historical neglect. Over a decade later, H. Leon McBeth's *The Baptist Heritage* did not demonstrate the role of state conventions in the early nineteenth century. McBeth did adamantly assert the preference of a convention approach over against a society approach:

> Whoever fails to grasp the differences between society and convention methods will never understand Northern and Southern Baptists. The convention concept is based upon churches, which send messengers (or delegates, as they were then called) and contributions to a central body to plan and carry out Christian ministries beyond the local churches. The convention (or association) usually covers a specific geographical area, as a county or state. Further, the convention may sponsor multiple ministries, limited only by its vision and resources, the same convention appointing different boards for foreign missions, home missions, Sunday School publications, Christian education, or whatever.[7]

Jesse C. Fletcher's *The Southern Baptist Convention: A Sesquicentennial History* provided a small reference to the organization of state conventions in the South as a byproduct of the Triennial Convention. Fletcher did not address whether the state conventions provided a historical precedent for the Southern Baptist Convention.[8] Both McBeth and Fletcher truncated the argument by not investigating this relationship. While there are good reasons for analyzing the diverse reasons for forming the convention, the structure already had significant

---

[6] Baker, *The Southern Baptist Convention and Its People 1607–1972*, 118–47.

[7] H. Leon McBeth, *The Baptist Heritage* (Nashville: Broadman Press, 1987) 347–48.

[8] Jesse C. Fletcher, *The Southern Baptist Convention: A Sesquicentennial History* (Nashville: Broadman and Holman, 1994) 37–39.

precedent. Although the Southern Baptist Convention had its origins over the issue of slavery, it progressively embraced an organizational system that also differed from the North. A more comprehensive system already functioned on the state level.

In Georgia, Adiel Sherwood interacted with the movement of Georgia Baptist organization and practice. He purposefully initiated the beginnings of a state convention. Like other progressive Baptist thinkers, Sherwood knew that the purposes of education and missions could not be accomplished through the old system of associations. Not enough money or interest existed in any one Georgia Baptist association to complete the tasks he or anyone else desired. By promoting greater unity between Georgia Baptist associations, missionaries could be sent and ministers could be educated.

A new state convention in Georgia united churches and redefined local associations. Serving as a form of a larger association, the Georgia Baptist Convention from its first decade completed the same goals as local associations. Ministerial aid was granted to prospective ministers. The convention also gave monetary funds to foreign missions and sent their own domestic missionaries to the Creek Indians. In a sense, the convention took the place of the association. At the local level, associations changed from organizations established to defend doctrinal integrity to local ministerial fellowships. The rise of an educated ministry and a state convention placed doctrinal discipline back into the churches and out of the control of the associations.

The Georgia Baptist Convention also incorporated new institutions within its system of alliances. The growth of auxiliary societies determined the identity of the convention. All business matters from every society were conducted in each yearly meeting. Unlike their Northern counterparts, Georgia Baptists saw no inconsistency or problem in making societies a part of their conventional structure. The pooling of resources became a Southern phenomenon and trademark, and Georgia Baptists represented this trend.

ISSUES OF HISTORICAL THEOLOGY

Several issues pertaining to historical theology have also surfaced in this work. Sherwood promoted some aspects of New England Calvinism in Baptist life in the South. His views of moral inability and Christ's atonement coincided with the evangelical form of Calvinism taught at Andover Seminary. (This modified form of Calvinism presented the metaphysical relationship of the work of the Holy Spirit in light of human sin by placing a distinction between natural and moral inability.) Sherwood also believed in a strict biblical literalism that helped alter the confessional structure of Georgia Baptists. Observable in his works, Sherwood, although a Reformed thinker, downplayed the role of confessional or systematic doctrine in order for his audience to accept an unsystematic, biblical literalism. This form of biblical interpretation later fit well within the goals of early Southern Baptist Landmarkism, an ecclesiological trend that attempted to create, or demonstrate, absolute continuity between true Christianity and Baptist polity. However, Sherwood provided more depth to his arguments than early Landmark leaders by utilizing this form of biblical hermeneutic in a more consistent manner. He argued for a pure church while avoiding the popular tendency to exclude non-Baptist views as completely heterodox.

Sherwood provided a link between New England Congregationalism and Baptists of the South. In the chapter 1, I establish Sherwood's link to New England. Not only did he import the organizational ideas of New England, but he also brought the normative theological perspectives of his predecessors with him. In Baptist life, he agreed with the theology of Andrew Fuller. In New England Congregational life, he held to the biblical and theological opinions of Timothy Dwight and his student, Moses Stuart. With these theological influences, Sherwood could maintain that sinners had the natural ability to believe with the human faculties but still lacked the moral ability to repent without the work of the Holy Spirit. In this popular formula of evangelical New England Calvinism, New England divines believed the theological paradox between total depravity and moral accountability was solved. Moral inability supposed that divine agency changed the disposition of the heart and thus brought a sinner willingly to comply with the conditions of faith. The theory of moral inability, as opposed to natural inability, encouraged evangelical Calvinists to offer open invitations for sinners to trust the gospel. Sherwood also believed in the Fullerite view of the atonement. Evangelical Calvinists all held to the same view of human inability, but they differed on the atonement. As Reformed thinkers, all Calvinists believed in the limited outcome of the atonement, or limited redemption. Yet, they differed on the plausible extent of the atonement. Sherwood represented the form of evangelical Calvinism filtering into the South that held to this modified view of the atonement—an atonement sufficient for all but efficient for the elect. By embracing Andrew Fuller's version of limited atonement, Sherwood, like many other Georgia Baptist preachers, could uphold God's intent to save his own, while assuring their audience that Christ's atoning work could be offered to all people.

Sherwood consistently preached a strict form of biblicism. In early life, his biblicism appeared as anti-creedal or anti-confessional, whereas it was considered normative in Southern Baptist life a generation later. He drew truth from Scripture differently than earlier Georgia Baptists. The older method of exposing biblical passages through the categorical framework of a confession changed to a more descriptive, unsystematic form of biblical exposition. Sherwood did not destroy the confessional framework of Georgia Baptists; he continued to endorse the practice of each new church and association to compose a constitution and confession. Yet, he did change the use of the confession in Georgia Baptist life. Within his polemic against the Primitive Baptists, Sherwood asserted that the use of confessions was to bind churches together on common beliefs, but they were not to be used to undermine the rights of the local churches in maintaining their own discipline. Confessions could not be applied to associations in the same manner as to members of a local church. Within a voluntary association, churches could only disassociate over matters of doctrine. They could not interfere with doctrinal discipline within the congregations. If a church departed from the faith, they were encouraged to leave their former association and fellowship was withdrawn.

Sherwood's literal biblicism also formed his ecclesiology. He held to a moderate form of early Landmarkism. In the 1850s, when Baptists defended the biblical principles that defined them, some Baptists interpreted their view of the church to an extent in which they completely separated from those who practiced infant baptism, both in pulpit affiliation and interdenominational meetings. Sherwood's view of the church intensified with other Baptists in the South, but not to this point of separation. Rather, he embraced and promulgated normative ecclesiological views of Southern Baptists, such as denominational distinctiveness, a succession of Baptist principles in church history, and religious liberty based on biblical principles.

DEDUCTIONS FOR SOUTHERN BAPTIST FOUNDATIONS

If Adiel Sherwood changed the course of Georgia Baptist history through consistent work in evangelism and denominational involvement, did he help to form a tradition that influenced the Southern Baptist Convention? The Georgia tradition in which Sherwood played an instrumental role reflected the overall identity of all Southern Baptists who gathered in Augusta in 1845. Baptists of the South experienced a theological shift, evident in the Primitive Baptist split in the 1830s. The theology of missionary Baptists made room for societies to promote education, missions, and Bible distribution. This same manner of interpretation defended the institution of slavery but was not necessarily allied with any racist view. In a larger sense, Sherwood represented a normative theology of most Southern Baptists.

The natural biblicism of Baptists in the South continued longer than in the North. Although Southern Baptists still regarded their confessions as important witnesses to faith, they learned to view them more dynamically within the context of a literal interpretation of the Bible. Within the Primitive and missionary Baptist struggle, both parties read their Bibles in a literal fashion and differed only in defining biblical injunctions. Their differences centered on how a believer should follow the implicit commands of Scripture. Missionary Baptists of the South believed the commands of Scripture included explicit and implicit aspects. They held to the letter and spirit of biblical injunctions, making explicit statements their primary source of direction while also leaving room for implicit commands. Between the North and South, the nature of explicit interpretation divided the denomination in 1845. Although their culture confirmed their belief system, Baptists in the South defended slavery on the same principle they enacted under the antimission controversy. From 1845 to 1865, Southern Baptists defended slavery as a biblical institution, an explicit example of Scripture.

From 1801 to 1845, Baptists of the South refined a simple form of biblicism by which they defined the legitimacy, or illegitimacy, of moral crusades and to which they adapted their use of confessions. The societies and structures that sprung from their denomination bore witness to a scriptural commission. After the Civil War, the convention grew while avoiding the perceived errors of their recent past. Before the war, they considered the unbiblical, rationalistic moralism of the abolitionists and the creedalism of the Primitive Baptists as detrimental to evangelical religion.

In the twentieth century, Southern Baptists still lived under this same form of tradition. When disputes arose over the validity of scriptural texts, Baptists sensed a disruption in the foundation of their identity. The question did not center on the nature of living up to the letter of their confession, but on being true to their hermeneutical tool—the Bible. Southern Baptists possessed a tradition that did not divorce confessions from scriptural texts. The adoption of the 1925, 1963, and 2000 confessions reflected the basic hermeneutic of Baptists. The plain, literal meaning of Scripture informed the confessional framework of Baptists, just as it represented Adiel Sherwood's contribution to Georgia Baptist life. He, like his contemporaries, allowed biblical literalism to form his beliefs and organize his practice.

BIBLIOGRAPHY

PRIMARY WORKS CITED

Books/Monographs

Boykin, Samuel. *History of the Baptist Denomination in Georgia: With Biographical Compendium and Portrait Gallery of Baptist Ministers and Other Georgia Baptists.* Atlanta: James P. Harrison and Company, 1881.

Fleming, Robert. *An Essay on the Baptism of John with an Introduction by Adiel Sherwood, D.D.* Athens GA: W. C. Richards, 1849.

Jeter, J. B., J. M. Pendleton, and A. Sherwood. *The True Mission of Baptists.* Nashville: South-Western Publishing House, 1859.

Sherwood, Adiel. *Gazeteer of the State of Georgia.* 4th edition. Macon GA: S. Boykin, 1860. Reprint, Atlanta: Cherokee Publishing Company, 1970.

———. *The Jewish and Christian Churches; or the Hebrew Theocracy and Christian Church Distinct Organizations.* St. Louis: T. W. Ustick, 1850.

———. *Notes on the New Testament, Practical and Explanatory.* New York: Sheldon, Blakeman and Company, 1857.

———. *The True and Spurious Churches Contrasted.* Philadelphia: King and Baird, 1845.

Sherwood, Julia L., and Samuel Boykin. *Memoir of Adiel Sherwood, D.D.* Philadelphia: Grant and Faires, 1884.

Sermons by Adiel Sherwood

Address by Prof. Sherwood. Washington GA: M. J. Kappel, 1840.

"The Careful Minister." In volume 1 of *The Georgia Pulpit: or Ministers' Yearly Offering.* Edited by Robert Fleming. Richmond: H. K. Ellyson, 1847.

"The Covenant of Redemption." In *The Georgia Pulpit: or Ministers' Yearly Offering.* Edited by Robert Fleming, 82–90. Richmond: H. K. Ellyson, 1847.

The Doom of those who Neglect the Gospel. Washington GA: News Office, 1833.
"The Identity of Primitive and Modern Missions: A Discourse." *Southern Baptist Preacher* (March 1840): 53–66.
Introductory Discourse Delivered before the Georgia Baptist Convention, April, 1858. Atlanta: Franklin Printing House, 1861.
Knowledge Necessary and Desirable for a Minister of the Gospel. Milledgeville GA: Camak and Ragland, 1830.
"What are the Mutual and Distinct Duties of Ministers and Members in the Government of Churches?" *Minutes of the General Association of the Baptist Denomination in Georgia.* Augusta: William J. Bunce, 1825.

Circulars by Adiel Sherwood
"Address to the Associations and Individuals." *Minutes of the General Association of the Baptist Denomination in Georgia.* Augusta: William J. Bunce, 1826.
"Circular." *Minutes of the General Association of the Baptist Denomination in Georgia.* Augusta: William J. Bunce, 1832.
"Circular." *Minutes of the Georgia Association.* Augusta: W. Lawson, 1831.
"Circular." *Minutes of the Sarepta Association.* Augusta: William J. Bunce, 1821; 1824.
"Circular to the Several Associations and Churches in the State." *Minutes of the Proceedings of the Eighth Anniversary of the Georgia Baptist Convention,* 1829.
Conversation in a Tent. Macon GA: John L. Jenkins and Co., 1861.
[As Nehemiah.] *Strictures on the Sentiments of the Kehukee Association, Originally Published in a Series of Essays in the Statesman.* 2d edition. Milledgeville GA: Camak & Ragland, 1829.

Journal Articles by Adiel Sherwood
"African Colonization." *Christian Repository* (October 1871): 272–74.
"Bigotry and Liberalism." *Christian Repository* (April 1875): 266–70.
"Connection between Means and End." *The Baptist Pulpit of the United States* (1853): 433–36.
"A Day's Ride in Georgia." *American Baptist Memorial* (1855): 10–11.
"Extract of a Letter from Rev. Mr. Sherwood to the Editor of the Columbian Star." *American Baptist Magazine* 8 (1828): 122–23.
"Georgia." *Baptist Memorial and Monthly Chronicle* (April 1842): 52–53.
"The Influence of the Baptist Denomination on Religious Liberty." *Christian Review* (September 1838): 333–42.
"Jesse Mercer." *Baptist Memorial and Monthly Chronicle* (April 1842): 107–10.

[As Adelphos.] "Little Jane Bussey." *Baptist Tract Magazine* (September 1828): 205–10.

"Ministerial Education in Georgia." *Christian Review* (December 1837): 579–84.

"Prejudice and Infidelity Overcome." *American Baptist Magazine* 9/12 (December 1829): 396–98.

"Rev. Edmund Shackleford." *Baptist Memorial and Monthly Chronicle* (October 1842): 298–99.

Newspaper Articles

Adelphos [Adiel Sherwood]. "Ministerial Education in Georgia." *Christian Index*, 21 December 1837, 821–22.

———. "Points Gained." *Religious Herald*, 25 April 1828, 61.

A Baptist. "Education of Ministers." *Christian Index*, 16 July 1831, 37.

———. "The General Baptist Association of the State of Georgia." *Columbian Star*, 17 August 1822, 2.

"The Baptist General Convention." *Baptist Missionary Magazine*, July 1823, 141.

Battle, E. "Education of Ministers." *Christian Index*, 13 August 1831, 107–108.

———. "Explanation." *Christian Index*, 8 October 1831, 229.

Brantly, W. T. "Manual Labor and Education." *Columbian Star*, 21 November 1829, 323–24.

Campbell, Jesse H. "Rev. A. Sherwood." *Christian Index*, 12 May 1843, 296.

"Columbian College, D.C., June 10, 1836, Circular." *Biblical Recorder*, 13 July 1836, 2.

"Death of Rev. Luther Rice." *Biblical Recorder*, 19 October 1836, 3.

Editor [Joshua Lawrence]. "The Address." *Primitive Baptist* (Tarsboro NC), 2 February 1837, 42.

Editor. "Minister's Meeting—'The Address.'" *Christian Index*, 8 December 1836, 753.

Editor. *Primitive Baptist*, 24 June 1837, 188.

"Education with Manual Labor." *Federal Union* (Milledgeville GA), 29 December 1831, 3.

"Education with Manual Labor." *Federal Union*, 2 February 1832, 2.

Erasmus. "Extracts from Sherwood's MSS History of Georgia Baptists: Treatment of Slaves." *Christian Index*, 13 October 1843, 644.

"Georgia." *Christian Index*, 18 May 1833, 307.

"Georgia Temperance Society." *Christian Index*, 19 March 1831, 192.

"Georgia Temperance Society." *Christian Index*, 19 January 1833, 41.

Hough, John. "Mechanical Labor Combined with Study." *Christian Index*, 12 March 1831, 164–65.

"Jasper County Temperance Society." *Columbian Star*, 26 December 1829, 405.

"The Laws of the Mercer University." *Christian Index*, 3 January 1839, 4.

"Letter to the Editor from Washington, Georgia." *Columbian Star*, 19 September 1829, 188–89.

Lexi [Adiel Sherwood]. "Religious Liberty: Family conversations, embracing the important part taken by Baptists, in the History of the past, in regard to the great principle of Soul-liberty (parts 1–6)." *Christian Index*, 9 January–13 February 1861.

————. "Religious Liberty and Slavery." *Christian Index*, 20 February 1861, 1.

————. "Religious Liberty and Infant Baptism." *Christian Index*, 27 February 1861, 1.

————. "Religious Liberty and Infant Baptism." *Christian Index*, 6 March 1861, 1.

"Manual Labor School under the Care of the Ga. Baptist Convention." *Christian Index*, 21 July 1832, 46.

Melanchthon [Adiel Sherwood] "Can an Association, without violating its own constitution, receive a promise from a church, to perform an act which would prostrate its own internal rights?" *Christian Index*, 12 November 1833, 71.

————. "Constitution of Churches and Associations." *Christian Index*, 3 November 1835, 2.

————. "Essays on the Reformation, Parts. I-X." *Religious Herald*, December 1828–May 1829.

————. "For 'A Young Member.'" *Christian Index*, 31 March 1835, 3.

————. "Is Discipline an Internal Right of the Church?" *Christian Index*, 14 September 1833, 38.

————. "Is Faith the Gift of God, or the Act of the Creature?" *Christian Index*, 25 February 1834, 31.

————. "Observations on Washing the Saint's Feet." *Christian Index*, 1 December 1835, 3.

————. "Offences." *Christian Index*, 28 October 1834, 3.

————. "Repentance a Distinctive Trait in Primitive Preaching." *Christian Index*, 25 March 1834, 47.

————. "Sabbath Monthly Meetings." *Christian Index*, 23 June 1835, 3.

————. "St. Peter's Successor, or When the Union or Communion is broken in that case, the Churches have agreed to put their keys into the hands of the Association." *Christian Index*, 3 December 1833, 83.

————. "To 'A Young Member.'" *Christian Index*, 29 October 1833, 63.

————. "To the Editor." *Christian Index*, 30 December 1834, 3.

————. "To Young Members." *Christian Index*, 23 December 1834, 3.

————. "Value of Learning to the Interpreter of the Bible." *Christian Index*, 22 October 1833, 58.

A Member of the Georgia. "Central Association—Objections to Corresponding with her Noticed." *Christian Index*, 29 July 1834, 116.

Mercer, Jesse. "The General Baptist Association of the State of Georgia." *Columbian Star*, 7 September 1822, 3.

———. "Mercer's Letters to White on the Atonement." *Christian Index*, August-December, 1830.

"Mercer Institute, Ga." *Christian Index*, 10 November 1832, 301.

"Mercer Institute, Greene County, Georgia." *Christian Index*, 10 November 1835, 3.

"Mercer University." *Christian Index*, 8 November 1838, 694–95.

Moseley, William. "Report." *Primitive Baptist*, 24 September 1836, 274.

Nehemiah [Adiel Sherwood]. "Strictures on the Kehukee Association." *Religious Herald,* 17 April–15 May 1829.

Novation [Adiel Sherwood]. "The Sect Every Where Spoken Against." *Christian Index*, 3 July–25 September 1861.

Orderly, Richard [Adiel Sherwood]. "My Guest." *Missionary* (Mt. Zion GA), 4 February 1822, 1.

———. "My Minister." *Missionary*, 31 December 1821, 1.

———. "My Neighbor—The Politician." *Missionary*, 15 July 1822, 1.

———. "My Prejudices." *Missionary*, 13 May 1822, 1.

———. "Our School Master." *Missionary*, 8 July 1822, 1.

———. "The Skeletons." *Missionary*, 1 April 1822, 1.

Overwest [Adiel Sherwood]. "Baptist College." *Christian Index*, 15 September 1835, 3.

———. "Christians, Keep your Temper. Nos. 1–6." *Christian Index*, 17 February–24 March 1835.

———. "The Dilemma." *Christian Index*, 14 April 1835, 3.

———. "The Eatonton Church was put out of the Ocmulgee Association for not restoring persons whom she had excluded." *Christian Index*, 3 June 1834, 37.

———. "Faith and Discipline has caused Secession." *Christian Index*, 26 January 1835, 3.

———. "Ocmulgee and Georgia Associations." *Christian Index*, 29 October 1833, 63.

———. "Skeleton—Nos. 2–5." *Christian Index*, 22 October–19 November 1833.

———. "Strange Proceedings, &c." *Christian Index*, 17 June 1834, 95.

———. "Truth is Mighty." *Christian Index*, 1 April 1834, 51.

———. "Truth is Prevailing." *Christian Index*, 1 December 1835, 2–3.

———. "Western Association Again." *Christian Index*, 19 August 1834, 125.

———. "Western Churches becoming jealous of their rights." *Christian Index*, 19 November 1833, 79.

"Proceedings of the Minister's Meeting at Forsyth, Ga., July, 1836." *Christian Index*, 28 July 1836, 451–53.

"Proceedings of the Second Minister's Meeting." *Christian Index*, 24 November 1836, 722–24.

"Professor A. Sherwood." *Christian Index*, 24 September 1841, 3.

"Professor Sherwood." *Christian Index*, 20 August 1841, 3.

"Rev. Adiel Sherwood." *Banner and Pioneer* (Louisville KY), 12 November 1846, 178.

"Savannah Missionary Society." *Christian Watchman and Baptist Register* (Boston), 6 May 1820, 2.

"The Secession of Churches from Associations." *Christian Index*, 13 August 1831, 102–103.

Sherwood, Adiel. "Address of Dr. Sherwood to Central Association." *Christian Index*, 7 November 1860, 1.

———. "The Apostolic Form." *Christian Index*, 11 November 1862, 1.

———. "Associational and Church Powers." *Baptist Champion* (Macon GA), 1 November 1859, 1–2.

———. "Associational Meetings: Should they Embrace the Sabbath or be held on Week Days?" *Christian Index*, 3 November 1858, 2–3.

———. "Central Association." *Christian Index*, 26 August 1834, 132.

———. "Central Association—Objections to Corresponding with her Noticed." *Christian Index*, 29 July 1834, 116.

———. "Circular Address of the Baptist State Convention at Buckhead, 1831." *Christian Index*, 19 August 1834, 122.

———. "Colportage: The Convention Ought to Encourage It." *Christian Index*, 17 April 1861, 2.

———. "Columbian College." *Christian Index*, 11 August 1836, 484.

———. "Columbian College.—Final Effort." *Christian Index*, 23 March 1837, 186.

———. "Communication from Columbian College." *Biblical Recorder*, 17 March 1838, 3.

———. "Covenant of Redemption." *Christian Index*, 24 November 1835, 1–2.

———. "A Dangerous Theory." *Christian Index*, 7 February 1878, 2.

———. "Desirable Knowledge." *Religious Herald*, 23 July 1830, 1.

———. "Don't Let the College Be Sold." *Christian Index*, 1 March 1838, 116.

———. "Eatonton, Ga." *Religious Herald*, 8 February 1828, 2.

———. "Education—with Manual Labour." *Georgia Journal* (Milledgeville GA), 22 December 1831, 3.

———. "Explanation and Defence." *Christian Index*, 3 April 1861, 1.

———. "The Freedman." *Missouri Baptist Journal* (Palmyra), 7 January 1867, 2.

———. "The Freedman." *Missouri Baptist Journal*, 17 July 1868, 1.

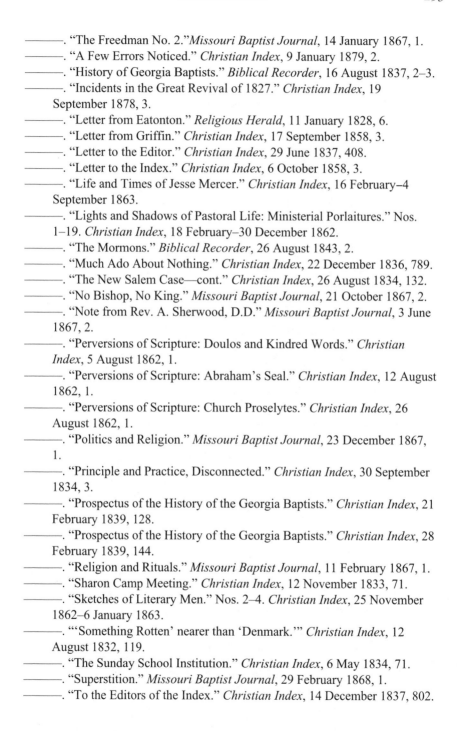

———. "The Freedman No. 2."*Missouri Baptist Journal*, 14 January 1867, 1.

———. "A Few Errors Noticed." *Christian Index*, 9 January 1879, 2.

———. "History of Georgia Baptists." *Biblical Recorder*, 16 August 1837, 2–3.

———. "Incidents in the Great Revival of 1827." *Christian Index*, 19 September 1878, 3.

———. "Letter from Eatonton." *Religious Herald*, 11 January 1828, 6.

———. "Letter from Griffin." *Christian Index*, 17 September 1858, 3.

———. "Letter to the Editor." *Christian Index*, 29 June 1837, 408.

———. "Letter to the Index." *Christian Index*, 6 October 1858, 3.

———. "Life and Times of Jesse Mercer." *Christian Index*, 16 February–4 September 1863.

———. "Lights and Shadows of Pastoral Life: Ministerial Porlaitures." Nos. 1–19. *Christian Index*, 18 February–30 December 1862.

———. "The Mormons." *Biblical Recorder*, 26 August 1843, 2.

———. "Much Ado About Nothing." *Christian Index*, 22 December 1836, 789.

———. "The New Salem Case—cont." *Christian Index*, 26 August 1834, 132.

———. "No Bishop, No King." *Missouri Baptist Journal*, 21 October 1867, 2.

———. "Note from Rev. A. Sherwood, D.D." *Missouri Baptist Journal*, 3 June 1867, 2.

———. "Perversions of Scripture: Doulos and Kindred Words." *Christian Index*, 5 August 1862, 1.

———. "Perversions of Scripture: Abraham's Seal." *Christian Index*, 12 August 1862, 1.

———. "Perversions of Scripture: Church Proselytes." *Christian Index*, 26 August 1862, 1.

———. "Politics and Religion." *Missouri Baptist Journal*, 23 December 1867, 1.

———. "Principle and Practice, Disconnected." *Christian Index*, 30 September 1834, 3.

———. "Prospectus of the History of the Georgia Baptists." *Christian Index*, 21 February 1839, 128.

———. "Prospectus of the History of the Georgia Baptists." *Christian Index*, 28 February 1839, 144.

———. "Religion and Rituals." *Missouri Baptist Journal*, 11 February 1867, 1.

———. "Sharon Camp Meeting." *Christian Index*, 12 November 1833, 71.

———. "Sketches of Literary Men." Nos. 2–4. *Christian Index*, 25 November 1862–6 January 1863.

———. "'Something Rotten' nearer than 'Denmark.'" *Christian Index*, 12 August 1832, 119.

———. "The Sunday School Institution." *Christian Index*, 6 May 1834, 71.

———. "Superstition." *Missouri Baptist Journal*, 29 February 1868, 1.

———. "To the Editors of the Index." *Christian Index*, 14 December 1837, 802.

————. "What the Baptists Have Done—N.T. Church." *Christian Index*, 4 March 1862, 1.

————. "What the Baptists Have Done—Religious Liberty." *Christian Index*, 18 March 1862, 1.

"Teachers' Convention." *Georgia Journal*, 29 December 1831, 3.

"Temperance." *Columbian Star*, 17 April 1830, 246–47.

"Temperance Cause Advancing." *Christian Index*, 1 October 1831, 213.

"Temperance Societies Admonished." *Columbian Star*, 11 July 1829, 29.

"Temperance Societies Admonished." *Columbian Star*, 15 August 1829, 108.

Testis [Adiel Sherwood]. "Reminiscences of Georgia." Nos. 1–23. *Christian Index*, 30 May 1860–20 March 1861.

"The Union of Labor and Study." *Columbian Star*, 20 November 1830, 333–34.

Watchman [Adiel Sherwood]. "It is a Contest for Principle." *Christian Index*, 17 December 1833, 90.

————. "A Revolution." *Christian Index*, 25 February 1834, 31.

Personal Letters/Manuscripts

Sherwood, Adiel. Letter to Elizabeth [Fellows]. Andover, Archival Letter Series (ALS), 23 April 1818. Georgia Baptist History Depository. Jack Tarver Library, Mercer University, Macon GA.

————. Letter to Rev. J. Ludovicus Brookes. Milledgeville, ALS, 15 May 1830. Special Collections. Ina Dillard Russell Library. Georgia College and State University, Milledgeville GA.

————. Letter to Jesse Mercer. Eatonton, ALS, 30 August 1831. Georgia Baptist History Depository. Jack Tarver Library, Mercer University, Macon GA.

————. Letter with no stated recipient. Upper Alton, ALS, 28 December 1844. Georgia Baptist History Depository. Jack Tarver Library, Mercer University, Macon GA.

Sherwood, Emma C. ALS, 6 August 1879. Duke University Rare Books Collection. Duke University, Durham NC.

SECONDARY WORKS

Books/Monographs

Andrews, Garnett. *Reminiscences of an Old Georgia Lawyer*. Atlanta: Cherokee Publishing Company, 1984.

Ansley, Mrs. J. J. *History of the Georgia Woman's Christian Temperance Union from its Organization, 1883 to 1907*. Columbus GA: Gilbert Printing Company, 1914.

Armitage, Thomas. *A History of the Baptists; Traced by Their Vital Principles and Practices, from the Time of our Lord and Savior Jesus Christ to the Year 1886.* New York: Bryan, Taylor and Company, 1887.

Baker, Robert A. *A Baptist Source Book with Particular Reference to Southern Baptists.* Nashville: Broadman Press, 1966.

————. *Relations Between Northern and Southern Baptists.* Fort Worth: Southwestern Baptist Theological Seminary, 1948.

————. *The Southern Baptist Convention and Its People 1607–1972.* Nashville: Broadman Press, 1974.

Barnes, William Wright. *The Southern Baptist Convention 1845–1953.* Nashville: Broadman Press, 1954.

Batts, H. Lewis, and Rollin S. Armour. *History of the First Baptist Church of Christ at Macon.* Macon GA: First Baptist Church, 1991.

Beebe, Gilbert. *A Compilation of Editorial Articles, Copied from the "Signs of the Times," Embracing a Period of Thirty-Five Years; in which is Reflected the Doctrine and Order of the Old School, or Primitive Baptists.* 2 volumes. Middleton NY: Benton L. Beebe, 1868.

Belcher, Joseph, editor. *The Complete Works of Andrew Fuller.* 2 volumes. Harrisonburg VA: Sprinkle Publications, 1988.

Benedict, David. *Fifty Years Among the Baptists.* New York: Sheldon and Company, 1860.

Bennett, Charles Alphaeus. *History of Manual and Industrial Education up to 1870.* Peoria IL: Chas. A. Bennett Co., 1926.

Berk, Stephen E. *Calvinism versus Democracy: Timothy Dwight and the Origins of American Evangelical Orthodoxy.* Hamden CT: Archon Book, 1974.

Berry, W. J. *The Kehukee Declaration and Black Rock Address, with Other Writings Relative to the Baptist Separation between 1825–1840.* Elon College NC: Primitive Publications, n.d.

Bonner, James C., and Lucien E. Roberts. *Studies in Georgia History and Government.* Athens: University of Georgia, 1940.

Boogher, Elbert W. G. *Secondary Education in Georgia, 1732–1858.* Philadelphia: I. F. Huntzinger Co., 1933.

Brand, Edward P. *Illinois Baptists, A History.* Bloomington IL: Pantagraph Printing and Sta. Co., 1930.

Burkitt, Lemuel, and Jesse Read. *A Concise History of the Kehukee Baptist Association.* Philadelphia: Lippincott, Grambo and Company, 1850.

Campbell, Jesse. *Georgia Baptists: Historical and Biographical.* Revised edition. Macon GA: J. W. Burke and Company, 1874.

Carroll, B. H., Jr. *The Genesis of American Anti-Missionism.* Louisville: Baptist Book Concern, 1902.

Carver, Saxon Rowe. *Ropes to Burma: the Story of Luther Rice.* Nashville: Broadman Press, 1961.

Clark, James G. *History of William Jewell College, Liberty, Clay County, Missouri.* St. Louis: Central Baptist Print, 1893.

Coulter, E. Merton. *Studies in Georgia History and Government.* Athens: University of Georgia, 1940.

Crowley, John G. *Primitive Baptists of the Wiregrass South.* Gainesville: University Press of Florida, 1998.

De Blois, Austen Kennedy. *The Pioneer School: A History of Shurtleff College.* New York: Fleming H. Revell, 1900.

Dillow, Myron D. *Harvesttime on the Prairie.* Franklin TN: Providence House Publishers, 1996.

Dodd, Damon C. *Marching Through Georgia: A History of the Free Will Baptists in Georgia.* N.p., 1977.

Encyclopedia of the History of Missouri. 5 volumes. St. Louis: Southern History Company, 1901.

An Examination of the Principles and Proceedings of the Bible Society of the Baptist Denomination. New York: Tract Society of the Methodist Episcopal Church, n.d.

Finney, Charles G. *Lectures on Revivals of Religion.* New York: Fleming H. Revell Company, 1868.

The First Baptist Church of Greensboro, Georgia: A Celebration and History of 175 years. N.p., 1996.

Flanders, Bertram Holland. *Early Georgia Magazines: Literary Periodicals to 1865.* Athens: University of Georgia Press, 1944.

Fletcher, Jesse C. *The Southern Baptist Convention: A Sesquicentennial History.* Nashville: Broadman and Holman Publishers, 1994.

Foster, Frank Hugh. *A Genetic History of New England Theology.* Chicago: University of Chicago Press, 1907.

Gardner, Robert G. *A Decade of Debate and Division: Georgia Baptists and the Formation of the Southern Baptist Convention.* Macon GA: Mercer University Press, 1995.

————. *A History of the Georgia Baptist Association, 1784–1984.* Atlanta: Georgia Baptist Historical Society, 1988.

Giltner, John H. *Moses Stuart: The Father of Biblical Science in America.* Atlanta: Scholar's Press, 1988.

Grimke, Thomas S. *Correspondence on the Principles of Peace, Manual Labor Schools, Etc.* Charleston: Observer Office Press, 1833.

Hardman, T. C. *History of the Sarepta Baptist Association of Georgia and Historical Sketches of Churches Composing the Association.* Athens: McGregor Company, 1943.

Harwell, Jack U. *An Old Friend with New Credentials: A History of the Christian Index.* Atlanta: *Christian Index*, 1972.

Hassell, Sylvester. *History of the Church of God, from the Creation to A.D. 1885; including especially the History of the Kehukee Primitive Baptist Association.* Middletown NY: Gilbert Beebe's Sons, 1886.

Hayne, Coe. *Vanguard of the Caravans: A Life-Story of John Mason Peck.* Philadelphia: Judson Press, 1931.

Hill, Mrs. A. P. *The Life and Services of Rev. John E. Dawson, D.D.* Atlanta: Franklin Steam Printing House, 1872.

Hillyer, S. G. *Reminiscences of Georgia Baptists.* Atlanta: Foote and Davies Company, 1902.

History, Faith, Views, Plans, Etc. of the Central Association; Embracing the Whole Ground of Difference Between Her and Those Associations From Which She Has Separated. Washington GA: *Christian Index,* 1836.

Jeter, Jeremiah B. *Memoir of Abner W. Clopton, A.M.* Richmond: Yale and Wyatt, 1837.

Jones, Anna Olive. *History of the First Baptist Church, Augusta, Georgia 1817–1967.* Columbia SC: R. L. Bryan Company, 1967.

Jones, Charles Edgeworth. *Education in Georgia—No. 5.* Washington, DC: Government Printing Office, 1889.

[Kayser, Elmer Louis]. *Luther Rice, Founder of Columbian College.* Washington, DC: George Washington University, 1966.

Knight, Edgar W., editor. *A Documentary History of Education in the South Before 1860.* Volumes 4–5. Chapel Hill: University of North Carolina Press, 1953.

Lumpkin, William L. *Baptist Foundations in the South.* Nashville: Broadman Press, 1961.

Mallary, Charles Dutton. *Memoirs of Elder Jesse Mercer.* New York: John Gray, 1844.

Marty, Martin E. *Pilgrims in Their Own Land: 500 Years of Religion in America.* New York: Penguin Books, 1984.

McBeth, H. Leon. *The Baptist Heritage.* Nashville: Broadman Press, 1987.

McGlothlin, William J. *Baptist Beginnings in Education: A History of Furman University.* Nashville: Sunday School Board of the Southern Baptist Convention, 1926.

Mercer, Jesse. *History of the Georgia Baptist Association.* Washington GA: Georgia Baptist Association, 1838.

———. *Ten Letters Addressed to the Rev. Cyrus White, in Reference to His Scriptural View of the Atonement.* Washington GA: News Office, 1830.

Ministers' Meeting: Proceedings of the Second Minister's Meeting Held at Covington, Newton County, October 29, 30, 31, and November 1, 1836. Washington GA: *Christian Index,* 1837.

Missouri Baptist Centennial. Columbia MO: E. W. Stephens Publishing Company, 1907.

Moore, Lamire Holden. *Southern Baptists in Illinois.* Nashville: Benson Printing Company, 1957.

Newton, J. W. *History of the Baptists of Georgia and the Ocmulgee Association.* Forsyth GA: self published, 1925.

An Old Pioneer [John Mason Peck]. *"Father Clark," or The Pioneer Preacher.* New York: Sheldon, Lamport and Blakeman, 1855.

Orr, Dorothy. *A History of Education in Georgia.* Chapel Hill: University of North Carolina Press, 1950.

Pascal, George W. *A History of North Carolina Baptists.* 2 volumes. Raleigh: General Board of North Carolina Baptist State Convention, 1930.

Peck, John Mason. *Forty Years of Pioneer Life: Memoir of John Mason Peck D.D.* Edited by Rufus Babcock. Philadelphia: American Baptist Publication Society, 1864. Reprint, Carbondale: Southern Illinois University Press, 1965.

Perkins, James H. *Annals of the West.* Edited by J. M. Peck. 2d edition. St. Louis: James R. Albach, 1850.

Peterson, Owen. *A Divine Discontent: The Life of Nathan S.S. Beman.* Macon GA: Mercer University Press, 1986.

Ragsdale, B. D. *The Founders of Mercer University: An Address at Penfield Chapel* Macon GA: Mercer University, 1933.

———. *The Story of Georgia Baptists.* 3 volumes. Atlanta: Foote and Davies Company, 1935.

Riley, B. F. *A History of the Baptists in the Southern States East of the Mississippi.* Philadelphia: American Baptist Publication Society, 1898.

———. "A History of Southern Baptists." Typed manuscript (microfiche). James P. Boyce Centennial Library. Southern Baptist Theological Seminary, Louisville KY.

Robinson, R. L. *History of the Georgia Baptist Association.* Atlanta: n. p., 1928.

Scomp, H. A. *King Alcohol in the Realm of King Cotton.* Blakely GA: Blakely Printing Company, 1888.

Smith, T. E. *History of the First Baptist Church of Milledgeville, Georgia, 1811–1975.* Atlanta: Cherokee Publishing Company, 1976.

———. *History of the Washington Baptist Association of Georgia.* Milledgeville GA: Doyle Middlebrooks, 1979.

Startup, Kenneth Moore. *The Root of All Evil: The Protestant Clergy and the Economic Mind of the Old South.* Athens: University of Georgia Press, 1997.

Sweet, William Warren, editor. *Religion on the American Frontier: The Baptists 1783–1830.* New York: Cooper Square Publishers, 1964.

Taylor, James B. *Memoir of Rev. Luther Rice, One of the First American Missionaries to the East.* Baltimore: Armstrong and Berry, 1840. Reprint, Nashville: Broadman Press, 1937.

Thompson, Evelyn Wingo. *Luther Rice: Believer in Tomorrow.* Nashville: Broadman Press, 1967.

Torbet, Robert G. *A History of the Baptists.* 3rd edition. Valley Forge: Judson Press, 1950.

Wade, John Donald. *Augustus Baldwin Longstreet: A Study of the Development of Culture in the South.* New York: Macmillan Company, 1924.

White, Charles L. *A Century of Faith.* Philadelphia: Judson Press, 1932.

White, Cyrus. *A Scriptural View of the Atonement.* Milledgeville GA: Statesman and Patriot, 1830.

Williams, William R. *Lectures on Baptist History.* Philadelphia: American Baptist Publication Society, 1877.

Wilson, Kenneth Lee. *The Man with Twenty Hands: John Mason Peck.* New York: Friendship Press, 1948.

Wyckoff, William H. *A Sketch of the Origin and some Particulars of the History of the Most Eminent Bible Societies.* 2d edition. New York: Lewis Colby and Co., 1847.

Dissertations

Gibson, L. T. "Luther Rice's Contribution to Baptist History." S.T.D. thesis, Temple University, 1944.

Haynes, Julietta. "A History of the Primitive Baptists." Ph.D. dissertation, University of Texas, 1959.

Lambert, Byron Cecil. "The Rise of the Anti-Mission Baptists: Sources and Leaders, 1800–1840." Ph.D. dissertation, University of Chicago, 1957.

Mathis, James Rhett. "'Can Two Walk Together Unless They Be Agreed?': The Origins of the Primitive Baptists, 1800–1840." Ph.D. dissertation, University of Florida, 1997.

McPherson, John Thomas. "John Mason Peck: A Conversionist Methodology for a Social Transformation on the American Frontier." Ph.D. dissertation, Southern Baptist Theological Seminary, 1985.

Taylor, Raymond Hargus. "The Triennial Convention, 1814–1845: A Study in Baptist Co-operation and Conflict." Th.D. dissertation, Southern Baptist Theological Seminary, 1960.

Tonks, Alfred Ronald. "A History of the Home Mission Board of the Southern Baptist Convention: 1845–1882." Th.D. dissertation, Southern Baptist Theological Seminary, 1967.

Journal Articles

Anderson, L. F. "The Manual Labor School Movement." *Educational Review* 46 (June–December 1913): 369–86.

Baker, Robert A. "Big Little-Known Southern Baptists: Adiel Sherwood." *Quarterly Review* 37 (January–March 1977): 17–22.

Bryant, James C. "An Historical Account of Theological Education at Mercer University," *Viewpoints* 15 (1996): 71–100.

Carswell, W. J. "Adiel Sherwood." *Viewpoints* 2 (1969): 93–107.

Giltner, John H. "The Fragmentation of New England Congregationalism and the Founding of Andover Seminary." *Journal of Religious Thought* 20/1 (1963–1964):27–42.

Harrison, Paul M. "John Mason Peck: 'American Baptist de Tocqueville.'" *American Baptist Quarterly* 3 (September 1984): 215–24.

Hudgins, Ira Durwood. "The Anti-Missionary Controversy Among Baptists." *Chronicle* 14 (October 1951): 147–63.

Jennings, H. Louise. "A First in Religious Journalism." *Foundations* 2 (January 1959): 40–50.

Jones, Terry L. "Benjamin Franklin Riley." *Baptist History and Heritage* (July 1970): 147–52, 169.

Lafar, Margret Freeman. "Lowell Mason's Varied Activities in Savannah." *Georgia Historical Quarterly* 28 (1944): 113–37.

Leavenworth, J. Lynn. "John Mason Peck's Ministry and the Flow of History." *Foundations* 17 (July–September 1974): 259–67.

Lynch, William O. "The Westward Flow of Southern Colonists before 1861." *Journal of Southern History* 9 (August 1943): 303–27.

Newsome, Jerry. "'Primitive Baptists': A Study in Name Formation or What's in a Word." *Viewpoints* 6 (1978): 63–69.

"Origin of the Anxious Seat," *Baptist Memorial, and Monthly Record* 9 (1850): 229.

Peterson, Owen. "Nathan S.S. Beman at Mt. Zion." *Georgia Historical Quarterly* 49 (1965): 157–70.

Poe, Harry L. "The History of the Anti-Missionary Baptists." *Chronicle* 2/2 (April 1939): 51–64.

Posey, Walter B. "Adiel Sherwood: Georgia's First Gazetteer." *Emory University Quarterly* 13 (March 1957): 17–26.

Proctor, Emerson. "Georgia Baptists: Polarization and Division, 1803–1838." *Viewpoints* 3 (1972): 31–40.

Ragsdale, Bartow Davis. "Early History of Baptist Education in Georgia," typed manuscript, p. 64. Special Collections. Jack Tarver Library, Mercer University, Macon GA, n.d.

S. [possibly Sherwood]. "White-ites." *Baptist Memorial and Monthly Chronicle* (March 1842): 77–78.

Sanders, Daniel P. "Frontier to Forefront: Adiel Sherwood and the Shaping of Georgia Baptists, 1818–1841." *Viewpoints* 12 (1990): 31–46.

Shurden, Walter B. "The Southern Baptist Synthesis: Is it Cracking?" *Baptist History and Heritage* (April 1981): 3–8.

Stephens, Bruce M. "Breaking the Chains of Literalism: The Christology of Moses Stuart." *Covenant Quarterly* (August 1992): 35–40.

Tyrrell, Ian R. "Drink and Temperance in the Antebellum South: An Overview and Interpretation." *Journal of Southern History* 48 (November 1982): 485–510.

Walker, Charles O. "The Development and Organization of the Georgia Baptist Convention, 1800–1842." *Viewpoints* 3 (1972): 5–30.

Wells, David F. "The Debate over the Atonement in 19th-Century America." 3 parts. In *Bibliotheca Sacra* 144 (1987): 123–43, 243–53, 363–76.

Wyatt-Brown, Bertram. "The Antimission Movement in the Jacksonian South: A Study in Regional Folk Culture." *Journal of Southern History* 36 (November 1970): 501–29.

Other Articles

Cathcart, William. "Thomas Baldwin, D.D." In volume 1 of *The Baptist Encyclopedia*, 63–64. Philadelphia: Louis H. Everts, 1881.

Johnson, Hansford D. "Adiel Sherwood." In *Encyclopedia of Southern Baptists,* 1199. Nashville: Broadman Press, 1958.

Lofton, George A. "Memorial Sermon of Dr. Adiel Sherwood. Delivered at Third Baptist Church, St. Louis, Mo. Oct. 12, 1879."

McBeth, Leon. "Southern Baptist Higher Education." In William Estep, *The Lord's Free People in a Free Land: Essays in Baptist History in Honor of Robert A. Baker.* Fort Worth: Southwestern Baptist Theological Seminary, 1976.

Noll, Mark. "The Contested Legacy of Jonathan Edwards in Antebellum Calvinism." In *Reckoning with the Past.* Grand Rapids: Baker Books, 1995.

"Thomas Baldwin." *Memoir of the Rev. John Stanford, D.D. with an Appendix by the Rev.John Williams, Thomas Baldwin and the Rev. Richard Furman.* New York: Swords, Stanford and Company, 1835.

WORKS BY ADIEL SHERWOOD NOT CITED

JOURNAL ARTICLES

"Accordance of the Teachings of the Apostles with those of Jesus Christ." *Christian Repository* (February 1873): 580–85.

"Acts 8:16; 10:48; 19:1–6." *Christian Repository* (March 1875): 193–95.

"Are the Jewish Organization and Christian Church Identical; or is the Latter but a Continuation of the Former?" *Christian Repository* (July 1875): 29–33.

"Baptist Statistics: Early churches and Missionary Societies." *Christian Repository* (February 1872): 613–14.

"The Baptist Triennial Convention: Personal Recollections." *Christian Repository* (January 1876): 28–34.

"The Bible vs. Tradition and Superstition." *Christian Repository* (December 1871): 444–47.

"Brief Notes on Certain Passages." *Christian Repository* (July 1873): 15–18.

"Brief Notice of John 3:5." *Christian Repository* (March 1874): 194–95.

"Children's Centennial Hymn." *Christian Repository* (May 1876): 382–84.

"The Conflict with Romanism." *Christian Repository* (June 1874): 413–17.

"The Covenant Named in Galatians 3:17." *Christian Repository* (27 April 1872): 749–52.

"The Covenants." *Christian Repository* (October 1877): 270–73.

"Credibility of History." *Christian Repository* (September 1872): 179–80.

"Doctrine of Baptisms." *Christian Repository* (December 1871): 443–44.

"Does the Christianity of the 19th Century Differ from the Apostolic Age?" *Christian Repository* (December 1876): 415–20.

"Georgia Baptists." *Christian Repository* (August 1876): 114–17.

"Indifference to Error." *Christian Repository* (May 1874): 342–45.

"The Jewish Church." *Christian Repository* (September 1873): 180–82.

"Memoir of Rev. Thomas Sumner Winn: Late of Liberty County, Ga." *American Baptist Magazine and Missionary Intelligencer* 2 (July 1819): 113–16.

"The New Testament Form of Government and its Superior Advantages." *Christian Repository* (November 1871): 332–37.

"Notes on Texts." *Christian Repository* (April 1877): 277–81.

"The Obedient, the Real Kindred of Jesus." *Christian Repository* (December 1877): 33–34.

"Peace and Truth." *Christian Repository* (April 1872): 745–49.

"Pedilavium—John 13:5–14." *Christian Repository* (January 1872): 498–500.

"Persistent Opposition to Immersion." *Christian Repository* (April 1874): 257–63.

"The Reign of Truth." *Christian Repository* (October 1875): 303–306.

"Religious Liberty: The Precursor of Civil Reform." *Christian Repository* (October 1872): 265–72.

"Remarks on the Divinity and Priesthood of Christ in the Epistle to the Hebrews." *Christian Repository* (October 1872): 277–78.

"Romans 5:7." *Christian Repository* (May 1872): 911.

"Romans 4:5." *Christian Repository* (January 1873): 494–97.

"Romans 6:3–5." *Christian Repository* (April 1872): 761–62.

"Romans 3:25." *Christian Repository* (July 1872): 15–18.

Newspaper Articles written by Adiel Sherwood

Adelphos [Adiel Sherwood]. "A Catechism of Law." *Religious Herald*, 18 May 1832, 76.

"Education for the Ministry: Female Societies." *Religious Herald*, 13 July 1832, 105.

"Two Remarks." *Christian Index*, 14 April 1835, 3.

Erasmus [Adiel Sherwood]. "Extracts from Sherwood's MSS History of Georgia Baptists: Religious Liberty." *Christian Index*, 2 June 1843, 340–41.

"Extracts from Sherwood's MSS History of Georgia Baptists: Savannah River Association." *Christian Index*, 30 June 1843, 401–402.

Sherwood, Adiel. "Addenda to Brother Hyde's Essay." *Central Baptist* (St. Louis MO), 12 January 1871, 1.

"Burman Mission." *Christian Index*, 3 March 1836, 118.

"A Call to the Ministry." *Missouri Baptist Journal*, 20 August 1866, 2.

"Characteristics of Primitive Christians." *Central Baptist*, 14 October 1869, 1.

"Different Denominations." *Central Baptist*, 8 October 1868, 1.

"Divorce." *Central Baptist*, 22 October 1868, 1.

"Excerpts from Mosheim's History." *Central Baptist*, 11 March 1869, 1.

"Excerpts from Mosheim—No.2." *Central Baptist*, 29 April 1869, 1.

"The First American Sunday School." *Missouri Baptist Journal*, 25 June 1860, 4.

"The Foundation of the Church." *Central Baptist*, 15 October 1868, 1.

"Government in the Church." *Missouri Baptist Journal*, 6 August 1866, 1.

"Habit and Desire." *Missouri Baptist Journal*, 13 June 1868, 1.

"Heart Religion." *Missouri Baptist Journal*, 22 February 1868, 1.

"Illogical Reasoning." *Central Baptist*, 31 December 1868, 1.

"Instincts and Impulses of our Nature." *Central Baptist*, 18 August 1870, 1.

"Is the Covenant of Circumcision referred to in Galatians 3:17?" *Central Baptist*, 28 October 1869, 1.

"Is the Religion of the Age the Apostolic Religion?" *Central Baptist*, 7 July 1870, 1.

"The Kingdom of Heaven and the Church." *Central Baptist*, 10 June 1869, 1.

"Knowledge of the Truth." *Central Baptist*, 12 April 1877, 1.

"Layman's Queries." *Central Baptist*, 24 June 1869, 1.

"Laxity in Admission Et Alia." *Central Baptist*, 10 March 1870, 1.

"Lay Preaching." *Missouri Baptist Journal*, 18 November 1867, 1.

"Maplehurst, or Campbellism Not Christianity: A Review." *Missouri Baptist Journal*, 5 August 1867, 2.

"Ministerial Levity." *Missouri Baptist Journal*, 13 May 0[?] 1867, 1.

"The Ministry." *Missouri Baptist Journal*, 30 September 1867, 1.

"The Mosaic and Christian Dispensations." *Central Baptist*, 27 December 1877, 1.

"National Sins, Sabbath Desecration." *Christian Index*, 22 April 1862, 3.

"New Doctrine." *Central Baptist*, 4 January 1872, 1.

"The Ordinances." *Central Baptist*, 22 October 1868, 1.

"Pastoral Visitation." *Central Baptist*, 5 May 1870, 1.

"Pastoral Visitation." *Central Baptist*, 12 May 1870, 1.

"Pliable Consciences." *Central Baptist*, 11 February 1867, 1.

"Proofs of Scripture History From Heathen Authors." *Central Baptist*, 20 December 1877, 1.

"Query: Should the Baptisms of a minister irregularly ordained and living in an unchristian manner be repeated?" *Central Baptist*, 3 June 1869, 1.

"Questions with Brief Answers." *Missouri Baptist Journal*, 20 June 1868, 1.

"Recollections of Georgia: Baptist Convention." *Christian Index*, 27 March 1861, 2.

"Remarks on Isaiah 4:1." *Christian Index*, 28 August 1863, 2.

"Reminiscences—V.R. Thornton." *Christian Index*, 19 August 1862, 2.

"Revelation Made to Paul." *Central Baptist*, 13 September 1877, 1.

"Revival of Religion." *Central Baptist*, 9 August 1877, 1.

"The Rights of the Churches." *Central Baptist*, 1 October 1868, 1.

"Sabbath Schools." *Missouri Baptist Journal*, 25 February 1867, 1.

"Sabbath Schools No. 3." *Missouri Baptist Journal*, 4 March 1867, 1.

"Sectarianism in Translation." *Christian Index*, 18 July 1878, 4.

"State Missions, the College, and the Journal." *Missouri Baptist Journal*, 15 February 1868, 1.

"Statistics of the Counties." *Missouri Baptist Journal*, 27 May 1867, 2.

"The St. Louis Association." *Missouri Baptist Journal*, 29 October 1866, 2.

"The Sunday School Institution." *Christian Index*, 6 May 1834, 71.

"Trip to Hot Springs, Arkansas." *Central Baptist*, 13 September 1877, 1.

"Truth is Mighty and Must Prevail." *Central Baptist*, 10 May 1877, 1.

"To a Mourner." *Missouri Baptist Journal*, 2 May 1868, 1.

"Too Liberal." *Missouri Baptist Journal*, 27 August 1866, 2.

"Universalism." *Christian Index*, 1 June 1863, 1.

"The Weeds and Underbrush: Educational Error." *Christian Index*, 5 June 1861, 1.

"When does a Man become Holy enough?" *Missouri Baptist Journal*, 31 September 1866, 1.

"Were the Apostles Baptized?" *Missouri Baptist Journal*, 25 June 1866, 4.

"What means may ministers employ the most effectually to bring the membership of our churches into active cooperation in the cause of Christ?" *Missouri Baptist Journal*, 9 September 1867, 2.

Watchman [Adiel Sherwood]. "Does the N.T. prescribe any model of Church Government?" *Christian Index*, 28 August–2 October 1861.

"A Glance at Matters and Things in a Series of Items." *Christian Index*, 5 December 1839, 785–86.

INDEX